Contents

Contributors

Project Manager
Ian Brookes

Editor
Alice Grandison

Editorial Assistance
Lynn Duke
Susan Dunsmore
Elaine O'Donoghue

Publishing Manager
Patrick White

Data Management
Patrick Gaherty

Prepress
Clair Cameron

Preface

by **Benjamin Zephaniah**

If you have bought this book or are just checking it out in a bookshop, you are probably interested in using poetry as a way of expressing your thoughts and feelings, or you may just want to change the world. You are not the only one; there are millions of us. People have always found poetry a particularly satisfying form of expression, and people like me continue to argue that in its oral form it is probably the oldest and most accessible art form known to mankind, and still we continue to use it in new and original ways. I started to create poetry because of my love of words; the rhythms of poetry excited me, and I was fascinated by the way words could be given various meanings depending on where they were placed on the page. When I walk into bookshops and libraries I still have to remind myself that there are only 26 letters in the alphabet, and that the books I see simply contain various arrangements of those 26 letters. How great the word! And this is just the English language!

A fellow poet once referred to me in a radio interview as a walking rhyming dictionary. What a great idea, I thought: a book full of rhymes! It wasn't until I began to phone friends to tell them of this new publishing idea I had that I was told that such things already existed. Having discovered them, I refused to use them. After all, why should I, the walking rhyming dictionary, require the use of such a book? Then I received one as a present (honest), and I have since learnt that they can be a great help when you are constructing tricky rhymes. I have found them most useful just when I feel that what I'm writing is not working. I am often surprised by their suggestions and then I find myself full of new ideas.

Chambers already have a reputation for producing great conventional dictionaries, but here they have adopted a completely new approach. Rhymes are grouped by the stressed syllables; phrases are given as well as individual words, and thousands of proper names have been included. So it's now official, you can rhyme *Johnny Cash* with *balderdash*, or *Ben Nevis* with *crevice*. The future is bright, it's a rapper's delight. By acknowledging words that have come into use via films, television, music, and other forms of popular culture, this new approach has brought the rhyming dictionary into the 21st century, so that experienced writers can enjoy finding new ways of doing things and younger writers will be familiar with many of its references.

Use this book as a starting point, a source for new ideas, and as a way of finishing those poems that will not be done by head-scratching alone, but remember there are no boundaries to the things that you can do in poetry. You have my permission to use words outside the list provided. By breaking the rules you may make new discoveries and you may very well find yourself contributing to a new edition of this very dictionary.

Benjamin Zephaniah

The Use of Rhyme

Is rhyme important?

Poetry does not have to rhyme. However, there are often good reasons for using rhyme to give your poem shape and structure. If you are writing poetry or songs to be performed in public, rhyme helps the audience to pick up the structure of the piece easily, a point which is important when the words are not written down.

Verses that rhyme are easier to remember than ones that don't. That is why rhymes are used in so many popular sayings. Your parents and grandparents probably told you rhymes to make you remember things, such as:

An apple a day
Keeps the doctor away.

Rhyme is also a great way to make people stop and take notice, especially when it is used in a creative or unusual way. The more unexpected and original the rhyme, the better. Writers such as Ogden Nash and W S Gilbert (of Gilbert and Sullivan fame) were expert at producing unexpected rhymes to give a comic effect, making *turtle* rhyme with *fertile* and *Hungary* rhyme with *ironmongery.*

Different forms of rhyme

Rhyme occurs when two lines of verse end with a similar sound. However, there are various different types of rhyme. Often there will be a stress or accent on the final syllable of the rhyming words. This is called "masculine rhyme" and is found, for example, when you rhyme *fox* with *socks*. However, you can also have rhymes when there is an extra unstressed syllable at the end of the line, such as when you rhyme *dancer* with *answer*. This is called "feminine rhyme". You can sometimes even have two unstressed syllables after the main stressed syllable, as in *charity* and *hilarity.*

Another form of rhyme happens when the ends of the words sound almost but not exactly identical. This is called "half-rhyme" or "near-rhyme". An example of this occurs if you rhyme *home* and *alone*. You will find that some pairs of letters, for example *m* and *n* or *d* and *t*, can be used almost interchangeably for rhyming purposes. Using half-rhymes greatly increases the number of words you can use to rhyme with any word. It also allows you to surprise and amuse by introducing unexpected words as rhymes.

Common rhyme schemes

Many types of verse use rhyme as an essential part of their structure. The simplest regular patterns or "rhyme schemes" involve using rhyme at the end of every two lines of a poem (AABBCCDD etc) or by using rhyme at the end of alternating lines of a poem (ABABCDCD etc). However, there are many ways of using rhyme in more elaborate patterns. The Elizabethan poet Edmund Spenser devised a verse-form (the Spenserian stanza) that interweaves three different sounds in the pattern ABABBCBCC, and there are any number of other patterns you could adopt.

One powerful rhyming technique is to repeat the same sound at the end of three, four, or even more successive lines of verse. Another variation is to use "internal rhyme" where the same sound is repeated at the middle and end of a line.

Some types of poem employ a specific pattern of rhymes to give them their structure. One of the most popular is the **sonnet**, a favourite of Shakespeare, which always has fourteen lines and follows a regular rhyme scheme (either ABBAABBA CDCDCD or ABABCDCD EFEFGG).

Another common verse form is the **limerick**. The limerick uses the pattern AABBA with the third and fourth lines being shorter than the others. The reappearance of the original rhyme in the last line often has a comic effect:

There once was a fellow called Patrick
Whose limbs were all made of elastic.
He could make buttered bread
While still lying in bed.
We were all quite astonished at that trick!

The comic possibilities of rhyme are also exploited by the **clerihew**. This type of poem uses a sequence of two rhyming couplets, often of different lengths:

Sir Francis Drake
Said "Make no mistake:
Playing bowls was much harder
Than defeating the Armada".

These are just a few of the ways that you can work with rhyme. However, you don't need to follow the patterns that other people have used, and it can often be more interesting to experiment with your own rhyme schemes. Enjoy your rhyming!

How to Use This Book

How the lists in the book are arranged

This book contains lists of words that rhyme. Each list is headed by a common word in bold type:

rabble
babble
dabble
gabble
scrabble

The lists of rhyming words are grouped together according to the main stressed syllable in a word. There are 19 different sections in the book corresponding to the 19 different vowel sounds used in Standard English. Thus all of the words in Section 8 have the sound *-er-* as their main stressed syllable, but within that section you will find lists of words that rhyme with *herb*, *work*, *word*, and so on.

Each section is divided into numbered subsections. Each subsection contains words that have the same consonant sound after the main vowel sound. Thus Subsection 8.2 contains words with the sound *-erb-*, Subsection 8.3 contains words with the sound *-erk-*, and so on.

Each subsection may also contain lists of words that have unstressed syllables at the end of the word. Thus under the list of words in Subsection 8.8 that rhyme with *term*, you will find lists of words that rhyme with *murmur*, words that rhyme with *thermal*, words that rhyme with *German*, and so on.

Where an explanation of the meaning of a word is required, this is supplied in brackets after the word:

tarry (= *like tar*)

Explanations are given to distinguish between easily confused words, or words that may be pronounced in different ways. For example, *tarry* only rhymes with *starry* when it means "like tar". When it means "to dawdle" it rhymes with *carry*.

Explanations are also given to show the full form of abbreviations:

VCR (= *video cassette recorder*)

How to find a rhyme for a word

Look up the word in the index at the back of the book. The index lists every word in alphabetical order and tells you where in the book you can find it. For example, if you look up the word *jammy* you will be told to look in Subsection 1.7.

Now go to the part of the book indicated by the index, using the subsection numbers at the top of each page to help you. You will find a list of words that rhyme with your word. The list may include not only common words, but also names of famous people and places, abbreviations, and common idioms or figures of speech, all of which may suggest a way of completing the rhyme. For example, you will find nine possible rhymes listed for *jammy*: *chamois*, *clammy*, *double whammy*, *gammy*, *hammy*, *mammy*, *Miami*, *Sammy* and *Tammy*.

The subsection may also contain lists of other words that have the same main stressed syllable, but a slightly different ending. Some of these lists may give near-rhymes for your word. For example, words in Subsection 1.7 that rhyme with *gammon* form near-rhymes with words that rhyme with *famine*.

Sometimes a note is added at the end of a list to give you a hint about how to add to the range of rhymes. For example, after the list of words in Subsection 1.13 that rhyme with *hatchet*, you are told:

> + You can also make rhymes for these words by using *it* after some words that rhyme with *catch*, as in *snatch it*.

Where you find a note like this, go to the list of words indicated, which should be in same subsection. Looking at the list of words that rhymes with *catch* offers you additional rhymes for *hatchet* such as *detach it*, *dispatch it*, *match it*, and so on.

You can also browse around the other lists in the section. These will not offer exact rhymes, but you may get some ideas for near-rhymes that will serve your purpose. For example, words in Section 8 that rhyme with *work* may form near-rhymes with words that rhyme with *shirt*.

Section 1
-A-

All the words in this section use the sound **-a-** (as in c*a*t, b*a*dger, Jap*a*n) in their main stressed syllable

1.1

cab
blab
crab
dab
drab
fab
flab
gab
gift of the gab
grab
hackney cab
jab
kebab
lab
minicab
nab
pick up the tab
scab
slab
stab
tab

blabber
Abba
jabber

rabble
babble
dabble
gabble
scrabble

collaborate
elaborate (= *to explain*)

shabby
abbey
Abby
cabby
crabby
flabby
Gab(b)y
scabby
tabby

rabid
crabbed

habit
cohabit
inhabit
rabbit

+ You can also make rhymes for these words by using *it* after some words that rhyme with *cab*, as in *dab it*

vocabulary
constabulary

1.2

back
aback
almanac
anorak
aphrodisiac
attack
back-to-back
bivouac
black
blow your stack
bric-ã-brac
Cadillac
cardiac
counterattack
crack
cul-de-sac
flak
get your own back
hack
haemophiliac
hard nut to crack
haversack
heart attack
hit the sack
hypochondriac
insomniac
in the black
Jack
jack
Jack Kerouac
knack
lack
laid-back
lumberjack
mac
Mach
pack
paperback
piggyback
quack
quarterback

rack
sac
sack
Sassenach
shack
slack
smack
snack
stack
steeplejack
stickleback
tack
track
unpack
water off a duck's back
whack
WRAC (= *Women's Royal Army Corps*)
yack (= *to talk*)
yak (= *a Tibetan ox*)
Za(c)k
zodiac

→ Many English speakers pronounce some words in section **2.3** (eg *Iraq*) in such a way that they rhyme with these words

backer
attacker
backpacker
cracker
Dakar
Dhaka
firecracker
hacker
knacker
lacquer
Michael Schumacher
packer
slacker
smacker

+ You can add to this list by adding *-er* to some words that rhyme with ***back***, as in ***blacker***

You can also make rhymes for these words by using ***her*** after some words that rhyme with ***back***, as in ***attack her***

tackle
cackle
crackle
cut the cackle
jackal
ramshackle
rugby-tackle
shackle
tabernacle

blacken
bracken
slacken

crackers
Caracas
maracas
nutcrackers

+ You can add to this list by adding *-s* to some words that rhyme with ***backer***, as in ***attackers***

tackier
Czechoslovakia
Slovakia
wackier

tacky
baccy
Jackie
lackey
wacky

backing
cracking
get cracking
nerve-(w)racking
packing
sacking
whacking

+ You can add to this list by adding *-ing* to some words that rhyme with ***back***, as in ***attacking***

jacket
bracket
cost a packet
packet
racket

+ You can also make rhymes for these words by using ***it*** after some words that rhyme with ***back***, as in ***crack it***

acne
Hackney

hackneyed
arachnid

slackness
blackness

jackpot
crackpot

tax
axe
battleaxe
fax
Filofax®
flax
Halifax
lax
Mad Max
Max
max
pax
relax
sax
sealing wax

slacks
wax

> **+** You can add to this list by adding *-s* to some words that rhyme with ***back***, as in ***cracks***

waxen
Anglo-Saxon
flaxen
Jackson
Jesse Jackson
klaxon
Michael Jackson
Saxon

axis
praxis (= *the practice of a profession*)

taxing
relaxing

> **+** You can add to this list by adding *-ing* to some words that rhyme with ***tax***, as in ***faxing***

waxed
overtaxed
relaxed

> **+** You can add to this list by adding *-(e)d* to some words that rhyme with ***tax***, as in ***faxed***

action
abstraction
attraction
contraction
delayed-action
dissatisfaction
distraction
extraction
faction
Fatal Attraction
fraction
inaction
interaction
reaction
satisfaction
subtraction
traction
transaction

act
abstract
artefact
attract
cataract
compact
contract (= *to become smaller*)
counteract
cracked
detract
distract
enact
exact
extract
fact
impact
inexact
intact
interact
jam-packed
matter-of-fact
overact
overreact
packed
pact
react
re-enact
refract
retract
subcontract
subtract
tact
tracked
tract
vacuum-packed
whacked

> **+** You can add to this list by adding *-ed* to some words that rhyme with ***back***, as in ***attacked***

actor
benefactor
contractor
detractor
factor
malefactor
protractor
reactor
subcontractor
tractor
windchill factor

> **+** You can also make rhymes for these words by using ***her*** after some words that rhyme with ***act***, as in ***attract her***

tractable
intractable
refractable
retractable

factory
olfactory
refractory
satisfactory
unsatisfactory

tactic
climactic
didactic
galactic
prophylactic

practical
impractical
tactical

distracted
impacted
protracted

+ You can add to this list by adding *-ed* to some words that rhyme with ***act***, as in ***attracted***

acting
distracting
exacting
play-acting

+ You can add to this list by adding *-ing* to some words that rhyme with ***act***, as in ***attracting***

active
attractive
hyperactive
inactive
interactive
overactive
proactive
radioactive
retroactive
unattractive
underactive

actress
benefactress

fracture
manufacture

actual
contractual
factual

spectacular
Dracula
vernacular

1.3

bad
ad
add
Baghdad
barking mad
bit of a lad
Brad
cad
Chad
clad
dad
fad
gad
glad
had
hopping mad
jihad
lad
Leningrad
like mad
mad
pad
plaid
rad
Riyadh
SAD (= *seasonal affective disorder*)
sad
Stalingrad
tad
Trinidad
Volgograd

ladder
adder
bladder
lowest rung of the ladder
stepladder
top rung of the ladder

+ You can add to this list by adding *-der* to some words that rhyme with ***bad***, as in ***sadder***

You can also make rhymes for these words by using ***her*** after some words that rhyme with ***bad***, as in ***add her***

haddock
paddock
shaddock

saddle
addle
paddle
side-saddle
straddle
unsaddle

madam
Adam

+ You can add to this list by adding ***'em*** to some words that rhyme with ***bad***, as in ***had 'em***

sadden
gladden
madden

daddy
baddie
caddie (= *a golfer's assistant*)
caddy (= *a container for tea*)
grandaddy
laddie
Paddy
paddy

nomadic
sporadic

radish
laddish
saddish

shadow
foreshadow
overshadow
saddo

badly
Bradley
gladly
madly
sadly

madman
ad-man
Bradman

badness
gladness
madness
midsummer madness
sadness

badge
cadge
hadj
Madge

magic
tragic

magically
tragically

agile
fragile

1.4

naff
blow the gaff
caff
carafe
decaf(f)
faff
gaff (= *a fishing pole*)
gaffe (= *a blunder*)
WAAF (= *Women's Auxiliary Air Force*)

+ You can also make rhymes for these words by using words in section **1.15** that rhyme with ***homeopath***

➔ Many English speakers pronounce some words in section **2.5** (eg *laugh*) in such a way that they rhyme with these words

gaffer
Jaffa
Staffa

baffle
raffle
snaffle

café
cybercafé
daffy

Mafia
daffier
raffia

graphic
demographic
geographic
photographic
pornographic
telegraphic
traffic
typographic

+ You can also make rhymes for these words by using word in section **1.15** that rhyme with ***telepathic***

geographical
autobiographical
biographical
typographical

graphics
affix

BAFTA
NAFTA (= *North American Free Trade Agreement*)

➔ Many English speakers pronounce some words in section **2.5** (eg *laughter*) in such a way that they rhyme with these words

1.5

bag
brag
crag
drag
fag
flag
gag
hag
Jag
jag
Jiffy® bag
lag
lose your rag
mag
nag
rag
saddlebag
sag
scallywag
slag
snag
stag
swag
tag
wag

dagger
cloak-and-dagger
ragga
stagger
swagger

+ You can add to this list by adding ***-ger*** to some words that rhyme with ***bag***, as in ***dragger***

You can also make rhymes for these words by using ***her*** after some words that rhyme with ***bag***, as in ***drag her***

haggard
laggard

+ You can add to this list by adding *-ed* to some words that rhyme with *dagger*, as in *staggered*

gaggle
haggle
straggle
waggle

dragon
fall off the wag(g)on
flagon
on the wag(g)on
pendragon
wag(g)on

diagonal
hexagonal
octagonal

antagonist
protagonist

maggot
braggart
faggot

baggy
craggy
jaggy
Maggie
saggy
scraggy
shaggy

ragged
jagged

nagging
unflagging

+ You can add to this list by adding *-ging* to some words that rhyme with *bag*, as in *bragging*

Magnus
Agnes

jaguar
Nicaragua

1.6

pal
Al
alimentary canal
cabal
Cal
canal
Chantal
corral
et al
gal
Hal
Sal
shall
Val

→ Many English speakers pronounce some words in section **2.8** (eg *morale*) in such a way that they rhyme with these words

ballet
Calais
chalet
valet

valour
Allah
Valhalla

salad
ballad

analogy
allergy
genealogy
metallurgy

gallon
Al(l)an
talon
Woody Allen

balance
imbalance
overbalance
valance

balanced
unbalanced
valanced
well-balanced

talent
gallant

gallery
calorie
high-calorie
low-calorie
salary
Valerie

callous
callus
Dallas
palace

galleon
Italian

rally
alley
Ally
dally
dilly-dally
galley
pally
Sally
sally
tally
valley

→ Many English speakers pronounce some words in section **2.8** (eg *finale*) in such a way that they rhyme with these words

metallic
Alec
Gallic
italic

valid
dallied

dilly-dallied
invalid (= *not valid*)
pallid
rallied
sallied
tallied

malice
Alice
aurora borealis
chalice
poisoned chalice

analysis
dialysis
paralysis
psychoanalysis

mallet
ballot
palate (= *the roof of the mouth*)
palette (= *a tray for mixing paint*)
pallet (= *a mattress*)

reality
abnormality
banality
brutality
confidentiality
eventuality
fatality
formality
generality
geniality
hospitality
illegality
immorality
immortality
impartiality
impracticality
individuality
informality
legality
locality
mentality
morality
mortality
municipality
nationality
neutrality
normality
originality
partiality
personality
plurality
practicality
principality
punctuality
sensuality
sentimentality
sexuality
speciality
spirituality
superficiality
technicality
totality
unpunctuality
vitality

shallow
callow
fallow
hallow
mallow
marshmallow
sallow
tallow

Alf
Ralph

Alma
halma
Palma

alto
contralto

valve
salve

stallion
battalion
galleon
medallion

1.7

jam
Abraham
ad nauseam
aerogram(me)
am
Amsterdam
anagram
battering ram
cam
centigram(me)
clam
cram
dam
damn
diagram
diaphragm
dram
electrocardiogram
epigram
exam
gram(me)
ham
histogram
hologram
jamb
kilogram(me)
kissogram
lamb
marjoram
milligram(me)
money for jam
monogram
not give a damn
Omar Khayyám
Pam
parallelogram
pram
pro-am
RAM (= *random access memory*)
ram
Rotterdam
Sam
scam
scram
sham
slam
spam
Surinam
swam
Tam
telegram

tram
Vietnam
Wham!
wham
yam

> ➕ You can also make rhymes for these words by using words in section **1.8** that rhyme with ***man***

hammer
Alabama
clamour
enamour
Franz Klammer
gamma
glamour
grammar
stammer
the slammer
yammer

> ➕ You can add to this list by adding ***-(m)er*** to some words that rhyme with ***jam***, as in ***crammer***

flammable
inflammable
nonflammable
programmable

enamoured
Muhammad

> ➕ You can add to this list by adding ***-ed*** to some words that rhyme with ***hammer***, as in ***stammered***

camel
enamel
mammal
Tamil

gammon
backgammon
salmon
with jam on

glamorous
amorous
clamorous

defamatory
amatory
declamatory
exclamatory

jammy
chamois
clammy
double whammy
gammy
hammy
mammy
Miami
Sammy
Tammy

dynamic
aerodynamic
ceramic
Islamic
panoramic

dynamics
aerodynamics
ceramics
thermodynamics

family
extended family
hammily
jammily
one-parent family

famine
cross-examine
examine
re-examine

contaminate
decontaminate
laminate

stamina
examiner

> ➕ You can also make rhymes for these words by using ***her*** after some words that rhyme with ***famine***, as in ***cross-examine her***

jamming
damning
lambing
spamming

> ➕ You can add to this list by adding ***-ming*** to some words that rhyme with ***jam***, as in ***cramming***

diameter
ammeter
parameter
pentameter

amber
Amber
clamber
samba

gamble
amble
bramble
gambol
preamble
ramble
scramble
shamble
unscramble

Zambia
Gambia

Bambi
namby-pamby

gambler
rambler
scrambler
unscrambler

gambling
rambling

scrambling
unscrambling

lamp
amp
camp
champ
clamp
cramp
damp
ramp
revamp
rubber-stamp
scamp
stamp
tramp
vamp

hamper
camper
damper
pamper
scamper
Tampa
tamper

+ You can add to this list by adding ***-er*** to some words that rhyme with ***lamp***, as in ***clamper***

You can also make rhymes for these words by using ***her*** after some words that rhyme with ***lamp***, as in ***clamp her***

ample
trample

→ Many English speakers pronounce some words in section **2.9** (eg *sample*) in such a way that they rhyme with these words

champion
campion
Grampian

tampon
crampon

+ You can also make rhymes for these words by using ***on*** after some words that rhyme with ***lamp***, as in ***stamp on***

1.8

man
Aberfan
also-ran
an
anchorman
angry young man
Ann(e)
artisan
ASEAN (= *Association of Southeast Asian Nations*)
ban
began
billy-can
bipartisan
bogeyman
bran
businessman
Caliban
cameraman
can
Cannes
caravan
carry the can
Catalan
catamaran
clan
Dan
Dian(n)e
divan
extractor fan
fan
flan
flash in the pan
frying pan
gran
handyman
Has(s)an
in the can
Isle of Man
Jan
Japan
jerrican
Joanne
Kirg(h)izstan
Kurdistan
ladies' man
Leanne
man-to-man
Marianne
marzipan
middleman
Milan
muscleman
Nan
newspaperman
non-partisan
Oman
open-plan
Oran
outran
overran
pan
Parmesan
partisan
Peter Pan
plan
ran
reran
Roseanne
Roxan(n)e
scan
sedan
self-made man
signalman
snowman
span
spick-and-span
Stan
Sudan

superman
tan
than
trimaran
van
weatherman
Yerevan
yuan

+ You can also make rhymes for these words by using words in section **1.7** that rhyme with ***jam***

→ Many English speakers pronounce some words in section **2.10** (eg *Iran*) in such a way that they rhyme with these words

manner
Anna
bandan(n)a
banner
Deanna
Diana
Fermanagh
Hannah
Havana
Indiana
Joanna
Louisiana
manor
Montana
planner
Pollyanna
Savannah
savanna(h)
scanner
spanner
Susanna(h)
tanner

+ You can also make rhymes for these words by using ***her*** after some words that rhyme with ***man***, as in ***fan her***

→ Many English speakers pronounce some words in section **2.10** (eg *Guyana*) in such a way that they rhyme with these words

channel
cross-Channel
flannel
panel

panelling
channelling

panellist
analyst
psychoanalyst

cannon
canon
Rhiannon
Shannon

cannery
granary
tannery

Britannia
cannier
pannier
Tanya

nanny
Annie
canny
cranny
Danny
Fanny
granny
Omani
trannie
uncanny

panic
Germanic
Hispanic
inorganic
Koranic
manic
mechanic
messianic
oceanic
organic
satanic
Titanic
titanic
volcanic

mechanical
botanical
puritanical
tyrannical

unanimous
magnanimous

planning
Bernard Manning
overmanning
undermanning

+ You can add to this list by adding ***-ning*** to some words that rhyme with ***man***, as in ***banning***

ban(n)ister
canister

vanish
banish
Spanish

planet
gannet
granite
Janet
pomegranate

+ You can also make rhymes for these words by using ***it*** after some words that rhyme with ***man***, as in ***ban it***

sanitary
interplanetary
planetary

vanity
Christianity
humanity
inanity
inhumanity
insanity
profanity
sanity
urbanity

bank
blank
clank
crank
dank
drank
flank
franc
Frank
frank
Girobank
Hank
lank
outflank
plank
point-blank
prank
rank
sank
shank
shrank
spank
stank
swank
tank
thank
Yank
yank

banker
anchor
Bianca
canker
Casablanca
hanker
lingua franca
rancour
Sri Lanka
supertanker
tanker

+ You can add to this list by adding *-er* to some words that rhyme with ***bank***, as in ***flanker***

You can also make rhymes for these words by using ***her*** after some words that rhyme with ***bank***, as in ***thank her***

ankle
rankle

lanky
cranky
Frankie
hanky
hanky-panky
manky
swanky
Yankee

spanking
ranking
telebanking

+ You can add to this list by adding *-ing* to some words that rhyme with ***bank***, as in ***tanking***

frankly
Bill Shankly
blankly
dankly
lankly
rankly

hand
ampersand
and
band
bland
borderland
brand
cash in hand
close at hand
contraband
crash-land
disband
Euroland
expand
fat of the land
Ferdinand
gland
grand
hand-to-hand
hinterland
inland
land
lend a hand
lie of the land
Maryland
misunderstand
motherland
near at hand
Newfoundland
no man's land
offhand
one-night stand
overland
pituitary gland
rand
Rio Grande
sand
second-hand
sleight of hand
stagehand
stand
strand
Swaziland
Switzerland
tanned
underhand
understand
unmanned
unplanned
withstand
Wonderland

+ You can add to this list by adding ***-ned*** to some words that rhyme with ***man***, as in ***banned***

→ Many English speakers pronounce some words in section **2.10** (eg *command*) in such a way that they rhyme with these words

panda
Amanda
backhander
bystander
candour
coriander
dander
gander
Icelander
Laplander
left-hander
meander
memoranda
Miranda
oleander
pander
philander
propaganda
right-hander
Rwanda
salamander
Uganda
veranda(h)

+ You can add to this list by adding ***-er*** to some words that rhyme with ***hand***, as in ***grander***

+ You can also make rhymes for these words by using ***her*** after some words that rhyme with ***hand***, as in ***understand her***

→ Many English speakers pronounce some words in section **2.10** (eg *slander*) in such a way that they rhyme with these words

standard
meandered
pandered
substandard

handle
candle
dandle
fly off the handle
mishandle
sandal
scandal
vandal

vandalize
scandalize

random
memorandum
tandem

+ You can add to this list by adding ***'em*** to some words that rhyme with ***hand***, as in ***stand 'em***

abandon
Rwandan
Ugandan

handy
Andy
bandy
brandy
Candy
candy
dandy
Indira Gandhi
Mahatma Gandhi
Mandy
Randy
Sandy
sandy
shandy

landed
backhanded
cack-handed
candid
candied
empty-handed
even-handed
expanded
heavy-handed
high-handed
left-handed
red-handed
right-handed

+ You can add to this list by adding ***-ed*** to some words that rhyme with ***hand***, as in ***branded***

candidly
single-handedly

landing
expanding
long-standing
misunderstanding
notwithstanding
outstanding
standing
understanding
upstanding

+ You can add to this list by adding ***-ing*** to some words that rhyme with ***hand***, as in ***branding***

brandish
outlandish

handbag
sandbag

grandly
blandly

Sandra
Cassandra

Andrea
Alexandria

handstand
bandstand
grandstand

hang
bang
boomerang
clang
fang
gang
go with a bang
harangue
meringue
orang-outan(g)
overhang
pang
rang
sang
slang
sprang
tang
twang

anger
banger
Bangor
clanger
cliffhanger
hangar
hanger
languor

+ You can also make rhymes for these words by using *her* after some words that rhyme with *hang*, as in ***harangue her***

angle
bangle
dangle
disentangle
entangle
jangle
mangle
quadrangle
rectangle
spangle
strangle
tangle
untangle
wangle
wide-angle
wrangle

tangled
newfangled

+ You can add to this list by adding *-d* to some words that rhyme with ***angle***, as in ***entangled***

mango
quango
tango

angling
dangling
gangling
jangling
wrangling

anguish
languish

angular
rectangular
triangular

manhandle
panhandle

manly
Stanley
unmanly

expanse
askance
finance
manse
Penzance
romance

→ Many English speakers pronounce some words in section **2.10** (eg *dance*) in such a way that they rhyme with these words

cancer
Cancer
necromancer
romancer

→ Many English speakers pronounce some words in section **2.10** (eg *answer*) in such a way that they rhyme with these words

ransom
handsome
king's ransom
transom

fancy
chancy
Clancy
flights of fancy
Nancy
nancy
necromancy
trancey

financial
circumstantial
insubstantial
substantial

financially
substantially

mansion
expansion

pant
ant
cant
commandant
decant
extant
gallivant
rant
recant
scant
sycophant

→ Many English speakers pronounce some words in section **2.10** (eg *plant*) in such a way that they rhyme with these words

banter
Atlanta
canter
decanter
manta
Santa
Tam o' Shanter

+ You can add to this list by adding *-er* to some words that rhyme with ***pant***, as in ***ranter***

phantom
bantam

scanty
Alicante
ante
anti
Dante
dilettante
shanty
vigilante

→ Many English speakers pronounce some words in section **2.10** (eg *auntie*) in such a way that they rhyme with these words

frantic
Atlantic
gigantic
pedantic
romantic
semantic
sycophantic
transatlantic
unromantic

antics
semantics

elephantine
Byzantine

tantrum
Antrim

pantry
gantry

pants
flying by the seat of one's pants
Hants
Northants
smarty-pants
underpants

+ You can add to this list by adding *-s* to some words that rhyme with ***pant***, as in ***ants***

panther
Samantha

philanthropist
misanthropist

spaniel
Daniel
Nathaniel

canyon
companion

annual
manual
Victor Emmanuel

annually
manually

bonanza
extravaganza
Mario Lanza
panzer
stanza

stanzas
Kansas

+ You can add to this list by adding *-s* to some words that rhyme with ***bonanza***, as in ***extravaganzas***

1.9

cap
bap
booby-trap
chap
clap
feather in one's cap
flap
gap
handicap
lap
Lapp
map
nap
overlap
pap
put on one's thinking cap
rap
sap
scrap
slap
snap
strap
take the rap
tap
thunderclap

trap
unwrap
wrap
yap
zap

rapper
Ayia Napa
clapper
dapper
sapper
slapper
trapper
whippersnapper
wrapper
zapper

> + You can add to this list by adding *-per* to some words that rhyme with *cap*, as in *flapper*
>
> You can also make rhymes for these words by using *her* after some words that rhyme with *cap*, as in *trap her*

apple
chapel
dapple
grapple

happy
chappie
flappy
gappy
happy-clappy
make it snappy
nappy
sappy
scrappy
snappy
unhappy
zappy

rapid
vapid

happily
sappily
scrappily
snappily
unhappily

happiness
sappiness
snappiness
unhappiness

wrapping
clapping
strapping
tapping

> + You can add to this list by adding *-ping* to some words that rhyme with *cap*, as in *snapping*

strapless
hapless

shrapnel
grapnel

lapse
collapse
elapse
perhaps
relapse

> + You can add to this list by adding *-s* to some words that rhyme with *cap*, as in *snaps*

caption
contraption

apt
adapt
chapped
handicapped
inapt
rapt
untapped

> + You can add to this list by adding *-ped* to some words that rhyme with *cap*, as in *trapped*

chapter
adapter
captor
raptor

capture
enrapture
rapture
recapture

1.10

Barra
Far(r)ah

Arab
carob

parable
arable

paragon
tarragon

barrel
apparel
carol
Carol(e)
Darryl
Lewis Carroll

Carolyn
Marilyn

Harold
double-barrelled

> + You can add to this list by adding *-led* to some words that rhyme with *barrel*, as in *carolled*

barren
Arran
baron

Darren
Karen
Sharon

apparent
transparent

embarrass
harass

embarrassed
harassed

carrot
carat
claret
garret
parrot

narrative
comparative

barrier
carrier
farrier
harrier

+ You can also make rhymes for these words by using *her* after some words that rhyme with *carry*, as in *marry her*

Marion
carrion

chariot
Harriet

carry
Barry
Carrie
Gar(r)y
Harry
harry
intermarry
Larry
marry
miscarry
parry
remarry
tarry (= *to dawdle*)

barbaric
Balearic
Tariq

married
arid
carried
harried
parried
tarried
unmarried

marriage
carriage
disparage
garage
hackney carriage
miscarriage
shotgun marriage
undercarriage

Harris
Paris

garrison
comparison

charity
barbarity
Charity
clarity
disparity
dissimilarity
familiarity
hilarity
irregularity
parity
peculiarity
polarity
popularity
regularity
similarity
solidarity
subsidiarity
unpopularity
vulgarity

arrow
barrow
harrow
Jarrow
marrow
narrow
sparrow
tarot
wheelbarrow

1.11

ass
alas
amass
bass (= *a fish*)
Calor Gas®
crass
en masse
gas
jackass
Kiribati
lass
mass
morass

→ Many English speakers pronounce some words in section **2.13** (eg *class*) in such a way that they rhyme with these words

Nasser
Mombasa
NASA (= *National Aeronautics and Space Administration*)

hassle
tassel

Vaseline®
gasoline

gassy
Cassie
chassis
Haile Selassie
Tallahassee

→ Many English speakers pronounce some words in section **2.13** (eg *classy*) in such a way that they rhyme with these words

classic
boracic
Jurassic
thoracic
Triassic

acid
flaccid
placid

classify
declassify
pacify

assassinate
fascinate

asset
basset
facet
tacit

acetate
incapacitate

capacity
audacity
incapacity
overcapacity
sagacity
tenacity
veracity
vivacity

massive
impassive
passive

massively
impassively
passively

Picasso
Burkina-Faso
El Paso

Alaska
Madagascar
Nebraska

+ You can also make rhymes for these words by using ***her*** after some words that rhyme with ***ask***, as in ***unmask her***

gasket
blow a gasket
mascot

→ Many English speakers pronounce some words in section **2.13** (eg *basket*) in such a way that they rhyme with these words

lambast
enthusiast

+ You can add to this list by adding ***-ed*** to some words that rhyme with ***ass***, as in ***amassed***

→ Many English speakers pronounce some words in section **2.13** (eg *last*) in such a way that they rhyme with these words

pasta
alabaster
aster

→ Many English speakers pronounce some words in section **2.13** (eg *master*) in such a way that they rhyme with these words

pasty
osteoplasty
rhinoplasty

→ Many English speakers pronounce some words in section **2.13** (eg *nasty*) in such a way that they rhyme with these words

plastic
bombastic
drastic
dynastic
ecclesiastic
elastic
enthusiastic
fantastic
gymnastic
iconoclastic
monastic
overenthusiastic
sarcastic
scholastic
spastic
unenthusiastic

sarcastically
drastically
enthusiastically
fantastically

1.12

smash
ash
balderdash
bash
brash
cache
cash
clash
crash
cut a dash
dash
flash
gash

gnash
hard cash
hash
have a bash
Johnny Cash
lash
mash
moustache
panache
pebbledash
quick as a flash
rash
rehash
sash
slapdash
slash
splash
stash
thrash
trash
Wall Street Crash

sachet
papier-mâché

rasher
flasher
Natasha
smasher

> You can add to this list by adding *-er* to some words that rhyme with ***smash***, as in ***basher***
>
> You can also make rhymes for these words by using ***her*** after some words that rhyme with ***smash***, as in ***splash her***

passion
ashen
compassion
fashion
parrot-fashion
ration

fashionable
rationable
unfashionable

national
international
irrational
multinational
rational
supranational

rationally
internationally
irrationally
nationally

nationalist
rationalist

nationalism
rationalism

nationalize
denationalize
rationalize

passionate
compassionate
dispassionate

old-fashioned
impassioned

> You can add to this list by adding *-ed* to some words that rhyme with ***passion***, as in ***rationed***

flashy
ashy
trashy

smashing
crashing
dashing
flashing

> You can add to this list by adding *-ing* to some words that rhyme with ***smash***, as in ***lashing***

flashback
cashback

rashly
Ashley

smashed
abashed
unabashed

> You can add to this list by adding *-ed* to some words that rhyme with ***smash***, as in ***flashed***

1.13

cat
acrobat
Anwar Sadat
aristocrat
at
autocrat
automat
bat
brat
bureaucrat
chat
Cheshire cat
copycat
cravat
Democrat
democrat
diplomat
drat
drowned rat
expat
fat
fat cat
flat
GATT (= *General Agreement on Tariffs and Trade*)
gnat
habitat
hat
just like that
mat

Matt
matt
Montserrat
Mount Ararat
Nat
Pat
pat
Photostat®
pit-a-pat
plait
Postman Pat
prat
Rabat
rat
rat-a-tat
resat
sat
scat
slat
spat
sprat
tat
that
thermostat
tit-for-tat
VAT
vat

pâté
latte
satay

matter
batter
bespatter
chatter
clatter
flatter
Jomo Kenyatta
latter
mad as a hatter
natter
patter
platter
Qatar
regatta
scatter
shatter
spatter
splatter

> + You can add to this list by adding ***-(t)er*** to some words that rhyme with ***cat***, as in ***fatter***
>
> You can also make rhymes for these words by using ***her*** after some words that rhyme with ***cat***, as in ***pat her***

battered
tattered

> + You can add to this list by adding ***-ed*** to some words that rhyme with ***matter***, as in ***shattered***

battle
cattle
chattel
embattle
half the battle
prattle
rattle
Seattle
tattle
tittle-tattle

latterly
Natalie
philately

atom
EURATOM (= *European Atomic Energy Community*)

> + You can add to this list by adding ***'em*** to some words that rhyme with ***cat***, as in ***at 'em***

flatten
baton
batten
fatten
General Patton
Lord Mountbatten
Manhattan
pattern
Staten

battery
cattery
flattery
Qatari

flattering
earth-shattering
shattering
smattering
unflattering

> + You can add to this list by adding ***-ing*** to some words that rhyme with ***matter***, as in ***splattering***

chatty
batty
Bugatti
catty
Cincinnati
fatty
James Hanratty
Hattie
Maserati
natty
Patty
ratty
scatty
tatty

static
acrobatic
Adriatic
aquatic
aristocratic
aromatic
Asiatic
asthmatic

attic
autocratic
automatic
axiomatic
bureaucratic
charismatic
climatic
democratic
diplomatic
dogmatic
dramatic
ecstatic
emphatic
enigmatic
erratic
fanatic
idiomatic
idiosyncratic
lymphatic
melodramatic
operatic
phlegmatic
pneumatic
pragmatic
problematic
psychosomatic
rheumatic
schematic
semiautomatic
symptomatic
systematic
thematic
traumatic
undemocratic
undiplomatic
unemphatic
unsystematic

fanatical
grammatical
mathematical
problematical
sabbatical

dramatically
automatically
democratically
emphatically
grammatically

mathematics
acrobatics

+ You can add to this list by adding *-s* to some words that rhyme with ***static***, as in ***rheumatics***

gratify
ratify

satin
Latin

+ You can also make rhymes for these words by using ***in*** after some words that rhyme with ***cat***, as in ***sat in***

gratitude
attitude
ingratitude
latitude
platitude

plateau
château
gâteau

plateaux
châteaux
gâteaux

catfish
flatfish

atlas
hatless

flatly
Clement Attlee

psychiatric
geriatric
hat trick
paediatric
Patrick

geriatrics
paediatrics

matrimony
patrimony

catch
attach
batch
detach
dispatch
hatch
latch
man of the match
match
meet one's match
patch
purple patch
scratch
slanging match
snatch
thatch

oystercatcher
Margaret Thatcher

+ You can add to this list by adding *-er* to some words that rhyme with ***catch***, as in ***dispatcher***

You can also make rhymes for these words by using ***her*** after some words that rhyme with ***catch***, as in ***snatch her***

catchy
patchy
scratchy

matching
catching
eye-catching

+ You can add to this list by adding *-ing* to some words that rhyme with ***catch***, as in ***snatching***

hatchet
ratchet

> ➕ You can also make rhymes for these words by using *it* after some words that rhyme with ***catch***, as in ***snatch it***

attachment
catchment
detachment

detached
semidetached
unattached

> ➕ You can add to this list by adding *-ed* to some words that rhyme with ***catch***, as in ***matched***

1.14

gather
blather
lather

1.15

homeopath
Kath
osteopath
psychopath

> ➕ You can also make rhymes for these words by using words in section **1.4** that rhyme with ***naff***

> ➔ Many English speakers pronounce some words in section **2.18** (eg *path*) in such a way that they rhyme with these words

telepathic
homeopathic
osteopathic
psychopathic

> ➕ You can also make rhymes for these words by using words in section **1.4** that rhyme with ***graphic***

1.16

cadaver
slaver

> ➔ Many English speakers pronounce some words in section **2.19** (eg *palaver*) in such a way that they rhyme with these words

travel
gavel
gravel
unravel

traveller
unraveller

travelling
unravelling

cavern
Cavan
Gavin
tavern

ravenous
cavernous

savage
ravage

lavish
ravish

gravity
cavity
depravity

1.17

jazz
as
Gaz
has
La Paz
razzmatazz
whereas

dazzle
Basil
basil
frazzle
razzle dazzle

chasm
enthusiasm
spasm

jazzy
snazzy

jasmine
Jasmine
Yasmin

Section 2
-AR-

All the words in this section use the sound **-ar-** (as in c*ar*t, b*ar*ber, al*ar*m) in their main stressed syllable

2.1

car
abattoir
Accra
afar
ajar
APR (= *annual percentage rate*)
are
Armagh
armoured car
au revoir
baa
bah
bar
bazaar
below par
bizarre
Bogotá
bra
budgerigar
catarrh
caviar(e)
char
cigar
czar
Daily Star
debar
ER
Eurostar®
fa(h)
far
GDR (= *German Democratic Republic*)
guitar
hurrah
hussar
isobar
jar
Kandahar
la(h)
Loire
ma
mar
MLR (= *minimum lending rate*)
motorcar
Myanmar
OCR (= *optical character reader*)
Omaha
OR (= *operating room*)
pa
papa
par
PR (= *public relations*)
R
R & R (= *rest and recreation*)
registrar
repertoire
reservoir
scar
seminar
shah
Shangri-La
SLR (= *single-lens reflex*)
spa
spar
star
Stranraer
superstar
ta
tar
ta-ta
tsar
um and aah
UNHCR (= *UN High Commissioner for Refugees*)
USSR
VCR (= *video cassette recorder*)
VTR (= *video tape recorder*)
Zanzibar

cacao
Bilbao

2.2

garb
barb

barber
harbour
macabre
Pearl Harbor

marble
garble
Kabul

garbled
marbled

Barbie
Abu Dhabi
Derby
derby
Robert Mugabe

Barbara
candelabra
Santa Barbara

2.3

mark
arc
ark
Bach
bark
black mark
clerk
Cutty Sark
dark
disembark
double-park
embark
hark
in the dark
Iraq
Jurassic Park
lark
leap in the dark
macaque
Mark
miss the mark
narc
nark
park
plaque
quark
remark
Sark
shark
spark
stark
trademark
watermark

marker
bookmarker
Charlie Parker
Lusaka
markka
nosy parker
Osaka
parka

+ You can add to this list by adding *-er* to some words that rhyme with ***mark***, as in ***darker***

sparkle
debacle
matriarchal
patriarchal

carcass
Marcus

+ You can also make rhymes for these words by using ***us*** after some words that rhyme with ***mark***, as in ***mark us***

narky
hierarchy
Iraqi
khaki
matriarchy
Nagasaki
oligarchy
patriarchy
sparky

marking
parking

+ You can add to this list by adding *-ing* to some words that rhyme with ***mark***, as in ***remarking***

marked
double-parked
unmarked

+ You can add to this list by adding *-ed* to some words that rhyme with ***mark***, as in ***sparked***

2.4

card
avant-garde
baaed
bard
battle-scarred
bodyguard
bombard
boulevard
charade
charred
discard
disregard
façade
guard
hard
Hyderabad
Islamabad
lard
leotard
Marquis de Sade
promenade
regard
retard
rock-hard
shard
yard

+ You can add to this list by adding *-red* to some words that rhyme with ***car***, as in ***barred***

larder
ardour
cicada
Douglas Bader
Granada
Lada

Lake Garda
Nevada
RADA (= *Royal Academy of Dramatic Art*)
Sierra Nevada
Torquemada

> + You can add to this list by adding *-er* to some words that rhyme with *card*, as in ***harder***
>
> You can also make rhymes for these words by using ***her*** after some words that rhyme with *card*, as in ***guard her***

garden
harden
Osama bin Laden
pardon

pardonable
hardenable
unpardonable

hardened
battle-hardened
pardoned

hardy
Bacardi®
foolhardy
Keir Hardie
Laurel and Hardy
tardy
Yardie

guarded
retarded
unguarded

> + You can add to this list by adding *-ed* to some words that rhyme with *card*, as in ***discarded***

bravado
avocado
Colorado
cruzado
incommunicado
The Mikado

cardboard
hardboard

large
barge
charge
discharge
enlarge
in charge
marge
overcharge
recharge
undercharge

enlarger
supercharger
turbo-charger

> + You can add to this list by adding *-r* to some words that rhyme with ***large***, as in ***charger***
>
> You can also make rhymes for these words by using ***her*** after some words that rhyme with ***large***, as in ***discharge her***

2.5

graph
autograph
barf
behalf
calf
cardiograph
cenotaph
chaff
choreograph
electrocardiograph
epitaph
giraffe
half
laugh
lithograph
monograph
paragraph
photograph
scarf
seismograph
staff
telegraph

> + You can also make rhymes for these words by using words in section **2.18** that rhyme with ***path***

> → Many English speakers pronounce some words in section **1.4** (eg *carafe*) in such a way that they rhyme with these words

staffing
laughing
overstaffing
understaffing

> + You can add to this list by adding *-ing* to some words that rhyme with ***graph***, as in ***chaffing***

craft
abaft
aft
daft
draft
draught
graft
handicraft
hovercraft
needlecraft

overdraft
overstaffed
raft
redraft
shaft
staffed
understaffed

> + You can add to this list by adding *-ed* to some words that rhyme with ***graph***, as in ***laughed***

after
grafter
happily ever after
hereafter
laughter
rafter
sought-after
thereafter

> → Many English speakers pronounce some words in section **1.4** (eg *BAFTA*) in such a way that they rhyme with these words

crafty
draughty

craftsman
draughtsman

2.6

saga
Aga®
lager

jargon
bargain

cargo
Chicago
embargo
lago
largo
Margo(t)
Santiago

2.7

Oahu
Binyamin Netanyahu

2.8

snarl
banal
Basle
Bhopal
corral
Guadalcanal
Jamal
Kamal
Karl
locale
marl
morale
Natal
Neanderthal
Roald Dahl
Thor Heyerdahl
Transvaal

gnarled
snarled

koala
Carla
gala
Guatemala
Kampala
Mahler
parlour

Harlem
slalom

> + You can add to this list by adding *'em* to some words that rhyme with ***snarl***, as in ***corral 'em***

Marlon
Guatemalan

Bali
barley
Bob Marley
Carly
Charlie
finale
Mali
Muhammad Ali
parley
Salvador Dali
Somali
Svengali

darling
starling

> + You can add to this list by adding *-(l)ing* to some words that rhyme with ***snarl***, as in ***corralling***

scarlet
Charlotte
Scarlett
starlet
starlit

Harlow
Carlow
Jean Harlow
Monte Carlo
St Malo

Charles
Arles
Ray Charles

> + You can add to this list by adding *-s* to some words that rhyme with ***snarl***, as in ***locales***

2.9

arm
alarm
Animal Farm

balm
calm
chance one's arm
charm
Dar es Salaam
disarm
embalm
farm
give one's right arm
grease someone's palm
Guam
harm
ma'am
palm
psalm
qualm
rearm

charmer
armour
Dalai Lama
drama
farmer
llama
melodrama
Osama
panorama
Parma
self-harmer
Vasco da Gama
Yokohama

+ You can add to this list by adding *-er* to some words that rhyme with ***arm***, as in ***embalmer***

You can also make rhymes for these words by using ***her*** after some words that rhyme with ***arm***, as in ***charm her***

barman
Carmen
Tutankhamen

pyjamas
Bahamas

+ You can add to this list by adding ***-s*** to some words that rhyme with ***charmer***, as in ***dramas***

army
balmy
barmy
macramé
origami
pastrami
salami
smarmy

charming
alarming
disarming
farming

+ You can add to this list by adding *-ing* to some words that rhyme with ***arm***, as in ***calming***

armed
becalmed
unarmed
unharmed

+ You can add to this list by adding *-ed* to some words that rhyme with ***arm***, as in ***charmed***

sample
example

alms
Brahms
Glamis
up in arms

+ You can add to this list by adding ***-s*** to some words that rhyme with ***arm***, as in ***charms***

2.10

barn
Afghanistan
Aga Khan
Aswan
Azerbaijan
Bhutan
darn
Don Juan
elan
Genghis Khan
Iran
Kazak(h)stan
Koran
Kublai Khan
Moshe Dayan
naan
Pakistan
Ramadan
San Juan
Sian
spin a yarn
Tadzhikistan
Taiwan
Teh(e)ran
Turkmenistan
Uzbekistan
yarn

banana
Botswana
Dana
Ghana
Guyana
gymkhana
iguana
Ivana
Juliana
Ljubljana
marijuana
nirvana

piranha
sultana
Tijuana
Tirana

blarney
Azerbaijani
Barney
Killarney
Pakistani

varnish
garnish
tarnish

garnet
Alf Garnett
Barnet
incarnate

soprano
oregano

demand
command
countermand
remand
reprimand

+ You can add to this list by adding *-ed* to some words that rhyme with ***barn***, as in ***darned***

slander
Alexander
commander

+ You can add to this list by adding *-er* to some words that rhyme with ***demand***, as in ***reprimander***

You can also make rhymes for these words by using ***her*** after some words that rhyme with ***demand***, as in ***reprimand her***

commanding
demanding
undemanding

+ You can add to this list by adding *-ing* to some words that rhyme with ***demand***, as in ***reprimanding***

dance
advance
Afrikaans
chance
enhance
entrance (= *to charm*)
France
glance
lance
prance
stance
trance

→ Many English speakers pronounce some words in section **1.8** (eg *askance*) in such a way that they rhyme with these words

dancer
answer
lancer

+ You can add to this list by adding *-r* to some words that rhyme with ***dance***, as in ***prancer***

You can also make rhymes for these words by using ***her*** after some words that rhyme with ***dance***, as in ***entrance her***

dancing
advancing
chancing
enhancing
entrancing
glancing
lancing
prancing

plant
aren't
aunt
can't
chant
confidante
débutant(e)
enchant
grant
implant
shan't
slant
supplant
transplant

→ Many English speakers pronounce some words in section **1.8** (eg *commandant*) in such a way that they rhyme with these words

auntie
slanty

→ Many English speakers pronounce some words in section **1.8** (eg *Dante*) in such a way that they rhyme with these words

slanting
enchanting

+ You can add to this list by adding *-ing* to some words that rhyme with ***plant***, as in ***granting***

branch
avalanche
blanch
Blanche
carte blanche
ranch

2.11

sharp
carp
harp
razor-sharp

2.12

mascara
Che Guevara
Clara
Guadalajara
Lara
Sahara
Sara
Tamara
Tara
tiara
Zara

aria
Gran Canaria
starrier

starry
Campari
Ferrari
Harare
Marie
safari
sari
tarry (= *like tar*)

scenario
impresario
Lothario
worst-case scenario

barring
jarring

+ You can add to this list by adding ***-ring*** to some words that rhyme with ***car***, as in ***starring***

guitarist
tsarist

Faro
Kilimanjaro

2.13

pass
bold as brass
brass
class
farce
fibreglass
first-class
glass
grass
hourglass
Madras
middle-class
outclass
overpass
second-class
snake in the grass
sparse
stained glass
supergrass
surpass
underclass
underpass
upper-class
working-class

passable
classable
impassable
surpassable
unsurpassable

castle
parcel

parson
arson
fasten
unfasten

classy
brassy
glassy
grassy

glasses
classes
eyeglasses
sunglasses

+ You can add to this list by adding ***-(e)s*** to some words that rhyme with ***pass***, as in ***farces***

ask
bask
Basque
cask
flask
mask
task
unmask

basket
breadbasket
casket

+ You can also make rhymes for these words by using ***it*** after some words that rhyme with ***ask***, as in ***mask it***

parsley
sparsely

grasp
clasp
gasp
rasp

last
aghast
Belfast
blast

blast from the past
breathe one's last
cast
caste
contrast
Elastoplast®
fast
Gormenghast
half-mast
hard-and-fast
mast
miscast
nail one's colours to the mast
opencast
outlast
overcast
past
repast
too good to last
unsurpassed
vast

+ You can add to this list by adding *-ed* to some words that rhyme with *pass*, as in ***surpassed***

master
bandmaster
broadcaster
castor
court disaster
disaster
headmaster
housemaster
newscaster
pastor
paymaster
plaster
postmaster
quartermaster
ringmaster
schoolmaster
scoutmaster
taskmaster

+ You can add to this list by adding *-er* to some words that rhyme with *last*, as in ***faster***

You can also make rhymes for these words by using ***her*** after some words that rhyme with *last*, as in ***blast her***

plastered
mastered

nasty
contrasty

lasting
broadcasting
casting
contrasting
everlasting
long-lasting

+ You can add to this list by adding *-ing* to some words that rhyme with *last*, as in ***fasting***

cast-off
blast-off

ghastly
lastly
vastly

2.14

mirage
arbitrage
barrage
camouflage
corsage
entourage
espionage
fuselage
massage
sabotage

2.15

harsh
marsh

→ Many English speakers pronounce some words in section **1.12** (eg *moustache*) in such a way that they rhyme with these words

partial
court-martial
impartial
marshal
martial

2.16

part
apart
applecart
art
Bart
cart
change of heart
chart
counterpart
dart
depart
heart
heart-to-heart
impart
outsmart
poles apart
scart
smart
start
state-of-the-art
tart
young at heart

starter
barter

charter
Djakarta
garter
Jimmy Carter
La Traviata
martyr
nonstarter
pro rata
Renata
self-starter
sonata
Sparta
stigmata
strata
Tartar
tartar

+ You can add to this list by adding *-er* to some words that rhyme with ***part***, as in ***smarter***

You can also make rhymes for these words by using ***her*** after some words that rhyme with ***part***, as in ***start her***

smarten
carton
hearten
kindergarten
spartan
tartan

heartening
disheartening
smartening

party
Abigail's Party
arty
chapati
hale and hearty
hearty
karate
multiparty
one-party
tarty

article
particle

downhearted
big-hearted
brokenhearted
cold-hearted
faint-hearted
half-hearted
hard-hearted
kind-hearted
light-hearted
lion-hearted
softhearted
stouthearted
tenderhearted
uncharted
warm-hearted
wholehearted

+ You can add to this list by adding *-ed* to some words that rhyme with ***part***, as in ***started***

parting
starting

+ You can add to this list by adding *-ing* to some words that rhyme with ***part***, as in ***smarting***

partly
smartly
tartly

heartless
artless

department
apartment
compartment

Sumatra
Frank Sinatra
Sartre

cartridge
partridge

march
arch
larch
March
parch
starch

archer
departure
Jeffrey Archer
marcher

starchy
Archie
Karachi

2.17

father
farther
founding father
rather

→ Many English speakers pronounce some words in section **1.14** (eg *lather*) in such a way that they rhyme with these words

2.18

path
aftermath
Bath
bath
hearth
lath

+ You can also make rhymes for these words by using words in section **2.5** that rhyme with ***graph***

Arthur
General MacArthur
Martha

2.19

carve
calve
halve
Slav
starve
suave
Yugoslav

lava
balaclava
Bratislava
cassava
Cava
guava
Java
larva
palaver

Harvey
Ravi

starving
calving
carving
halving

halves
calves
go halves
scarves

2.20

Okinawa
Peshawar

2.21

Mars
handlebars
parse
vase

+ You can add to this list by adding *-s* to some words that rhyme with *car*, as in *bars*

plaza
Gaza

Swazi
Benghazi
kamikaze

Section 3
-AY-

All the words in this section use the sound **-ay -** (as in b*ay*, pl*ay*er, aw*ay*) in their main stressed syllable

3.1

day
A
a (= *emphatic form of the indefinite article*)
AA
AAA (= *American Athletic Association*)
AEA (= *Atomic Energy Authority*)
affray
aka (= *also known as*)
allay
alleyway
all work and no play
anyway
array
astray
away
BA
bay
betray
blasé
BMA (= *British Medical Association*)
Bombay
Botany Bay
bouquet
bray
Cabaret
cabaret
caraway
carriageway
castaway
child's play
CIA
clay
CNAA (= *Council for National Academic Awards*)
convey
CSA (= *Child Support Agency*)
DA (= *District Attorney*)
day-to-day
decay
defray
delay
disarray
dismay
disobey
display
DNA
Dorian Gray
Doris Day
dossier
émigré
Ernest Hemingway
ETA (= *estimated time of arrival*)
everyday
FA (= *Football Association*)
faraway
Fay(e)
flay
foldaway
foul play
fray
gainsay
Galloway
gay
Gay(e)
General Pinochet
getaway
giveaway
going-away
grey
halfway
hay
hey
Hogmanay
hooray
Hudson Bay
Hyacinth Bucket
IAEA (= *International Atomic Energy Agency*)
IBA (= *Independent Broadcasting Authority*)
IFA (= *independent financial adviser*)
interplay
inveigh
IPA (= *International Phonetic Alphabet*)
IRA (= *Irish Republican Army*)
J
Jay
jay
K
Kay(e)

LA
Lady Jane Grey
lamé
latter-day
lay
LEA (= *Local Education Authority*)
live for the day
MA (= *Master of Arts*)
Malay
Mandalay
Marseilles
matinée
May
may
MBA (= *Master of Business Administration*)
Michael Faraday
midday
Milky Way
mislay
Monterey
motorway
née
negligée
neigh
Nineveh
NRA (= *National Rifle Association*)
obey
OK
out-of-the-way
outstay
outweigh
overstay
PA
parquet
passageway
passé
pay
pay one's way
play
portray
pray
present-day
prey
protégé
PTA
RA (= *Royal Academy*)
railway
Ray
ray
RDA (= *recommended daily allowance*)
red-letter day
relay
repay
replay
résumé
ricochet
RNA (= *ribonucleic acid*)
RSA (= *Royal Scottish Academy*)
RSPCA
runaway
St-Tropez
Santa Fe
save the day
say
SEA (= *Single European Act*)
seize the day
SFA (= *Scottish Football Association*)
slay
sleigh
spay
splay
spray
stay
Stornoway
straightaway
stray
survey
sway
TA (= *Territorial Army*)
take-home pay
tearaway
the devil to pay
they
today
tourniquet
tray
UDA (= *Ulster Defence Association*)
UK
underlay
USA
V&A (= *Victoria and Albert Museum*)
VOA (= *Voice of America*)
waterway
way
waylay
WBA (= *World Boxing Association*)
WEA (= *Workers' Educational Association*)
weigh
whey
workaday
yea
yesterday
YMCA
YWCA

layer
bricklayer
Eritrea
Marbella
player
purveyor
ratepayer
soothsayer
surveyor
taxpayer

+ You can add to this list by adding ***-er*** to some words that rhyme with ***day***, as in ***betrayer***

You can also make rhymes for these words by using ***her*** after some words that rhyme with ***day***, as in ***betray her***

payable
conveyable

decayable
defrayable
playable
portrayable
repayable
surveyable
swayable
unplayable
unsayable
weighable

betrayal
portrayal

Himalayan
Eritrean
Ghanaian
Guinean

conveyance
abeyance

archaic
Judaic
mosaic
prosaic

saying
greying
paying
playing
surveying

> + You can add to this list by adding *-ing* to some words that rhyme with *day*, as in *betraying*

laity
deity
spontaneity

payoff
lay-off
play-off

spray-on
crayon
rayon

Mayo
mayo
Montevideo

3.2

labour
neighbour
sabre
toss the caber

able
Abel
cable
disable
enable
fable
gable
label
Mabel
sable
stable
table
Tower of Babel
unable
under the table
unstable

fabled
disabled

> + You can add to this list by adding *-(le)d* to some words that rhyme with *able*, as in *labelled*

labouring
neighbouring

rabies
scabies

baby
Abie
crybaby
maybe

3.3

make
ache
awake
bake
bellyache
brake
break
cake
drake
fake
flake
for God's sake
for goodness' sake
for heaven's sake
for Pete's sake
forsake
give-and-take
hake
Jake
lake
mistake
on the make
opaque
overtake
partake
quake
rake
rattlesnake
remake
retake
sake
shake
sheik(h)
Sir Francis Drake
slake
snake
stake
steak
take
undertake
wake

baker
acre
bookmaker
breaker
cabinet-maker
caretaker
clockmaker
dressmaker
holidaymaker
housebreaker

icebreaker
Jamaica
lawmaker
maker
matchmaker
meet one's maker
moneymaker
pacemaker
Quaker
shirtmaker
shoemaker
strikebreaker
taker
troublemaker
undertaker
watchmaker

> + You can add to this list by adding ***-r*** to some words that rhyme with ***make***, as in ***partaker***
>
> You can also make rhymes for these words by using ***her*** after some words that rhyme with ***make***, as in ***forsake her***

breakable
mistakable
shakeable
unbreakable
unmistakable
unshakeable

taken
awaken
bacon
bring home the bacon
forsaken
godforsaken
Jamaican
mistaken
overtaken
partaken
reawaken
retaken
shaken
undertaken
waken

takeaway
breakaway

shaky
achy
flaky
wakey wakey

shaking
aching
awaking
backbreaking
baking
bellyaching
braking
breaking
breathtaking
caking
decision-making
dressmaking
epoch-making
faking
flaking
forsaking
ground-breaking
heartbreaking
housebreaking
in the making
leave-taking
loss-making
lovemaking
making
mistaking
moneymaking
muckraking
non-profit-making
overtaking
painstaking
partaking
profit-making
quaking
raking
record-breaking
remaking
retaking
slaking
snaking
staking
stocktaking
taking
undertaking
waking

takeover
makeover

stakeout
breakout
takeout

make-up
break-up
shake-up
take-up

baked
caked
half-baked

> + You can add to this list by adding ***-d*** to some words that rhyme with ***make***, as in ***faked***

3.4

shade
accolade
Adelaide
afraid
aid
aide
arcade
bade
balustrade
barricade
Belgrade
blade
blockade
braid
brigade
brocade
cascade
cavalcade
centigrade

chambermaid
cockade
colonnade
crusade
custom-made
decayed
degrade
dissuade
downgrade
escapade
esplanade
evade
fade
first-aid
forbade
fusillade
glade
grade
grenade
handmade
home-made
inlaid
invade
Jade
jade
laid
lemonade
made
maid
make the grade
man-made
marinade
marmalade
masquerade
mislaid
motorcade
overlaid
overpaid
paid
palisade
parade
persuade
pervade
prepaid
raid
ready-made
remade
renegade
repaid
retrograde
Rollerblade®
serenade
Sinéad
spade
staid
stockade
suede
tailor-made
they'd
tirade
trade
unafraid
underpaid
unmade
unpaid
upbraid
upgrade
wade
waylaid
well-made
well-paid

+ You can add to this list by adding *-ed* to some words that rhyme with ***day***, as in ***delayed***

heyday
Mayday
payday

trader
Ada
cicada
crusader
Darth Vader
Grenada
invader
persuader
raider
wader

+ You can also make rhymes for these words by using ***her*** after some words that rhyme with ***shade***, as in ***evade her***

degradable
biodegradable
evadable
upgradable

cradle
ladle

maiden
Aden
Aidan
doom-laden
laden

stadia
nadir

stadium
radium

Canadian
Barbadian

radiant
gradient

lady
My Fair Lady
Sadie
shady

faded
computer-aided
jaded
shaded
unaided

+ You can add to this list by adding *-(e)d* to some words that rhyme with ***shade***, as in ***traded***

fading
aiding
degrading
grading
shading
trading
upgrading

+ You can add to this list by adding *-ing* to some words that rhyme with ***shade***, as in ***braiding***

tornado
Toledo

Adrian
Adrienne
Hadrian

age
assuage
backstage
cage
disengage
engage
enrage
gauge
offstage
on-stage
over-age
page
Pa(i)ge
rage
rampage
rattle someone's cage
sage
stage
under-age
upstage
wage

wager
John Major
major
pager
old stager
sergeant-major
teenager

+ You can add to this list by adding *-r* to some words that rhyme with ***age***, as in ***rampager***

You can also make rhymes for these words by using ***her*** after some words that rhyme with ***age***, as in ***page her***

courageous
advantageous
contagious
outrageous

+ You can also make rhymes for these words by using ***us*** after some words that rhyme with ***age***, as in ***upstage us***

courageously
advantageously
contagiously
outrageously

raging
ageing
assuaging
caging
disengaging
engaging
enraging
gauging
paging
rampaging
staging
upstaging
waging

waged
aged (as in *aged 10*)
engaged
middle-aged
unwaged

+ You can add to this list by adding *-d* to some words that rhyme with ***age***, as in ***rampaged***

shades
AIDS
Crusades

+ You can add to this list by adding *-s* to some words that rhyme with ***shade***, as in ***parades***

3.5

safe
chafe
Ralph
strafe
unsafe
waif

+ You can also make rhymes for these words by using words in section **3.16** that rhyme with ***faith***

wafer
chafer
safer
UEFA (= *Union of European Football Associations*)

3.6

vague
Craig
Earl Haig
Hague
plague
renege
The Hague

bagel
Hegel
inveigle

pagan
Copenhagen
Ronald Reagan

Las Vegas
plague us
Tagus

Fagin
Menachem Begin

lumbago
sago
San Diego
Tierra del Fuego
Trinidad and Tobago

fragrant
flagrant
vagrant

3.7

mail
Abigail
abseil
ail
ale
assail
avail
bail
bale
bewail
Braille
curtail
dale
derail
entail
exhale
fail
fairytale
fight tooth and nail
fingernail
flail
frail
full-scale
Gail
gale
hail
hale
impale
inhale
jail
kale
male
monorail
nail
nightingale
pail
pale
ponytail
prevail
quail
rail
regale
resale
Richter Scale
sail
sale
scale
shale
snail
stale
tail
tale
they'll
trail
travail
unveil
vale
veil
wail
whale

sailor
Elizabeth Taylor
inhaler
jailer
Leila
loudhailer
Michaela
tailor
trailer
Venezuela
whaler
wholesaler

> + You can add to this list by adding *-(e)r* to some words that rhyme with ***mail***, as in ***frailer***
>
> You can also make rhymes for these words by using *her* after some words that rhyme with ***mail***, as in ***regale her***

available
assailable
saleable
unassailable
unavailable

Australia
azalea
dahlia
paraphernalia
regalia

alien
Alien
Australian
episcopalian
Pygmalion

daily
Benjamin Disraeli
capercaillie
ceilidh
Eilidh
gaily
Hayley
Israeli
scaly
ukulele

sailing
mailing
plain sailing
scaling
unavailing
unfailing
unveiling
whaling

> + You can add to this list by adding *-ing* to some words that rhyme with ***mail***, as in ***trailing***

railings
palings

+ You can add to this list by adding *-s* to some words that rhyme with ***sailing***, as in ***failings***

failed
veiled

+ You can add to this list by adding *-(e)d* to some words that rhyme with ***mail***, as in ***bewailed***

ailment
derailment

scales
Gaels
telesales
Wales

+ You can add to this list by adding *-s* to some words that rhyme with ***mail***, as in ***prevails***

3.8

game
acclaim
aim
became
blame
came
claim
dame
declaim
defame
disclaim
exclaim
fame
flame
frame
inflame
in heaven's name
lame
maim
much the same
name
old flame
overcame
proclaim
put to shame
reclaim
rename
same
shame
tame
what's-her-name
what's-his-name

+ You can also make rhymes for these words by using words in section **3.9** that rhyme with ***pain***

gamer
disclaimer

+ You can add to this list by adding ***-(e)r*** to some words that rhyme with ***game***, as in ***framer***

You can also make rhymes for these words by using ***her*** after some words that rhyme with ***game***, as in ***name her***

layman
Bremen
Damon
Eamonn
shaman
stamen

payment
claimant
down payment
non-payment
overpayment
prepayment
repayment
underpayment

famous
ignoramus
Seamus
world-famous

+ You can also make rhymes for these words by using ***us*** after some words that rhyme with ***game***, as in ***blame us***

Amy
cockamamie
gamy
Jamie

famed
above-named
ashamed
unashamed
unclaimed
unnamed
untamed

+ You can add to this list by adding ***-(e)d*** to some words that rhyme with ***game***, as in ***named***

namely
gamely
lamely
tamely

shameless
aimless
blameless
nameless

games
fan the flames
James
Jesse James

+ You can add to this list by adding *-s* to some words that rhyme with ***game***, as in ***names***

3.9

pain
abstain
aeroplane
arraign
ascertain
attain
Bahrain
bane
brain
Cain
campaign
cane
Cellophane®
chain
champagne
Charlemagne
Charmaine
Citizen Kane
cocaine
complain
constrain
contain
counterpane
crane
Dame Margot Fonteyn
Dane
deign
detain
disdain
domain
down the drain
drain
Duane
El Alamein
Elaine
entertain
explain
feign
gain
Germaine
germane
grain
humane
hurricane
Hussein
hydroplane
inane
inhumane
insane
Jane
John Wayne
lain
lane
Lorraine
main
Maine
maintain
mane
Mark Twain
mundane
obtain
ordain
pane
pertain
plain
plain Jane
plane
polyurethane
profane
rain
raise Cain
refrain
regain
reign
rein
remain
restrain
retain
retrain
right as rain
Saddam Hussein
sane
scatterbrain
Seine
Shane
slain
Spain
sprain
stain
strain
sustain
terrain
train
Ukraine
underlain
urbane
vain
vane
varicose vein
vein
wane
windowpane
with might and main

+ You can also make rhymes for these words by using words in section **3.8** that rhyme with ***game***

trainer
campaigner
container
entertainer
Gaynor
retainer
strainer

+ You can add to this list by adding ***-er*** to some words that rhyme with ***pain***, as in ***abstainer***

You can also make rhymes for these words by using ***her*** after some words that rhyme with ***pain***, as in ***restrain her***

attainable
containable
obtainable
retainable
retrainable
sustainable
trainable
unattainable
uncontainable
unobtainable
unsustainable

anus
heinous
Uranus

+ You can also make rhymes for these words by using *us* after some words that rhyme with ***pain***, as in ***entertain us***

mania
Albania
crania
kleptomania
Lithuania
Mauritania
megalomania
nymphomania
Pennsylvania
pyromania
Romania
Ruritania
Tasmania
the Lusitania
Transylvania

cranium
geranium
titanium
uranium

Romanian
Albanian
Iranian
Jordanian
Lithuanian
Mauritanian
Mediterranean
Panamanian
Pennsylvanian
Ruritanian
subterranean
Tasmanian
Transylvanian
Ukrainian

spontaneous
extraneous
instantaneous
miscellaneous
simultaneous

rainy
Ayatollah Khomeini
Bahraini
brainy
Eugenie
grainy
zany

maniac
brainiac
dipsomaniac
kleptomaniac
megalomaniac
nymphomaniac
pyromaniac

training
entertaining
reigning
remaining
retraining

+ You can add to this list by adding ***-ing*** to some words that rhyme with ***pain***, as in ***restraining***

trained
ingrained
nothing ventured,
  nothing gained
pained
potty-trained
restrained
self-contained
strained
sustained
unexplained
untrained

+ You can add to this list by adding ***-ed*** to some words that rhyme with ***pain***, as in ***remained***

strange
arrange
change
chop and change
exchange
free-range
interchange
long-range
mange
medium-range
range
rearrange
short-change
short-range

danger
endanger
hydrangea
manger
ranger
stranger

+ You can add to this list by adding ***-r*** to some words that rhyme with ***strange***, as in ***arranger***

You can also make rhymes for these words by using ***her*** after some words that rhyme with ***strange***, as in ***change her***

changeable
arrangeable

exchangeable
interchangeable

mangy
rangy

changing
arranging
exchanging
interchanging
ranging
rearranging
short-changing
unchanging
wide-ranging

deranged
estranged
prearranged
unchanged

+ You can add to this list by adding *-d* to some words that rhyme with ***strange***, as in ***changed***

painful
disdainful
gainful

painfully
disdainfully
gainfully

mainly
humanely
inhumanely
insanely
plainly
sanely
ungainly
urbanely
vainly

painless
brainless

attainment
arraignment
ascertainment
containment
detainment
entertainment

brainstorm
rainstorm

paint
acquaint
ain't
complaint
constraint
faint
feint
quaint
repaint
restraint
saint
self-restraint
taint
try the patience of a saint

untainted
unacquainted

+ You can add to this list by adding *-ed* to some words that rhyme with ***paint***, as in ***tainted***

faintly
quaintly
saintly

remains
pick someone's brains
rack one's brains
Staines

+ You can add to this list by adding *-s* to some words that rhyme with ***pain***, as in ***veins***

3.10

ape
cape
crêpe
drape
escape
gaffer tape
gape
grape
in shape
insulating tape
jape
masking tape
measuring tape
nape
out of shape
parcel tape
rape
reshape
scrape
Sellotape®
shape
tape

paper
blotting paper
caper
crêpe paper
draper
flypaper
glasspaper
greaseproof paper
newspaper
notepaper
sandpaper
scraper
skyscraper
taper
tapir
toilet paper
vapour
wallpaper
wastepaper
wrapping paper
writing paper

+ You can also make rhymes for these words by using ***her*** after some words that rhyme with ***ape***, as in ***escape her***

capable
escapable
incapable
inescapable
shapable

staple
maple
papal

staples
maples
Naples

capon
misshapen

rapist
escapist

3.11

face
abase
about-face
ace
anyplace
at a snail's pace
base
bass (= *deep voice*)
brace
breathing space
case
chase
commonplace
cyberspace
database
debase
deface
disgrace
displace
efface
embrace
encase
face-to-face
Grace
grace
interface
in-your-face
lace
Mace®
mace
make a face
marketplace
misplace
not a hair out of place
outer space
pace
pillowcase
place
plaice
pull a face
race
replace
retrace
slap in the face
space
steeplechase
trace
unlace
waste of space

racer
chaser

+ You can add to this list by adding *-r* to some words that rhyme with *face*, as in *defacer*

You can also make rhymes for these words by using *her* after some words that rhyme with *face*, as in *embrace her*

mason
basin
chasten
freemason
hasten
Jason
stonemason
washbasin
wash-hand basin

+ You can also make rhymes for these words by using *in* after some words that rhyme with *face*, as in *place in*

adjacent
complacent

bases
oases
précis (= *summaries*)

racy
Count Basie
Kevin Spacey
lacy
pac(e)y
spacey
Stac(e)y
Trac(e)y

racing
abasing
all-embracing
bracing
casing
chasing
debasing
defacing
disgracing
displacing
effacing
embracing
encasing
facing
gracing
interfacing
lacing
misplacing
north-facing
pacing
placing
replacing
retracing
self-effacing
south-facing
spacing
steeplechasing
tracing
unlacing

basis
oasis

racist
antiracist
bassist
non-racist

evasive
abrasive
invasive
non-invasive
persuasive
pervasive

wayside
Speyside
Tayside

say-so
peso

graceful
caseful
disgraceful

gracefully
disgracefully

faceless
baseless
graceless
spaceless
traceless

basement
casement
debasement
displacement
effacement
encasement
outplacement
placement
replacement

taste
aftertaste
baby-faced
baste
chaste
cut-and-paste
distaste
foretaste
hard-faced
haste
no accounting for taste
paste
poker-faced
posthaste
red-faced
shamefaced
straight-faced
straitlaced
waist
waste

+ You can add to this list by adding *-d* to some words that rhyme with *face*, as in *embraced*

taster
paster
turkey baster
waster

tasty
hasty
pasty (= *pale*)

pasting
basting
time-wasting
wasting

Hastings
Battle of Hastings
pastings

tasteful
distasteful
wasteful

3.12

beige
Liège

Asia
Australasia
Eurasia

→ Many English speakers pronounce some words in section **3.18** (eg *aphasia*) in such a way that they rhyme with these words

Asian
abrasion
Australasian
Caucasian
equation
Eurasian
evasion
invasion
occasion
persuasion
quadratic equation

3.13

racial
facial
interracial
multiracial
palatial
spatial

nation
abbreviation
abdication
aberration
abomination
acceleration
acclamation
accommodation
accumulation
accusation
adaptation
adjudication
administration
admiration
adoration
adulation
adulteration
affectation
affiliation
affirmation
afforestation
aggravation

agitation
allegation
alliteration
allocation
Alsatian
alteration
altercation
amputation
animation
annexation
annihilation
anticipation
application
appreciation
appropriation
approximation
arbitration
articulation
artificial insemination
asphyxiation
aspiration
assassination
assignation
assimilation
association
authorization
automation
aviation
beatification
brutalization
calculation
cancellation
capitalization
carnation
castration
casualization
celebration
cessation
characterization
circulation
citation
civilization
clarification
classification
cohabitation
collaboration
combination
commemoration
commendation
commiseration
communication
compensation
compilation
complication
computation
computerization
concentration
conciliation
condemnation
condensation
confederation
configuration
confirmation
confiscation
confrontation
congregation
conjugation
connotation
consecration
conservation
consideration
consolation
consolidation
constellation
consternation
constipation
consultation
contamination
contemplation
continuation
conurbation
conversation
cooperation
coordination
copulation
coronation
corporation
correlation
corroboration
creation
cremation
Croatian
cross-examination
crustacean
culmination
cultivation
Dalmatian
damnation
decentralization
decimalization
declaration
decoration
dedication
defamation
deflation
deforestation
deformation
degeneration
degradation
dehydration
deindustrialization
delegation
deliberation
demarcation
demobilization
demonstration
denationalization
denomination
denunciation
depopulation
deportation
depravation
deprecation
depreciation
deprivation
deputation
deregulation
derivation
desalination
desecration
desegregation
designation
desolation
desperation
destination
deterioration
determination
detonation
detoxification
devaluation
devastation
deviation
dictation
dilapidation

dilation
discrimination
disinclination
disinformation
disintegration
dislocation
disorganization
disorientation
dispensation
disqualification
dissertation
dissipation
diversification
documentation
domination
donation
duplication
duration
edification
education
ejaculation
elation
electrification
elevation
elimination
emancipation
emendation
emigration
equivocation
escalation
estimation
evacuation
evaluation
evaporation
evocation
exaggeration
examination
exasperation
excavation
exclamation
excommunication
exhalation
exhortation
expectation
explanation
exploitation
exploration
exportation
expropriation
extermination
extrapolation
fascination
federation
fermentation
fixation
flotation
fluctuation
formation
fornication
fortification
foundation
frustration
further education
generalization
generation
gentrification
germination
gestation
globalization
gradation
graduation
gratification
gyration
habitation
Haitian
hallucination
harmonization
hesitation
hibernation
higher education
humiliation
hyperinflation
identification
illumination
illustration
imagination
imitation
immigration
immunization
impersonation
implementation
implication
importation
impregnation
improvisation
inauguration
incantation
incarceration
incarnation
incineration
inclination
incubation
indentation
indication
indignation
indoctrination
infatuation
infiltration
inflammation
inflation
information
inhalation
initiation
innovation
inoculation
insemination
insinuation
inspiration
installation
instigation
instrumentation
insubordination
insulation
integration
interpretation
interrogation
intimidation
intonation
intoxication
investigation
invitation
in vitro fertilization
irradiation
irrigation
irritation
isolation
jollification
jubilation
justification
laceration
lamentation
legalization
legation
legislation

levitation
liberation
limitation
liquidation
litigation
location
lubrication
magnification
manifestation
manipulation
masturbation
matriculation
mediation
medication
meditation
menstruation
migration
misappropriation
miscalculation
misinformation
mispronunciation
misrepresentation
mistranslation
mitigation
moderation
modernization
modification
modulation
mortification
motivation
mouth-to-mouth
 resuscitation
multiplication
mutation
mutilation
nationalization
naturalization
navigation
negation
negotiation
nomination
normalization
notation
notification
no-win situation
obfuscation
obligation
observation
occupation
operation
oration
ordination
organization
orientation
ostentation
ovation
overgeneralization
overpopulation
ovulation
pagination
pale imitation
participation
penetration
perforation
permutation
personification
perspiration
pigmentation
plantation
polarization
pollination
poor relation
population
precipitation
predestination
preoccupation
preparation
presentation
preservation
prevarication
privation
privatization
probation
proclamation
procrastination
procreation
proliferation
pronunciation
propagation
protestation
provocation
publication
punctuation
purification
qualification
quotation
radiation
ramification
ratification
rationalization
reafforestation
recitation
reclamation
recommendation
reconciliation
recreation
recrimination
recuperation
reflation
reforestation
reformation
refrigeration
refutation
regeneration
regimentation
regionalization
registration
regulation
rehabilitation
reincarnation
reinterpretation
reiteration
relation
relaxation
relegation
relocation
remuneration
renovation
reorganization
reparation
repatriation
representation
repudiation
reputation
reservation
resignation
respiration
restoration
resuscitation
retaliation
reunification
revelation
reverberation
rotation

salvation
sanitation
saturation
sedation
segmentation
segregation
self-deprecation
self-determination
self-preservation
sensation
separation
sequestration
simplification
simulation
situation
sophistication
specialization
specification
speculation
stagflation
stagnation
standardization
starvation
station
sterilization
sticky situation
stimulation
stipulation
strangulation
stratification
subordination
suffocation
superannuation
supplication
synchronization
syncopation
taxation
temptation
termination
titillation
tit(t)ivation
toleration
transformation
translation
transplantation
transportation
trepidation
tribulation
undulation
unification
urbanization
vacation
vaccination
validation
valuation
variation
vegetation
veneration
ventilation
verification
vexation
vibration
victimization
vilification
vindication
violation
visualization
vocation

stationer
probationer
vacationer

sensational
coeducational
conversational
denominational
educational
gravitational
navigational
non-denominational
occupational
operational
recreational
representational
vocational

stationary
deflationary
inflationary
probationary
stationery

palpitations
congratulations
Great Expectations
machinations
telecommunications

+ You can add to this list by adding *-s* to some words that rhyme with ***nation***, as in ***sensations***

gracious
audacious
capacious
curvaceous
efficacious
fallacious
flirtatious
loquacious
ostentatious
perspicacious
pugnacious
rapacious
sagacious
salacious
sebaceous
spacious
tenacious
ungracious
vivacious
voracious

satiate
ingratiate

3.14

date
abate
abbreviate
abdicate
accelerate
accentuate
accommodate
accumulate
activate
adjudicate
adulterate
advocate (= *to recommend*)
affiliate
aggravate
agitate
Alexander the Great

alienate
allocate
alternate
amalgamate
amputate
animate (= *to enliven*)
annihilate
annotate
anticipate
appreciate
appropriate (= *to take*)
approximate (= *to be close*)
arbitrate
articulate (= *to speak clearly*)
asphyxiate
assimilate
associate (= *to connect with*)
ate
authenticate
automate
await
backdate
bait
bantamweight
berate
bicarbonate
blind date
calculate
calibrate
candidate
capitulate
captivate
carbonate
castigate
castrate
Catherine the Great
celebrate
chlorinate
circulate
circumnavigate
coagulate
cogitate
collate
commemorate
commentate
commiserate
communicate
compensate
complicate
concentrate
confiscate
congratulate
congregate
conjugate
consecrate
consolidate
consummate
contemplate
cooperate
coordinate (= *to match*)
copperplate
correlate
corroborate
counterweight
crate
create
cremate
cultivate
debate
debilitate
decapitate
decelerate
decimate
decorate
defecate
deflate
deliberate (= *to ponder*)
delineate
denigrate
deprecate
depreciate
deregulate
desecrate
designate
deteriorate
detonate
devastate
dictate
differentiate
dilate
directorate
disintegrate
dislocate
disorientate
disseminate
dissociate
domesticate
dominate
donate
duplicate (= *to make a copy of*)
educate
eight
elevate
elongate
elucidate
emanate
emancipate
emasculate
emigrate
emirate
emulate
encapsulate
enervate
enumerate
enunciate
equate
equivocate
eradicate
escalate
estate
estimate (= *to guess*)
evacuate
evaluate
evaporate
exacerbate
exaggerate
exasperate
excavate
excommunicate
exonerate
expiate
expostulate
expropriate
expurgate
extirpate
extrapolate
extricate
fabricate
fate
featherweight

fête
first-rate
flagellate
fluctuate
flyweight
formulate
freight
frustrate
fumigate
gait
gate
germinate
graduate
grate
gravitate
great
gyrate
hallucinate
hate
heavyweight
hesitate
hibernate
hundredweight
hyphenate
ice-skate
illustrate
imitate
immigrate
impersonate
implicate
impregnate
inaugurate
incarcerate
incinerate
incorporate
incubate
inculcate
indoctrinate
infiltrate
inflate
infuriate
innate
innovate
inoculate
insinuate
instigate
insulate
integrate
interpolate
interrogate
intimate (= *to suggest*)
intimidate
inundate
invalidate
investigate
invigilate
invigorate
irate
irradiate
irrigate
irritate
isolate
Kate
Kuwait
lacerate
late
legislate
legitimate
levitate
liberate
liquidate
locate
lubricate
luxuriate
magistrate
mandate
marinate
mate
mediate
meditate
menstruate
middleweight
migrate
miscalculate
moderate (= *to ease*)
modulate
motivate
mutate
mutilate
narrate
nauseate
navigate
necessitate
negate
negotiate
nominate
numberplate
obviate
one over the eight
operate
orchestrate
orientate
originate
ornate
oscillate
out-of-date
overcompensate
overestimate
overrate
overstate
overweight
ovulate
palpate
palpitate
paperweight
pate (= *head*)
penetrate
percolate
perforate
permeate
perpetrate
perpetuate
placate
plate
pollinate
pontificate
postulate
potentate
precipitate
predate
predominate
prevaricate
procrastinate
procreate
proliferate
propagate
prostrate
pulsate
punctuate
radiate
rate
reactivate
reanimate
recapitulate

reciprocate
re-create
recuperate
redecorate
reflate
refrigerate
regulate
regurgitate
reinstate
rejuvenate
relate
relocate
remunerate
renovate
repatriate
replicate
reprobate
repudiate
resonate
resuscitate
retaliate
reverberate
roller-skate
rotate
salivate
sate
saturate
second-rate
sedate
segregate
sell-by date
separate (= *to part*)
skate
slate
solid-state
spate
speculate
stagnate
state
straight
strait
subjugate
sublimate
subordinate (= *to make subservient*)
substantiate
suffocate
sulphate
suppurate
tabulate
tempt fate
tête-à-tête
third-rate
titillate
tit(t)ivate
tolerate
trait
translate
truncate
ulcerate
underestimate
underrate
underweight
undulate
update
up-to-date
urinate
use-by date
vacate
vaccinate
vacillate
validate
vegetate
ventilate
vibrate
wait
weight
welterweight

later

accelerator
adjudicator
administrator
agitator
alligator
alternator
animator
arbitrator
calculator
cater
collaborator
commentator
coordinator
crater
creator
cultivator
curator
data
decorator
demonstrator
denominator
detonator
dictator
dumb waiter
elevator
equator
escalator
excavator
freighter
gaiter
generator
gladiator
grater
illustrator
imitator
impersonator
incinerator
incubator
indicator
innovator
instigator
interrogator
investigator
invigilator
legislator
liberator
mater
mediator
narrator
navigator
numerator
operator
pater
percolator
perpetrator
peseta
radiator
refrigerator
regulator
respirator
skater
spectator
speculator
traitor
translator

ventilator
vibrator
waiter

+ You can add to this list by adding ***-(e)r*** to some words that rhyme with ***date***, as in ***straighter***

You can also make rhymes for these words by using ***her*** after some words that rhyme with ***date***, as in ***hate her***

debatable
inflatable
translatable
untranslatable

fatal
antenatal
postnatal
prenatal

verbatim
ultimatum

+ You can add to this list by adding ***'em*** to some words that rhyme with ***date***, as in ***hate 'em***

straighten
Len Deighton
Satan
straiten

latent
blatant
patent

blatantly
latently
patently

compensatory
regulatory

status
apparatus
hiatus

+ You can also make rhymes for these words by using ***us*** after some words that rhyme with ***date***, as in ***hate us***

matey
eighty
Haiti
Katie
Kuwaiti
slatey
weighty

fated
agitated
animated
antiquated
associated
bated
belated
calculated
carbonated
celebrated
coin-operated
complicated
constipated
corrugated
cultivated
decaffeinated
deflated
dehydrated
dilapidated
educated
elasticated
elated
electroplated
elevated
emaciated
emancipated
exaggerated
exhilarated
frustrated
gold-plated
graduated
ill-fated
inebriated
infatuated
inflated
integrated
interrelated
intoxicated
invigorated
isolated
liberated
opinionated
outdated
overrated
perforated
performance-related
polyunsaturated
prefabricated
premeditated
related
serrated
silver-plated
simulated
situated
sophisticated
unadulterated
unaffiliated
unappreciated
uncomplicated
uncontaminated
uncoordinated
uncorroborated
uncultivated
undated
underpopulated
uneducated
uninitiated
unrelated
unsophisticated
unsubstantiated
variegated
zero-rated

+ You can add to this list by adding ***-d*** to some words that rhyme with ***date***, as in ***hated***

waiting
accommodating
aggravating
alternating
appreciating
calculating
captivating
debilitating
deprecating
depreciating
devastating
enervating
exasperating
excruciating
exhilarating
fascinating
frustrating
grating
humiliating
ice-skating
illuminating
infuriating
ingratiating
intoxicating
invigorating
irritating
lady-in-waiting
liberating
mating
operating
penetrating
rating
roller-skating
scintillating
skating
stimulating
suffocating
unhesitating
weighting

+ You can add to this list by adding *-ing* to some words that rhyme with *date*, as in *waiting*

native
creative
dative
stative

daytime
playtime

NATO
Plato
potato

grateful
fateful
hateful
ungrateful

lately
greatly
irately
sedately
stately

stateless
dateless
weightless

statement
abatement
overstatement
reinstatement
understatement

lateness
greatness
irateness
sedateness

matron
patron

matriarch
patriarch

3.15

bathe
lathe
swathe

scathing
bathing

3.16

faith
Faith
in good faith
wraith

+ You can also make rhymes for these words by using words in section **3.5** that rhyme with ***safe***

pathos
bathos

3.17

save
aftershave
behave
beyond the grave
brave
cave
concave
crave
Dave
dig one's own grave
early grave
engrave
enslave
forgave
from the cradle to the grave
gave
grave
knave
microwave
misbehave
nave
pave
rant and rave
rave
shave
slave
stave
they've
waive
wave

quaver
demisemiquaver
disfavour

engraver
favour
flavour
life-saver
raver
saver
savour
semiquaver
shaver
waver

+ You can add to this list by adding *-r* to some words that rhyme with ***save***, as in ***braver***

You can also make rhymes for these words by using ***her*** after some words that rhyme with ***save***, as in ***forgave her***

flavourless
savourless

raven
Avon
clean-shaven
graven
haven
shaven
unshaven

bravery
quavery
savoury
slavery
unsavoury

wavering
flavouring
unwavering

+ You can add to this list by adding *-ing* to some words that rhyme with ***quaver***, as in ***favouring***

Moldavia
Octavia
Scandinavia

navy
Davy
gravy
wavy

saving
craving
energy-saving
engraving
enslaving
face-saving
life-saving
paving
raving
shaving
staving
time-saving
waving
waiving

Mavis
Bette Davis
Miles Davis
Steve Davis

depraved
well-behaved

+ You can add to this list by adding *-d* to some words that rhyme with ***save***, as in ***behaved***

bravely
gravely

saviour
behaviour
misbehaviour

3.18

gaze
AAA (= *Amateur Athletic Association*)
ablaze
amaze
appraise
baize
blaze
bolognese
braise
craze
daze
erase
faze
glaze
graze
halcyon days
haze
laze
liaise
maize
malaise
mayonnaise
maze
nowadays
one of these days
paraphrase
phase
phrase
polonaise
praise
raise
raze
reappraise
rephrase
the good old days
the Krays
to coin a phrase
waifs and strays

+ You can add to this list by adding *-s* to some words that rhyme with ***day***, as in ***plays***

laser
blazer
eraser
Fraser
razor

+ You can add to this list by adding ***-r*** to some words that rhyme with ***gaze***, as in ***appraiser***

You can also make rhymes for these words by using ***her*** after some words that rhyme with ***gaze***, as in ***praise her***

nasal
appraisal
Hazel
hazel

brazen
emblazon
raisin

glazier
Anastasia
aphasia
brazier
crazier
euthanasia
Fantasia
hazier
lazier
Malaysia

→ Many English speakers pronounce some words in section **3.12** (eg *Australasia*) in such a way that they rhyme with these words

lazy
crazy
Daisy
daisy
hazy
Maisie

phrasing
amazing
appraising
blazing
braising
crazing
dazing
double-glazing
erasing
fazing
gazing
glazing
grazing
liaising
navel-gazing
phasing
praising
raising
razing
reappraising
rephrasing

dazed
crazed
glazed
phased
unfazed

+ You can add to this list by adding ***-d*** to some words that rhyme with ***gaze***, as in ***praised***

Section 4
-AIR-

All the words in this section use the sound **-air-** (as in ch*air*, f*air*y, desp*air*) in their main stressed syllable

4.1

rare
affair
aftercare
air
anywhere
au pair
aware
Ayr
bare
bear
beware
beyond compare
billionaire
blare
Burke and Hare
camelhair
care
chair
Cher
Cla(i)re
commissionaire
compare
County Clare
dare
debonair
declare
Delaware
despair
devil-may-care
disrepair
doctrinaire
earthenware
eclair
ensnare
everywhere
fair
fair and square
fanfare
fare
flair
flare
forbear
forswear
Fred Astaire
glare
go spare
Hair
hair
hare
heir
impair
in good repair
Jane Eyre
Kildare
kitchenware
lair
laisser-faire
legionnaire
mare
mayor
midair
millionaire
multimillionaire
open-air
ovenware
pair
pare
pear
prayer
premiere
prepare
questionnaire
repair
rocking chair
scare
share
silverware
snare
solitaire
spare
square
stair
stare
swear
tableware
tear (= *to rip*)
their
there
the worse for wear
they're
thoroughfare
Tony Blair
unaware
underwear
unfair
Vanity Fair
walk on air
Walter De La Mare
wear
Weston-super-Mare
where
yeah

4.2

scared
black-haired
brown-haired
curly-haired
dark-haired
fair-haired
grey-haired
laird
Logie Baird
long-haired
prepared
red-haired
short-haired
straight-haired
unimpaired
unprepared
white-haired

> + You can add to this list by adding *-(e)d* to some words that rhyme with ***rare***, as in ***dared***

4.3

rarely
barely
debonairly
fairly
squarely
unfairly

airlift
chairlift
stairlift

airless
careless
hairless

airline
hairline

4.4

chairman
repairman
vice-chairman

4.5

cairn
bairn
Nairn
Pitcairn

fairness
awareness
bareness
squareness
unawareness
unfairness

4.6

carer
bearer
Éamon de Valera
Eire
pallbearer
Riviera
Sara(h)
seafarer
wayfarer

> + You can add to this list by adding ***-(e)r*** to some words that rhyme with ***rare***, as in ***fairer***
>
> You can also make rhymes for these words by using ***her*** after some words that rhyme with ***rare***, as in ***compare her***

bearable
repairable
unbearable

Aries
caries

area
Bavaria
Bulgaria
malaria
planetaria

aerial
secretarial

barium
aquarium
planetarium

Aryan
agrarian
antiquarian
authoritarian
barbarian
Bavarian
Bulgarian
Caesarean
centenarian
disciplinarian
egalitarian
grammarian
humanitarian
Hungarian
libertarian
librarian
nonagenarian
octogenarian
ovarian
parliamentarian
proletarian
sectarian
septuagenarian
sexagenarian
totalitarian
utilitarian
vegetarian
veterinarian

sectarianism
egalitarianism
vegetarianism

> + You can add to this list by adding ***-ism*** to some words that rhyme with ***Aryan***, as in ***agrarianism***

various
Aquarius

gregarious
hilarious
multifarious
nefarious
precarious
Sagittarius
vicarious

variously
hilariously
multifariously
nefariously
precariously
vicariously

secretariat
proletariat

vary
airy
airy-fairy
Azeri
Canary
canary
chary
contrary (= *perverse*)
dairy
fairy
General Galtieri
hairy
Mary
prairie
scary
Tipperary
unwary
wary

daring
airing
bearing
caring
child-bearing
despairing
hard-wearing
overbearing
profit-sharing
raring
seafaring
sparing
swearing
uncaring
unsparing
wearing

+ You can add to this list by adding *-ing* to some words that rhyme with *rare*, as in *repairing*

sparingly
despairingly
glaringly
overbearingly

heiress
mayoress
millionairess

Pharaoh
bolero
Rio de Janeiro
sombrero

4.7

stairway
airway
fairway

4.8

theirs
downstairs
split hairs
unawares
upstairs
wares

+ You can add to this list by adding *-s* to some words that rhyme with *rare*, as in *stairs*

Section 5
-E-

All the words in this section use the sound **-e-** (as in b*e*t, cr*e*dit, impr*e*ss) in their main stressed syllable

5.1

web
at a low ebb
ebb
Maghreb
pleb
Zagreb

pebble
rebel
treble

Debbie
Entebbe

Deborah
zebra

5.2

neck
beck
bedeck
bottleneck
check
cheque
Czech
deck
discotheque
double-check
Eurocheque
fleck
get it in the neck
halterneck
heck
high-tech
millstone round one's neck
nervous wreck
pain in the neck
peck
polo neck
quarterdeck
Quebec
spec
speck
Toulouse-Lautrec
trek
turtleneck
up to one's neck
V-neck
wreck

wrecker
Boris Becker
double-decker
exchequer
Mecca
Rebecca
single-decker
spell-checker
trekker
woodpecker

+ You can also make rhymes for these words by using ***her*** after some words that rhyme with ***neck***, as in ***check her***

freckle
Dr Jekyll
heckle
shekel
speckle

beckon
Brecon
reckon

second
beckoned
nanosecond
reckoned
split-second

reckless
feckless
necklace

flex
annex
circumflex
convex
ex
multiplex
Oedipus Rex
pecs
perplex
Rex
sex
specs
Tex-Mex
unisex
vex
X

+ You can add to this list by adding *-s* to some words that rhyme with ***neck***, as in ***checks***

dyslexia
alexia
anorexia
sexier

sexy
apoplexy

anorexic
dyslexic

complexity
convexity
perplexity

text
from one day to the next
hypertext
next
teletext
vexed

+ You can add to this list by adding *-ed* to some words that rhyme with ***flex***, as in ***annexed***

section
affection
antivivisection
by-election
collection
complexion
connection
convection
correction
cross-section
defection
deflection
dejection
detection
direction
disaffection
ejection
election
erection
imperfection
infection
injection
inspection
insurrection
interjection
intersection
introspection
objection
perfection
projection
protection
recollection
re-election
reflection
rejection
resurrection
selection
subsection
vivisection

perfectionist
antivivisectionist
projectionist
protectionist
vivisectionist

sect
affect
after-effect
architect
aspect
bisect
circumspect
collect
connect
correct
defect (= *to desert one's country*)
deflect
detect
dialect
direct
disconnect
disinfect
disrespect
dissect
effect
eject
elect
erect
expect
genuflect
incorrect
indirect
infect
inflect
inject
inspect
intellect
interconnect
interject
intersect
knock-on effect
misdirect
neglect
object (= *to make an objection*)
perfect (= *to make perfect*)
project
prospect
protect
recollect
redirect
re-elect
reflect
reject
respect
resurrect
retrospect
select
self-respect
subject (= *to cause to experience something*)
suspect
unchecked
Utrecht
wrecked

+ You can add to this list by adding *-ed* to some words that rhyme with ***neck***, as in ***checked***

sector
collector
connector
conscientious objector
defector
detector
director
elector
executive director
film director
Hannibal Lecter
Hector
hector
inspector
managing director
nectar
nonexecutive director
objector
projector
prospector
protector
rector
reflector
respecter
selector
spectre
vector

+ You can also make rhymes for these words by using *her* after some words that rhyme with *sect*, as in *respect her*

respectable
collectable
connectable
correctable
delectable
detectable
disrespectable
electable
erectable
injectable
inspectable

vasectomy
hysterectomy
mastectomy

expectant
disinfectant

pectoral
electoral

rectory
directory
ex-directory
refectory
trajectory

hectic
apoplectic
dialectic
eclectic

expected
affected
collected
dejected
directed
disaffected
disconnected
erected
rejected
selected
unaffected
unconnected
undetected
unexpected
unprotected
unsuspected
well-respected
write-protected

+ You can add to this list by adding *-ed* to some words that rhyme with *sect*, as in *respected*

rectify
objectify

unsuspecting
directing
erecting
rejecting
self-respecting

+ You can add to this list by adding *-ing* to some words that rhyme with *sect*, as in *projecting*

detective
collective
corrective
defective
directive
effective
elective
ineffective
introspective
invective
irrespective
objective
perspective
prospective
protective
reflective
respective
retrospective
selective
subjective

effectively
collectively
objectively
respectively
retrospectively

respectful
disrespectful
neglectful

directly
correctly
incorrectly
indirectly

spectra
Electra

spectrum
plectrum

lecture
architecture
conjecture

effectual
ineffectual
intellectual

secular
molecular

consecutive
executive

5.3

bed
ahead
arrowhead
BEd (= *Bachelor of Education*)
behead
black bread
bled
bottle-fed
bread
bred
brown bread
centre spread
cut someone dead
dead
DipEd (= *Diploma in Education*)
dread
drop dead
Ed
ed
embed
Fed
fed
figurehead
fled
flowerbed
force-fed
Fred
gainsaid
gingerbread
go-ahead
go to someone's head
head
Holyhead
ill-bred
infrared
instead
knock 'em dead
lead (= *the metal*)
led
letterhead
like a bear with a sore head
lose one's head
MEd (= *Master of Education*)
misled
misread (= *past tense of misread*)
naan bread
Ned
not right in the head
out of one's head
overhead
paint the town red
Peterhead
pitta bread
quadruped
read (= *past tense of read*)
red
riverbed
said
see red
shed
shred
sled
sliced bread
soda bread
sped
spread
stead
stone-dead
streets ahead
Ted
the best thing since sliced bread
the Med
thoroughbred
thread
tread
underfed
unsaid
unshed
watershed
wed
well-bred
well-fed
well-read
white bread
wholemeal bread
Z

shredder
Cheddar
header

> + You can add to this list by adding ***-(d)er*** to some words that rhyme with ***bed***, as in ***spreader***
>
> You can also make rhymes for these words by using ***her*** after some words that rhyme with ***bed***, as in ***wed her***

medal
back-pedal
meddle
pedal
peddle
soft-pedal
treadle

deaden
Armageddon
leaden
redden

pedantry
sedentary

ready
already
Eddie
eddy
Freddie
heady
oven-ready
rough-and-ready
steady
Teddy

teddy
unsteady

edible
credible
incredible
inedible

dedicate
medicate
predicate (= *to proclaim*)

dedicated
medicated
predicated

dreaded
bareheaded
bigheaded
clear-headed
cool-headed
empty-headed
hard-headed
headed
hotheaded
leaded
level-headed
light-headed
muddleheaded
pig-headed
unleaded
wrong-headed

+ You can add to this list by adding ***-(d)ed*** to some words that rhyme with ***bed***, as in ***wedded***

readily
headily
steadily
unsteadily

sediment
impediment

wedding
bedding
heading
steading

+ You can add to this list by adding ***-(d)ing*** to some words that rhyme with ***bed***, as in ***spreading***

edit
credit
discredit
subedit

+ You can also make rhymes for these words by using ***it*** after some words that rhyme with ***bed***, as in ***said it***

editor
creditor
subeditor

headboard
breadboard

meddler
peddler
pedlar

deadly
medley

headline
breadline
deadline

wedlock
deadlock
dreadlock

bedpan
deadpan

Cedric
Frederic(k)

bedroom
headroom

edge
allege
dredge
hedge
ledge
on edge
pledge
Reg
sedge
sledge
veg
wedge

ledger
dredger

edgy
Reggie
veggie

double-edged
alleged
fully-fledged

+ You can add to this list by adding ***-d*** to some words that rhyme with ***edge***, as in ***wedged***

overheads
loggerheads
newlyweds
tear to shreds
zeds

+ You can add to this list by adding ***-s*** to some words that rhyme with ***bed***, as in ***threads***

5.4

chef
BAF (= *British Athletic Federation*)
cf (= *compare*)
clef
deaf
eff
F
Geoff

IMF (= *International Monetary Fund*)
IVF
RAF
ref
Rudolf Nureyev
stone-deaf
tone-deaf
treble clef
UHF (= *ultrahigh frequency*)
UNICEF
USAF (= *United States Air Force*)
VHF (= *very high frequency*)
WWF (= *Worldwide Fund for Nature; World Wrestling Federation*)

+ You can also make rhymes for these words by using words in section **5.16** that rhyme with ***death***

zephyr
heifer

reference
cross-reference
deference
preference

left
bereft
cleft
deft
theft
weft

5.5

leg
an arm and a leg
beg
break a leg
egg
Eigg
keg
Meg
nest egg
Peg
peg
Winnipeg

beggar
Arnold Schwarzenegger

leggy
Peggy

eggs
boiled eggs
dregs
fried eggs
hard-boiled eggs
on one's last legs
poached eggs
scrambled eggs
soft-boiled eggs
sure as eggs is eggs

+ You can add to this list by adding ***-s*** to some words that rhyme with ***leg***, as in ***begs***

5.6

tell
Adele
Alexander Graham Bell
Annabel(l)e
ASL (= *American Sign Language*)
befell
bell
Belle
belle
Brunel
caramel
caravel
carousel
cartel
cell
Charles Parnell
citadel
clientele
compel
Danielle
decibel
Del
dispel
dwell
EFL (= *English as a foreign language*)
Estelle
excel
expel
farewell
fell
foretell
Gabrielle
gazelle
gel
Gisèle
give someone hell
hell
hotel
HTML (= *hypertext markup language*)
impel
Isabel(le)
jell
Jezebel
kiss and tell
knell
L
lapel
like a bat out of hell
like hell
Mel
Michelle
misspell
motel
Nell
NFL (= *National Football League*)
Noël
Noel(l)e
not have a hope in hell
outsell
parallel
pell-mell
personnel
propel

quell
Raquel
Ravel
razor-shell
rebel (= *to revolt*)
repel
Scafell
sell
shell
smell
sound as a bell
spell
swell
Tinkerbell
tortoiseshell
unwell
URL (= *uniform resource locator*)
well
XL (= *extra large*)
yell

melee
Pele

seller
Arabella
Bella
bestseller
bookseller
cellar
Cinderella
Daniella
Della
dweller
Ella
Fenella
fortune-teller
Isabella
Nelson Mandela
Nigella
propeller
Prunella
rubella
salmonella
saltcellar
speller
Stella
storyteller
teller
umbrella
yeller

> + You can also make rhymes for these words by using ***her*** after some words that rhyme with ***tell***, as in ***smell her***

vellum
antebellum
cerebellum

> + You can add to this list by adding ***'em*** to some words that rhyme with ***tell***, as in ***smell 'em***

melon
Ellen
felon
Ferdinand Magellan
Helen
watermelon

Melanie
felony
miscellany

jealous
zealous

> + You can add to this list by adding ***-s*** to some words that rhyme with ***seller***, as in ***cellars***
>
> You can also make rhymes for these words by using ***us*** after some words that rhyme with ***tell***, as in ***sell us***

pellet
zealot

jelly
belly
Delhi
deli
Ellie
Gene Kelly
Grace Kelly
Kelly
Machiavelli
Ned Kelly
Nellie
New Delhi
not on your nelly
Shelley
smelly
tagliatelle
telly
welly

relic
angelic
psychedelic

eligible
ineligible
intelligible
unintelligible

relegate
delegate (= *to depute*)

telling
bestselling
compelling
dwelling
evil-smelling
gelling
selling
shelling
spelling
sweet-smelling
swelling
welling

> + You can add to this list by adding ***-ing*** to some words that rhyme with ***tell***, as in ***smelling***

wellington
Duke Ellington
Duke of Wellington
Wellington

trellis
Ellis
Ruth Ellis

hellish
embellish
relish

yellow
bedfellow
bellow
cello
fellow
Longfellow
mellow
Othello
schoolfellow

elk
whelk

held
beheld
jet-propelled
unparalleled
upheld
weld
withheld

> + You can add to this list by adding *-ed* to some words that rhyme with *tell*, as in *smelled*

elder
Imelda
welder
Zelda

welding
gelding

self
do-it-yourself
elf
herself
himself
itself
myself
oneself
shelf
yourself

selfish
elfish
shellfish
unselfish

elm
helm
overwhelm
realm

helmet
pelmet

help
self-help
whelp
yelp

Elsie
Chelsea

belt
at full pelt
Celt
conveyor belt
dealt
dwelt
felt
Franklin D Roosevelt
heartfelt
knelt
melt
misspelt
pelt
smelt
spelt
svelte
tighten one's belt
under one's belt
welt

shelter
belter
delta
helter-skelter
smelter
swelter
welter

> + You can also make rhymes for these words by using ***her*** after some words that rhyme with ***belt***, as in ***smelt her***

belch
squelch

health
Commonwealth
ill-health
stealth
wealth

healthy
stealthy
unhealthy
wealthy

twelve
delve
shelve

Kelvin
Melvin

Elvis
pelvis

elves
ourselves
selves
shelves
themselves
yourselves

Seychelles
H G Wells
wedding bells

> + You can add to this list by adding *-s* to some words that rhyme with *tell*, as in *smells*

5.7

gem
AGM (= *annual general meeting*)
AM (= *amplitude modulation*)
am (= *ante meridiem, before noon*)
ATM (= *automated teller machine*)
Bethlehem
CAM (= *computer-aided manufacture*)
condemn
diadem
Eminem
ERM (= *Exchange Rate Mechanism*)
FHM
FM (= *frequency modulation*)
GM (= *genetically modified*)
hem
IBM
Jerusalem
La Bohème
Lib Dem
M
NUM
phlegm
PM
pm (= *post meridiem, after noon*)
REM
rpm
stem
them
wpm (= *words per minute*)

+ You can also make rhymes for these words by using words in section **5.8** that rhyme with ***pen***

Emma
dilemma
Gemma
tremor

lemon
Yemen

lemony
anemone
Yemeni

demonstrate
remonstrate

memory
emery

jemmy
semi

epidemic
academic
endemic
polemic

chemical
biochemical
petrochemical
polemical

blemish
Flemish

demo
memo

member
December
dismember
non-member
November
remember
September

tremble
assemble
dissemble
reassemble
resemble

gremlin
Kremlin

solemnity
indemnity

hemp
temp

redemption
exemption

tempt
attempt
contempt
exempt
last-ditch attempt
pre-empt
unkempt

5.8

pen
again
amen
Ben
born-again
cayenne
comedienne
den
fen
gen
glen
Glen(n)
Gwen
hen
ISBN (= *International Standard Book Number*)
ITN
Ken
ken
LAN (= *local area network*)
Len
men
N
once again
Phnom Penh
pigpen
playpen
RN (= *Royal Navy*)
ten
then
UN
USN (= *United States*

Navy)
WAN (= *wide area network*)
when
wren
yen

> + You can also make rhymes for these words by using words in section **5.7** that rhyme with ***gem***

henna
antenna
Ayrton Senna
Jenna
Siena
tenner
tenor
Vienna

kennel
fennel

tenant
flight lieutenant
lieutenant
pennant

generate
degenerate (= *to deteriorate*)
regenerate
venerate

perennial
bicentennial
biennial
centennial

penny
any
a pretty penny
Benny
Jenny
Kenny
Kilkenny
Lenny
many
Penny
spend a penny
ten-a-penny

schizophrenic
allergenic
carcinogenic
hallucinogenic
hypoallergenic
photogenic
telegenic
transgenic

tennis
Den(n)is
Glenys
menace
The Merchant of Venice
Venice

venison
Alfred Lord Tennyson

rennet
Elizabeth Bennet
Senate
tenet

obscenity
serenity

Kenneth
zenith

end
amend
append
apprehend
ascend
at a loose end
attend
befriend
bend
blend
Bridgend
commend
comprehend
condescend
contend
defend
depend
descend
dirty weekend
distend
dividend
emend
extend
fend
friend
intend
lend
make someone's hair stand on end
mend
offend
on the mend
Ostend
overspend
People's Friend
portend
pretend
recommend
rend
round the bend
send
Southend
spend
superintend
suspend
tend
to the bitter end
transcend
trend
upend
weekend
wend

gender
agenda
bartender
bender
blender
Brenda
contender
defender
engender
fender
Glenda
Gwenda
hacienda
lender
moneylender
offender

render
sender
slender
spender
splendour
surrender
suspender
tender

> + You can add to this list by adding *-er* to some words that rhyme with ***end***, as in ***pretender***
>
> You can also make rhymes for these words by using ***her*** after some words that rhyme with ***end***, as in ***offend her***

dependable
amendable
commendable
emendable
expendable
extendable

tendon
Brendan

attendance
dependence
independence
nonattendance
overdependence
resplendence
transcendence

tendency
ascendancy
dependency
resplendency
transcendency

pendant
ascendant
attendant
defendant
dependant
dependent
independent
interdependent
overdependent
resplendent
superintendent

tremendous
horrendous
stupendous

> + You can also make rhymes for these words by using ***us*** after some words that rhyme with ***end***, as in ***send us***

tremendously
horrendously
stupendously

trendy
bendy
Wendy

splendid
intended
offended
open-ended
overextended
suspended
undefended
unintended

> + You can add to this list by adding *-ed* to some words that rhyme with ***end***, as in ***pretended***

ending
condescending
defending
heartrending
impending
lending
never-ending
offending
parascending
pending
spending
unbending
uncomprehending
unending

> + You can add to this list by adding *-ing* to some words that rhyme with ***end***, as in ***pretending***

crescendo
decrescendo
diminuendo
innuendo
kendo
Nintendo®

endless
friendless

revenge
avenge
Stonehenge

strength
at arm's length
full-length
length

strengthen
lengthen

fence
coincidence
commence
condense
consequence
decadence
defence
dense
diffidence
diligence
disobedience
dispense
eloquence
eminence
evidence
excellence
expense

frankincense
hence
immense
impertinence
impotence
impudence
incense
incontinence
inference
innocence
insolence
intense
intransigence
magnificence
negligence
offence
omnipotence
pence
penitence
permanence
pestilence
precedence
pretence
providence
recompense
residence
self-defence
sense
suspense
tense
thence
turbulence
vehemence
violence
whence

censor
condenser
Lech Walesa
sensor

+ You can add to this list by adding *-r* to some words that rhyme with *fence*, as in *denser*

pencil
stencil
utensil

sensory
dispensary
extrasensory

census
consensus

+ You can also make rhymes for these words by using ***us*** after some words that rhyme with *fence*, as in ***incense us***

sensible
comprehensible
defensible
incomprehensible
indefensible
insensible
ostensible
reprehensible

sensibly
comprehensibly
defensibly
incomprehensibly
indefensibly
insensibly
ostensibly
reprehensibly

density
immensity
intensity
propensity

pensive
apprehensive
comprehensive
counteroffensive
defensive
expensive
extensive
inexpensive
inoffensive
intensive
labour-intensive
offensive

pensively
apprehensively
comprehensively
defensively
expensively
extensively
inexpensively
inoffensively
intensively
offensively

senseless
defenceless

densely
immensely
intensely
tensely

essential
confidential
consequential
deferential
differential
existential
exponential
inconsequential
inessential
influential
nonessential
potential
preferential
presidential
providential
quintessential
residential
reverential
sequential
torrential
vice-presidential

essentially
confidentially
consequentially
deferentially
inconsequentially
potentially
providentially
quintessentially
reverentially

mention
abstention
apprehension
Ascension
attention
bone of contention
comprehension
condescension
contention
contravention
convention
declension
detention
dimension
dissension
extension
hypertension
inattention
incomprehension
intention
intervention
invention
misapprehension
pension
pretension
prevention
retention
suspension
tension

pensionable
mentionable
unmentionable

conventional
intentional
one-dimensional
three-dimensional
two-dimensional
unconventional
unintentional

well-intentioned
above-mentioned
aforementioned
ill-intentioned
undermentioned

+ You can add to this list by adding *-ed* to some words that rhyme with ***mention***, as in ***pensioned***

pretentious
conscientious
contentious
licentious
sententious
tendentious
unpretentious

tent
accent (= *to stress*)
ascent
assent
augment
bent
cement
cent
circumvent
consent
content
dent
descent
discontent
disorient
dissent
event
extent
ferment
foment
forewent
fragment (= *to shatter*)
frequent (= *to visit*)
gent
Ghent
Gwent
happy event
heaven-sent
indent
intent
invent
Kent
lament
leant
Lent
lent
meant
misrepresent
misspent
nonevent
orient
overspent
peppercorn rent
percent
present (= *to introduce*)
prevent
reinvent
relent
rent
repent
represent
resent
scent
segment (= *to divide*)
sent
spent
torment
underwent
vent
went

The following words will also tend to rhyme with these when they come at the end of a line:
accident
accompaniment
acknowledg(e)ment
advertisement
argument
astonishment
banishment
belligerent
beneficent
betterment
bewilderment
complement
compliment
condiment
consequent
continent
corpulent
decadent
detriment
development
diffident

diligent
dissident
document
element
eloquent
embarrassment
embezzlement
embodiment
enlightenment
entanglement
entitlement
environment
establishment
excellent
excrement
exigent
filament
fraudulent
grandiloquent
imminent
impenitent
implement
impotent
imprisonment
improvident
impudent
incident
increment
indolent
innocent
insolent
instrument
intelligent
intransigent
irreverent
magnificent
management
measurement
monument
negligent
nourishment
omnipotent
opulent
ornament
parliament
penitent
permanent
precedent
predicament
presentiment
punishment
recipient
redolent
regiment
reticent
sacrament
sentiment
settlement
somnolent
subsequent
supplement
temperament
tenement
testament
tournament
turbulent
vehement
virulent

enter
centre
dissenter
epicentre
inventor
Jobcentre
magenta
placenta
presenter
re-enter
tormentor

+ You can add to this list by adding ***-er*** to some words that rhyme with ***tent***, as in ***lamenter***

You can also make rhymes for these words by using ***her*** after some words that rhyme with ***tent***, as in ***resent her***

presentable
preventable
unpresentable

+ You can add to this list by adding ***-able*** to some words that rhyme with ***tent***, as in ***fermentable***

mental
accidental
coincidental
continental
dental
departmental
detrimental
elemental
environmental
experimental
fundamental
gentle
governmental
incidental
incremental
instrumental
intercontinental
judg(e)mental
lentil
monumental
occidental
oriental
ornamental
parental
regimental
rental
sentimental
temperamental
transcendental
transcontinental
unsentimental

mentally
accidentally
fundamentally
incidentally

+ You can add to this list by adding ***-ly*** to some words that rhyme with ***mental***, as in ***monumentally***

instrumentalist
environmentalist
fundamentalist
Orientalist
sentimentalist

sentence
repentance

documentary
complementary
complimentary
elementary
parliamentary
rudimentary
supplementary
testamentary
uncomplimentary
unparliamentary

momentous
portentous

+ You can also make rhymes for these words by using ***us*** after some words that rhyme with ***tent***, as in ***resent us***

tentative
argumentative
preventative
representative
unrepresentative

plenty
aplenty
twenty

demented
contented
discontented
regimented
unrepresented

+ You can add to this list by adding ***-ed*** to some words that rhyme with ***tent***, as in ***resented***

dissenting
unrelenting

+ You can add to this list by adding ***-ing*** to some words that rhyme with ***tent***, as in ***resenting***

entity
identity
nonentity

incentive
attentive
disincentive
inattentive
inventive
preventive
retentive

memento
lento
pimento
Sacramento

eventful
resentful
uneventful

gently
Bentley
contently
intently

contentment
resentment

entry
gentry
re-entry
sentry

French
bench
blench
clench
drench
quench
retrench
stench
tench
trench
wench
wrench

venture
adventure
backbencher
misadventure

+ You can also make rhymes for these words by using ***her*** after some words that rhyme with ***French***, as in ***drench her***

tenth
nth

menu
pull-down menu
venue

strenuous
disingenuous
ingenuous
tenuous

lens
cleanse
telephoto lens
WRNS
zoom lens

+ You can add to this list by adding ***-s*** to some words that rhyme with ***pen***, as in ***dens***

cleanser
cadenza
influenza

5.9

step
crêpe
Dieppe
Johnny Depp
overstep

PEP
pep
prep
rep
steppe
yep

pepper
high-stepper
leper

leopard
shepherd

separable
inseparable
irreparable

tepid
intrepid

reception
apperception
conception
contraception
deception
exception
Immaculate Conception
inception
interception
misconception
perception
preconception
self-deception

kept
accept
adept
crept
except
inept
intercept
leapt
overslept
slept
swept
well-kept
wept

+ You can add to this list by adding *-ed* to some words that rhyme with *step*, as in *pepped*

septic
antiseptic
aseptic
epileptic
Eurosceptic
sceptic

5.10

error
sierra
terror

Herod
Gerard

peril
Beryl
Cheryl
Errol
imperil
Meryl

necessarily
ordinarily
temporarily
voluntarily

herald
Ella Fitzgerald
Gerald

errand
gerund

deterrent
inherent

cherry
berry
bury
Derry
ferry
Gerry
glacé cherry
Kerry
Londonderry
make merry
merry
Perry
sherry
Terry
very

cleric
atmospheric
Derek
derrick
Eric
esoteric
generic

Erica
America

clerical
hysterical
numerical
spherical

hysterically
numerically

terrify
verify

merriment
experiment

terrace
Nerys

perish
cherish

merit
demerit
disinherit
ferret
inherit

sincerity
asperity
austerity
dexterity
insincerity
posterity
prosperity
severity
temerity

5.11

dress
acquiesce

address
anybody's guess
assess
bad press
baroness
battledress
Bess
bless
Caithness
caress
chess
coalesce
compress
confess
convalesce
couldn't-care-less
cress
deaconess
depress
digress
dispossess
distress
DSS (= *Department of Social Security*)
duress
excess
express
finesse
guess
HMS
impress
Inverness
IRS (= *Internal Revenue Service*)
Jess
largesse
less
lioness
Loch Ness
manageress
mess
nevertheless
NHS
nonetheless
NUS (= *National Union of Students*)
OAS (= *Organization of American States*)
obsess
OHMS (= *On Her Majesty's Service*)
oppress
overdress
peeress
Porgy and Bess
POS (= *point of sale*)
possess
press
princess
profess
progress
PS
reassess
redress
regress
repossess
repress
RS (= *Royal Society*)
Rudolf Hess
S
SAS
second-guess
shepherdess
Shimon Peres
Skegness
SOS
stewardess
stress
success
suppress
Tess
transgress
trouser press
undress
unless
US
USS (= *United States Ship*)
VHS
watercress
yes

The following words will also tend to rhyme with these when they come at the end of a line:

absent-mindedness
assertiveness
backwardness
barrenness
bashfulness
bitterness
carelessness
cautiousness
cleanliness
cleverness
clumsiness
colourless
consciousness
drowsiness
eagerness
easiness
effectiveness
effortless
emptiness
expressionless
featureless
gentleness
giddiness
governess
greediness
holiness
humourless
idleness
indebtedness
inventiveness
jauntiness
judiciousness
lawlessness
laziness
limitless
liveliness
loneliness
manliness
meaningless
merciless
motionless
nastiness
nervousness
nosiness
odourless
openness
penniless
pitiless
powerless

precociousness
pretentiousness
quietness
selfishness
shabbiness
silliness
sorceress
stubbornness
suddenness
tenderness
thoroughness
ticketless
togetherness
unpleasantness
untidiness
usefulness
valueless
wariness
weariness
wickedness
wilderness

dresser
aggressor
assessor
compressor
confessor
lesser
Odessa
possessor
predecessor
professor
successor
TESSA
Tessa
Vanessa

> + You can add to this list by adding *-(e)r* to some words that rhyme with ***dress***, as in ***guesser***
>
> You can also make rhymes for these words by using ***her*** after some words that rhyme with ***dress***, as in ***impress her***

wrestle
Cecil
nestle
pestle
TESL (= *Teaching English as a Second Language*)
trestle
vessel

lesson
delicatessen
lessen

essence
acquiescence
adolescence
convalescence
effervescence
excrescence
fluorescence
incandescence
luminescence
obsolescence
phosphorescence
quiescence
quintessence

crescent
acquiescent
adolescent
antidepressant
convalescent
effervescent
fluorescent
incandescent
incessant
luminescent
phosphorescent
quiescent

pessary
accessory

messy
Bessie
dressy
Jesse
Jessie

accessible
expressible
inaccessible
inexpressible
irrepressible

message
presage

decimal
infinitesimal

dressing
blessing
depressing
distressing
prepossessing
pressing
unprepossessing
window-dressing

> + You can add to this list by adding *-ing* to some words that rhyme with ***dress***, as in ***guessing***

excessive
aggressive
depressive
expressive
impressive
inexpressive
manic-depressive
obsessive
oppressive
possessive
progressive
regressive
repressive
successive

excessively
aggressively
progressively

> + You can add to this list by adding *-ly* to some words that rhyme with ***excessive***, as in ***obsessively***

desk
burlesque
grotesque
picturesque
statuesque

fresco
alfresco
Tesco
UNESCO

stressful
successful
unsuccessful

wrestling
nestling

yes-man
chessman

rest
abreast
arrest
attest
behest
bequest
best
blessed
blest
breast
Bucharest
Budapest
chest
contest
crest
depressed
detest
digest
distressed
divest
do one's level best
feather one's own nest
guest
hard-pressed
hornet's nest
infest
interest
invest
jest
lest
love nest
Mae West
manifest
Marie Celeste
Mid-West
molest
nest
north-northwest
northwest
oppressed
overdressed
pest
professed
protest
quest
reinvest
request
second-best
self-confessed
self-possessed
south-southwest
southwest
suggest
suppressed
test
Trieste
unimpressed
unrest
unstressed
vest
well-dressed
west
wrest
zest

+ You can add to this list by adding ***-ed*** to some words that rhyme with ***dress***, as in ***impressed***

pester
Chester
Esther
fester
Hester
investor
jester
Leicester
Lester
polyester
protester
semester
sequester
sou'-wester
Sylvester
trimester

+ You can add to this list by adding ***-er*** to some words that rhyme with ***rest***, as in ***tester***

You can also make rhymes for these words by using ***her*** after some words that rhyme with ***rest***, as in ***detest her***

western
Charlton Heston
Mid-Western
north-northwestern
northwestern
Preston
south-southwestern
southwestern

contestant
decongestant

bestial
celestial

domestic
majestic

vested
congested
double-breasted
flat-chested
single-breasted
tried-and-tested
uncontested
undigested
untested

+ You can add to this list by adding *-ed* to some words that rhyme with ***rest***, as in ***detested***

destine
clandestine
intestine
predestine

jesting
arresting
testing

+ You can add to this list by adding *-ing* to some words that rhyme with ***rest***, as in ***detesting***

festive
digestive
restive
suggestive

kestrel
ancestral
orchestral

pedestrian
equestrian

question
beyond question
congestion
digestion
indigestion
suggestion
without question

tempestuous
incestuous

5.12

pleasure
countermeasure
displeasure
leisure
measure
tape measure
treasure

measurable
immeasurable
pleasurable

5.13

fresh
afresh
Bangladesh
crèche
enmesh
flesh
Marrakesh
mesh
refresh
thresh

fresher
high-pressure
pressure
refresher
thresher

session
accession
aggression
compression
concession
confession
decompression
depression
digression
discretion
expression
freshen
immunosuppression
impression
indiscretion
intercession
manic depression
obsession
oppression
possession
procession
profession
progression
recession
regression
repression
secession
self-expression
self-possession
succession
suppression

professional
confessional
obsessional
processional
unprofessional

concessionary
discretionary

fleshy
Bangladeshi

5.14

set
abet
aid and abet
alphabet
Annette
Antoinette
baronet
barrette
Bernadette
beset
bet
Brett
brunette
cadet
cassette
cigarette
clarinet
Claudette
close-set
Colette
coquette
Corvette
courgette
croquette
debt
diskette
duet
epaulette
epithet
etiquette

forget
fret
gazette
Georgette
get
Internet
Intranet
Jean(n)ette
jet
Juliet
kitchenette
Lafayette
laundrette
layette
let
Lynette
maisonette
Marie Antoinette
marionette
met
minaret
minuet
motet
Nanette
Net
net
netiquette
no sweat
octet
Odette
overate
parapet
Paulette
pet
Phuket
pipette
pirouette
play hard to get
preset
quadruplet
quartet
quintet
regret
reset
Romeo and Juliet
rosette
roulette
septet
serviette
sextet
silhouette
Somerset
statuette
sublet
suffragette
sweat
thickset
threat
Tibet
turbojet
upset
usherette
vet
vignette
wet
whet
yet
Yvette

letter
better
carburettor
debtor
fetter
for the better
go-getter
Greta
Henrietta
Loretta
newsletter
operetta
setter
sweater
trendsetter
typesetter
Valetta
vendetta

+ You can add to this list by adding *-ter* to some words that rhyme with ***set***, as in ***wetter***

You can also make rhymes for these words by using ***her*** after some words that rhyme with ***set***, as in ***get her***

regrettable
forgettable
unforgettable

settle
Dettol®
fettle
grasp the nettle
kettle
metal
mettle
nettle
petal
Popocatepetl
unsettle

threaten
Breton
cretin
Tibetan

petty
Betty
confetti
Hetty
jetty
machete
spaghetti
sweaty
yeti

athletic
aesthetic
anaesthetic
apathetic
apologetic
ascetic
cosmetic
diabetic
emetic
energetic
frenetic
genetic
hermetic
kinetic
magnetic
pathetic

phonetic
poetic
prophetic
sympathetic
synthetic
unapologetic
unsympathetic

poetical
alphabetical
arithmetical
heretical
hypothetical
theoretical

genetically
alphabetically
apathetically
apologetically
athletically
cosmetically
energetically
frenetically
hermetically
hypothetically
pathetically
phonetically
poetically
prophetically
sympathetically
synthetically
theoretically
unapologetically
unsympathetically

athletics
aesthetics
cybernetics
genetics
phonetics

+ You can add to this list by adding *-s* to some words that rhyme with ***athletic***, as in *cosmetics*

indebted
fetid

+ You can add to this list by adding *-ted* to some words that rhyme with ***set***, as in ***netted***

betting
abetting
bloodletting
netting
setting
upsetting
vetting

+ You can add to this list by adding *-ting* to some words that rhyme with ***set***, as in *forgetting*

ghetto
falsetto
libretto
Rigoletto
Soweto
stiletto

set-up
get-up
het up
let-up

fretful
forgetful
regretful

Petra
et cetera

Betsy
tsetse

fetch
etch
lech
retch
sketch
stretch
vetch
wretch

stretcher
lecher

+ You can add to this list by adding *-er* to some words that rhyme with ***fetch***, as in ***sketcher***

You can also make rhymes for these words by using ***her*** after some words that rhyme with ***fetch***, as in ***sketch her***

lecherous
treacherous

lechery
treachery

sketchy
stretchy
tetchy

fetching
etching

+ You can add to this list by adding *-ing* to some words that rhyme with ***fetch***, as in ***sketching***

5.15

tether
altogether
at the end of one's tether
blether
feather
get-together
Heather
heather
leather
together
under the weather
weather

whether

feathery
heathery
leathery

5.16

death
Beth
breath
Elizabeth
flog to death
hang on like grim death
Lady Macbeth
Macbeth
Nazareth
Seth
worried to death

+ You can also make rhymes for these words by using words in section **5.4** that rhyme with *chef*

5.17

clever
endeavour
ever
forever
however
never
never-never
same as ever
sever
Trevor
whatever
whatsoever
whenever
wherever
whichever
whoever
whosoever

level
bedevil
bevel
daredevil
devil
go to the devil
high-level
low-level
Neville
revel
top-level

reveller
leveller

prevalence
benevolence
malevolence

prevalent
benevolent
malevolent

cleverly
Beverley

seven
Aneurin Bevan
Devon
eleven
Evan
heaven
in seventh heaven
Kevin
leaven
Severn

seventh
eleventh

reverence
irreverence
severance

heavy
bevvy
bevy
levy
top-heavy

crevice
Ben Nevis

brevity
levity
longevity

5.18

pleasant
omnipresent
peasant
pheasant
present (= *here*)
unpleasant

pleasantly
presently
unpleasantly

president
nonresident
resident
vice-president

Lesley
Elvis Presley
John Wesley
Leslie

Section 6
-EE-

All the words in this section use the sound **-ee-** (as in gr*ee*n, ch*ee*ky, ind*ee*d) in their main stressed syllable

6.1

tree

A & E (= *accident and emergency*)
AB (= *able-bodied seaman*)
ABC
absentee
AD
ADC (= *aide-de-camp*)
agree
Ali G
ANC (= *African National Congress*)
asap
B
B & B
BBC
BC
be
Bea
bee
bonhomie
bootee
bourgeoisie
BSc
BSE
BST (= *British Standard Time*)
bug-free
bumblebee
C
CAB (= *Citizens' Advice Bureau*)
CAD (= *computer-aided design*)
CAP (= *Common Agricultural Policy*)
Capri
CB (= *citizens' band*)
CBE (= *Commander of the (Order of the) British Empire*)
cc
CD
CFC
Cherie
chimpanzee
CID
C-in-C (= *Commander-in-Chief*)
CJD
CND
COD
C of E (= *Church of England*)
CSE (= *Certificate of Secondary Education*)
CV
D
DC
decree
deep-sea
degree
detainee
devotee
disagree
divorcee
DOE (= *Department of the Environment*)
DTP (= *desktop publishing*)
Dundee
duty-free
DVD
E
ECG
ECT
EDP (= *electronic data processing*)
EEC
EFT (= *electronic funds transfer*)
eg
ELT (= *English Language Teaching*)
ENT (= *ear, nose and throat*)
EOC (= *Equal Opportunities Commission*)
escapee
ESP (= *extrasensory perception*)
EST (= *Eastern Standard Time*)
ET
Euro-MP
evacuee
examinee
fait accompli
fee
filigree
first-degree

flea
flee
foresee
formulae
free
fricassee
FTP (= *file transfer protocol*)
G
Galilee
GB
GCE
GCSE
GDP (= *gross domestic product*)
gee
glee
GMT
GNP (= *gross national product*)
GP
guarantee
he
HGV
HIV
HMG (= *Her Majesty's Government*)
HNC
HND
HP
HRT
HTTP (= *hypertext transfer protocol*)
ID
ie
interest-free
internee
interviewee
ISP (= *Internet Service Provider*)
IT
ITV
jamboree
JP
jubilee
KB (= *kilobyte*)
kedgeree
key
KGB
knee
LCD (= *liquid crystal display*)
lea
lead-free
LED (= *light-emitting diode*)
Lee
low-key
LP
LSD
lychee
Marie
marquee
marrowfat pea
MBE
MC
MD (= *managing director*)
ME
me
MEP
mg (= *milligram(me)*)
mi
MOD
monoski
MOT
mother-to-be
MP
mpg (= *miles per gallon*)
MSc
MSG (= *monosodium glutamate*)
MSP (= *Member of the Scottish Parliament*)
NB
NME
nominee
NSPCC
NUT
OAP
OBE
OD
OECD (= *Organization for Economic Cooperation and Development*)
off-key
OHP (= *overhead projector*)
OTC (= *Officers' Training Corps*)
OTT
oversee
P
p & p
PAYE
payee
PC
PE
pea
pedigree
PG
PhD
plc
plea
PMT
PT
PVC
QC
QED
quay
RAC
R & D (= *research and development*)
RC (= *Roman Catholic*)
RE
re (= *about*)
referee
refugee
rent-free
repartee
RIP
Robert E Lee
RP (= *Received Pronunciation*)
RRP (= *recommended retail price*)
RSPB
RSPCC
RSVP
RUC (= *Royal Ulster Constabulary*)
rupee
RV (= *Revised Version*)

SAE
scot-free
scree
SDLP
SDP
SE
sea
see
SET (= *selective employment tax*)
settee
she
ski
SNP (= *Scottish National Party*)
spree
sugar-free
T
tax-free
TB
te
tea
tee
Tennessee
thee
three
Tiree
TLC
TNT
toll-free
Torquay
trainee
Tralee
trouble-free
trustee
TV
TVP (= *textured vegetable protein*)
twee
Tweedledee
UAE (= *United Arab Emirates*)
UHT
USP (= *unique selling proposition*)
UV
V
VAT
VC
vCJD (= *variant-CJD*)
VIP
virtuosi
vis-à-vis
water-ski
WC
we
wee
whoopee
WP (= *word processing; word processor*)
WPC
ye
yippee
Z

The following words will also tend to rhyme with these when they come at the end of a line:

aborigine
absurdity
abundantly
academy
accompany
accordingly
accountability
accountancy
accuracy
accurately
acrimony
actively
actually
actuary
adequacy
adequately
Admiralty
admittedly
adultery
adversary
adversity
agency
agony
alacrity
Albany
alchemy
alimony
allegedly
allegory
alternately
alternatively
amnesty
anarchy
anatomy
ancestry
anchovy
Anglesey
angrily
anomaly
Ant(h)ony
antipathy
anxiously
apathy
apostrophe
apparently
appropriately
approximately
arbitrary
archery
arguably
aristocracy
armoury
artery
artistry
assuredly
atrophy
attentively
auditory
autopsy
auxiliary
aviary
avidly
Aylesbury
balcony
bankruptcy
basically
beautifully
beneficiary
Bethany
bigamy
bigotry
biodiversity
biology
biopsy
blackberry
blasphemy

blissfully
bloodthirsty
blustery
bodily
breviary
brilliantly
broccoli
brotherly
budgetary
buoyancy
bureaucracy
burglary
busily
butchery
calamity
Calgary
calligraphy
calumny
candidacy
canopy
Canterbury
capably
captaincy
carefully
carelessly
carpentry
casually
casualty
catastrophe
category
cautiously
cavalry
ceaselessly
celebrity
celery
celibacy
cemetery
centrally
century
ceremony
certainly
chaplaincy
chastity
cheerfully
chemistry
chiropody
chivalry
Cicely
clemency
colliery
colony
comedy
comfortably
commercially
commonly
company
complacency
compulsory
conceivably
conciliatory
concurrently
conditionally
confectionery
confederacy
confidently
congratulatory
consciously
consequently
conservatory
conspiracy
constituency
consultancy
contemporary
contingency
contrary
controversy
corollary
coronary
Coventry
cowardly
cranberry
credulity
Cromarty
crotchety
culinary
currency
currently
custody
customary
cutlery
dangerously
debauchery
deceptively
decidedly
deliberately
delicacy
delicately
delinquency
deliriously
democracy
dentistry
deputy
derogatory
desperately
despondency
destiny
desultory
diametrically
dictionary
differently
difficulty
digitally
dignitary
diplomacy
disciplinary
discrepancy
discriminatory
disorderly
distastefully
diversity
Dorothy
dreadfully
dromedary
drudgery
dynasty
dysentery
dystrophy
earnestly
easterly
eatery
ebony
economically
ecstasy
efficacy
efficiency
effortlessly
effrontery
elderly
electrically
electronically
elegantly
elegy
embassy
embroidery

Emily
eminently
emissary
emotionally
empathy
emphatically
enemy
energy
enmity
enormously
entirely
entirety
enviously
epitome
equally
estuary
ethically
ethnically
eulogy
evenly
eventually
evidently
exceedingly
excellency
exceptionally
excitedly
exemplary
expectancy
expediency
expertly
explanatory
explicitly
exquisitely
extraordinarily
extraordinary
fabulously
facsimile
faculty
faithfully
falconry
fallacy
famously
fantasy
fatally
fatherly
fearlessly
February
fidgety
fiendishly
figuratively
finally
finicky
flagrantly
fluently
foolishly
forcibly
forestry
forgery
fortunately
frantically
frequency
frequently
functionary
funnily
furiously
gaiety
galaxy
gallantry
gaudily
generally
generously
genially
gentlemanly
genuinely
Germany
gimmicky
gingerly
Glastonbury
glossary
gluttony
gooseberry
gossipy
graciously
gradually
graphically
gratefully
gratuitously
gravelly
grievously
grocery
grudgingly
gruesomely
grumpily
guardedly
guiltily
haberdashery
habitually
half-heartedly
hallucinatory
handsomely
haphazardly
harmony
hastily
hazily
heartily
heavenly
heavily
helpfully
helplessly
heraldry
hereditary
heredity
heresy
heroically
hesitancy
hideously
historically
homeopathy
homily
honestly
honorary
hopefully
hopelessly
horizontally
horribly
hosiery
hospitably
humanly
humorously
humourlessly
Hungary
hungrily
hurriedly
husbandry
hypocrisy
idiocy
idiosyncrasy
idolatry
illegitimacy
illegitimately
illiberally
illogically
illusory
imagery

imaginary
immediacy
immediately
immodestly
immodesty
immorally
imperceptibly
imperfectly
impersonally
importantly
impotency
inadequacy
inadequately
inadvertently
incendiary
inclemency
increasingly
incredibly
independently
individually
industry
inefficacy
inefficiency
inevitably
inextricably
infamy
infancy
infantry
infinitely
infirmary
infirmity
inflammatory
inflationary
inhospitably
inhumanly
injury
innumeracy
insanitary
insignificantly
insolvency
instantly
intangibly
integrity
intentionally
intermediary
intimacy
intimately
intravenously
intricacy
introductory
invariably
inventory
invisibly
involuntary
inwardly
irony
itinerary
ivory
January
jealously
jealousy
jeopardy
Jeremy
jerkily
jewellery
jittery
jokily
jokingly
jovially
joyfully
judiciary
justifiably
Kennedy
knowingly
laboratory
lamentably
languidly
larceny
lavatory
lavishly
laxity
legacy
legality
legally
legitimacy
legitimately
leisurely
lengthily
leprosy
lethargy
liberally
liberty
library
lifelessly
lingerie
literally
literary
liturgy
locally
logically
longingly
lovely
luminary
lunacy
luxury
mahogany
majesty
malady
Malagasy
mammary
mandatory
manfully
manifestly
marginally
Marjorie
markedly
masonry
masterly
mastery
materially
mediocrity
melody
menagerie
mercenary
mercifully
merrily
messily
mightily
migratory
military
mimicry
ministry
miserably
miserly
misery
moderately
modestly
modesty
momentary
monarchy
monastery
monetary
monogamy
moodily

morally
morbidly
mortuary
mulberry
mutually
naivety
narrowly
nastily
naturally
needlessly
negatively
negligently
neighbourly
nervously
niggardly
noiselessly
noisily
Normandy
northerly
nostalgically
notably
noticeably
novelty
nudity
nugatory
numeracy
obesity
obituary
obligatory
observatory
obstinacy
obviously
occasionally
odyssey
Offaly
ominously
openly
orally
orderly
ordinarily
ordinary
originally
outwardly
overwhelmingly
pageantry
palmistry
panicky
panoply
papacy
papery
paramilitary
parody
partially
particularly
patiently
peccary
peculiarly
pecuniary
penalty
Penelope
penitentiary
penury
peony
peppery
perceptibly
peremptory
perfectly
perfunctory
perilously
perpetually
personally
persuasively
pharmacy
philanthropy
philosophy
physically
piously
piracy
pitifully
plaintively
planetary
pleasantly
pleasantry
pleurisy
poetry
poignancy
pointedly
policy
politically
polygamy
popularly
positively
posthumously
potency
poverty
powdery
practically
precipitately
predatory
predictability
predictably
predominantly
preferably
pregnancy
preliminary
preparatory
presidency
presumably
previously
primacy
primarily
primary
privacy
privately
probably
probity
prodigy
profitably
profundity
progeny
prohibitively
prominently
property
prophecy
proprietary
provisionally
psychiatry
puberty
publicly
pulmonary
punctually
purgatory
purposely
quandary
quantity
quietly
rapidly
rarity
raspberry
reactionary
reasonably
recipe
redundancy
reformatory

regency
relatively
religiously
remarkably
remedy
repeatedly
repertory
reportedly
repository
reputedly
respectably
respiratory
reverie
rhapsody
rivalry
Romany
Rosalie
rosary
Rosemary
rosemary
Salisbury
salutary
sanctity
sanctuary
sanitary
savagely
Saxony
scantily
scarcity
scholarly
scruffily
scrupulously
scullery
secondary
secondly
secrecy
secretly
sesame
seventy
sexually
shabbily
shadowy
shakily
shamefully
shamelessly
showery
Shrewsbury
Sicily
signatory
significantly
silently
silvery
similarly
simile
simultaneously
sinewy
singularly
sisterly
sketchily
sleepily
slippery
slovenly
socially
solidly
soliloquy
solitary
solvency
sophistry
sorcery
southerly
sovereignty
specifically
statutory
stealthily
Stephanie
stonily
strategy
strawberry
strenuously
structurally
stupidly
sub judice
subsequently
subsidiary
subsidy
subtlety
suddenly
successfully
sugary
suitably
summarily
suppository
supremacy
surprisingly
swimmingly
sympathy
symphony
synergy
syrupy
tacitly
tactfully
tactlessly
tangibly
tapestry
tardily
tastefully
tastelessly
tearfully
technically
telepathically
telepathy
temporary
tenancy
tenderly
tentatively
terminally
terribly
terrifically
territory
tertiary
testily
testimony
thankfully
thanklessly
therapy
thingummy
thoroughly
thoughtfully
thoughtlessly
timidly
Timothy
tomfoolery
totally
tragedy
tragically
transitory
travesty
treasury
trilogy
Tripoli
Tuscany
typically
tyranny
ultimately

unanimously
unconditionally
unconsciously
understandably
undoubtedly
uneconomically
unfortunately
unhurriedly
unimportantly
unintentionally
unitary
universally
university
unknowingly
unlovely
unnaturally
unpredictability
unreasonably
unscrupulously
unsubtlety
unsuccessfully
unsuitably
unsurprisingly
untypically
unusually
unwillingly
unwittingly
upholstery
uppity
urgently
urinary
usefully
uselessly
usually
usury
vacancy
vacantly
vagary
vagrancy
valency
valiantly
velvety
vertically
veterinary
villainy
violently
virtually
visibly
visionary
visually
vitally
vividly
vociferously
volubly
voluntary
wallaby
warranty
watery
westerly
wilfully
willingly
wittily
wittingly
womanly
Zachary

idea
Lea(h)
Mia
Nicosia
Ria
sightseer
skier
Sophia
trachea

> **+** You can add to this list by adding ***-(e)r*** to some words that rhyme with ***tree***, as in ***freer***
>
> You can also make rhymes for these words by using ***her*** after some words that rhyme with ***tree***, as in ***free her***

agreeable
disagreeable
foreseeable
unforeseeable

Liam
mausoleum

> **+** You can add to this list by adding ***'em*** to some words that rhyme with ***tree***, as in ***free 'em***

Ian
Aegean
Caribbean
Crimean
epicurean
European
Fijian
Hebridean
Jacobean
Korean
paean
plebeian
Pyrenean
Tanzanian

seeing
being
sightseeing
skiing
wellbeing

> **+** You can add to this list by adding ***-ing*** to some words that rhyme with ***tree***, as in ***fleeing***

Leo
Cleo
Rio
Theo
trio

6.2

amoeba
RIBA (= *Royal Institute of British Architects*)
The Queen of Sheba

feeble
enfeeble
Keble

+ You can make rhymes for these words by using words in section **6.18** that rhyme with *evil*

keyboard
seaboard

Libra
zebra

6.3

week
antique
batik
beak
bezique
bleak
boutique
cheek
chic
clique
creak
creek
critique
eke
freak
geek
Greek
hide-and-seek
leak
leek
Martinique
meek
midweek
Mozambique
mystique
oblique
off-peak
peak
peek
physique
pique
reek
seek
shriek
Sikh
sleek
sneak
speak
squeak
streak
teak
technique
tweak
unique
weak
wreak

kneecap
recap

e-card
keycard

speaker
asylum-seeker
beaker
Costa Rica
eureka
loudspeaker
sneaker
streaker
Topeka
Ulrika

+ You can add to this list by adding *-er* to some words that rhyme with *week*, as in *weaker*

You can also make rhymes for these words by using *her* after some words that rhyme with *week*, as in *seek her*

beacon
archdeacon
Costa Rican
deacon
Mozambican
pecan
Puerto Rican
weaken

sneaky
cheeky
creaky
freaky
leaky
peaky
squeaky
streaky

speaking
creaking
French-speaking

+ You can add to this list by adding *-ing* to some words that rhyme with *week*, as in *sneaking*

weekly
bi-weekly
bleakly
meekly
sleekly
weakly

equal
sequel
unequal

6.4

seed
accede
agreed
aniseed
bead
bleed
bottle-feed
breast-feed
breed
cede
centipede
concede
creed
deed
exceed
feed
force-feed
freed

greed
guaranteed
he'd
heed
high-speed
impede
indeed
intercede
knead
knock-kneed
lead (= *to guide*)
millipede
mislead
misread (= *to read wrongly*)
need
plead
precede
proceed
read
recede
reed
secede
she'd
speed
stampede
succeed
supersede
Swede
swede
tweed
we'd
weak-kneed
weed

> ➕ You can add to this list by adding ***-d*** to some words that rhyme with ***tree***, as in ***refereed***

reader
Aida
bleeder
breeder
cedar
cheerleader
Freda
leader
mind-reader
newsreader
proofreader
ringleader

> ➕ You can add to this list by adding ***-er*** to some words that rhyme with ***seed***, as in ***speeder***
>
> You can also make rhymes for these words by using ***her*** after some words that rhyme with ***seed***, as in ***freed her***

readable
machine-readable
pleadable
unreadable

needle
wheedle

Eden
Anthony Eden
Sweden

media
encyclop(a)edia
greedier
mass media
multimedia
needier
seedier
speedier
weedier

medium
tedium

median
comedian
tragedian

obedient
disobedient
expedient
ingredient

immediate
intermediate

greedy
beady
needy
seedy
speedy
weedy

orthopa(e)dic
encyclop(a)edic

greedily
seedily
speedily

lead-in
Dunedin

> ➕ You can also make rhymes for these words by using ***in*** after some words that rhyme with ***seed***, as in ***succeed in***

reading
breeding
leading
misleading
preceding
speeding
succeeding

> ➕ You can add to this list by adding ***-ing*** to some words that rhyme with ***seed***, as in ***feeding***

torpedo
libido
lido
speedo
tuxedo

needless
heedless
seedless

siege
besiege
liege

DJ
Vijay

region
Glaswegian
legion
Norwegian

gee-gee
Fiji
squeegee

strategic
paraplegic
quadriplegic

Bognor Regis
aegis

weeds
Leeds
tweeds

> + You can add to this list by adding *-s* to some words that rhyme with ***seed***, as in ***needs***

6.5

chief
aperitif
bas-relief
beef
belief
brief
corned beef
debrief
disbelief
grief
handkerchief
leaf
motif
overleaf
reef
relief
roast beef
sheaf
Tenerife
thief

> + You can also make rhymes for these words by using words in section **6.16** that rhyme with ***teeth***

prefect
defect (= *a flaw*)

beefy
leafy

briefing
debriefing
leafing

chiefly
briefly

6.6

league
fatigue
intrigue

eager
meagre
Riga

legal
beagle
eagle
illegal
regal

legally
eagerly
illegally
meagrely
regally

6.7

steal
Achilles' heel
Anil
appeal
automobile
conceal
congeal
daisywheel
deal
eel
feel
ferris wheel
genteel
he'll
heal
heel
imbecile
Ismail
keel
Kiel
kneel
Lille
Lucille
meal
Neil
peal
peel
reel
repeal
reveal
seal
she'll
Sir Robert Peel
snowmobile
spiel
squeal
stainless steel
steel
Sunil
the Bastille
three-course meal
veal
we'll
weal
wheel
zeal

> → Many English speakers pronounce some words in section **7.4** (eg *ordeal*) in such a way that they rhyme with these words

dealer
concealer
feeler
Jamila
newsdealer
Sheila
tequila
three-wheeler

+ You can add to this list by adding *-er* to some words that rhyme with ***steal***, as in ***squealer***

You can also make rhymes for these words by using ***her*** after some words that rhyme with ***steal***, as in ***conceal her***

Celia
Amelia
camellia
Cecilia
Cordelia
Delia
Ophelia
steelier

freely
mealy
steely
touchy-feely
tweely
wheelie

feeling
appealing
ceiling
Darjeeling
double-dealing
free-wheeling
revealing
unappealing
unfeeling
wheeling and dealing

+ You can add to this list by adding *-ing* to some words that rhyme with ***steal***, as in ***concealing***

dealings
peelings

+ You can add to this list by adding ***-s*** to some words that rhyme with ***feeling***, as in ***ceilings***

beeline
feline

field
afield
battlefield
four-wheeled
high-heeled
Huddersfield
ill-concealed
left-field
low-heeled
midfield
shield
three-wheeled
two-wheeled
unconcealed
wedge-heeled
well-heeled
wield
yield

+ You can add to this list by adding *-ed* to some words that rhyme with ***steal***, as in ***concealed***

6.8

dream
A Midsummer Night's Dream
beam
blaspheme
bream
clotted cream
cream
deem
double cream
downstream
esteem
extreme
gleam
harem
Ibrahim
ice-cream
kibbutzim
let off steam
midstream
ream
redeem
regime
scheme
scream
seam
seem
self-esteem
single cream
sour(ed) cream
steam
stream
supreme
team
teem
theme
upstream
whipped cream
whipping cream

+ You can also make rhymes for these words by using words in section **6.9** that rhyme with ***clean***

female
e-mail

dreamer
femur

Hiroshima
Iwo Jima
lemur
Lima
Redeemer
steamer
streamer

> + You can add to this list by adding *-(e)r* to some words that rhyme with ***dream***, as in ***schemer***
>
> You can also make rhymes for these words by using ***her*** after some words that rhyme with ***dream***, as in ***esteem her***

demon
seaman

anaemia
creamier
dreamier
leukaemia
seamier
septicaemia
steamier

dreamy
creamy
seamy
steamy

seeming
gleaming
redeeming
teeming

> + You can add to this list by adding *-ing* to some words that rhyme with ***dream***, as in ***screaming***

seemingly
screamingly

Seymour
Timor

seemly
extremely
supremely
unseemly

6.9

clean
Aberdeen
Aileen
answering machine
aquamarine
aubergine
bean
been
beguine
Benin
between
big screen
black-eyed bean
bottle-green
broad bean
butter bean
caffeine
canteen
Charlene
clementine
Colleen
contravene
convene
cuisine
Dean
dean
demean
dopamine
dry-clean
eighteen
Eileen
emerald-green
evergreen
fifteen
fine bean
foreseen
fourteen
gabardine
gelatine
Gene
gene
Geraldine
glean
glycerine
go-between
Goose Green
green
grenadine
guillotine
Hallowe(')en
has-been
Idi Amin
in-between
intervene
iodine
Jacqueline
jade-green
James Dean
Janine
Jean
jellybean
Jolene
Josephine
Justine
Kathleen
keen
kerosene
kidney bean
knitting machine
latrine
lean
lima bean
limousine
machine
magazine
margarine
marine
Martine
Maxine
mean
mezzanine
Mr Bean
Nadine
naphthalene
navy bean
nectarine
nicotine

nineteen
nitroglycerine
obscene
overseen
oxyacetylene
pinto bean
polythene
preen
quarantine
Queen
queen
quinine
ravine
Roisin
routine
runner bean
sardine
scene
screen
seen
serene
seventeen
sewing machine
sheen
Shereen
silver screen
sixteen
small screen
soya bean
spleen
spring-clean
string bean
submarine
tambourine
tangerine
teen
terrine
thirteen
trampoline
tureen
ultramarine
umpteen
unclean
unforeseen
unseen
vaccine
velveteen
vending machine
village green
washing machine
wean
wide screen
Yitzhak Rabin

+ You can also make rhymes for these words by using words in section **6.8** that rhyme with ***dream***

cleaner
Angelina
arena
Argentina
ballerina
Bosnia-Herzegovina
Catriona
Christina
concertina
Cortina
Davina
demeanour
Edwina
Georgina
Gina
hyena
Katrina
Lena
Marina
marina
Martina
Messalina
misdemeanour
Nina
Pasadena
Pristina
retsina
Ribena®
Rowena
Sabrina
Saint Helena
Selina
semolina
Serena
Sheena
subpoena
Tina
Wilhelmina
Zena

+ You can add to this list by adding ***-er*** to some words that rhyme with ***clean***, as in ***keener***

You can also make rhymes for these words by using ***her*** after some words that rhyme with ***clean***, as in ***seen her***

penal
duodenal
renal
venal

scenery
bicentenary
centenary
greenery
machinery
plenary
tercentenary

Venus
genus
intravenous

+ You can also make rhymes for these words by using ***us*** after some words that rhyme with ***clean***, as in ***seen us***

Slovenia
Armenia
schizophrenia

menial
congenial
genial
venial

Slovenian
Armenian

lenient
convenient
inconvenient

teeny
Bikini
bikini
genie
Jean(n)ie
meanie
Mussolini
Puccini
Queenie
Rene
Santorini
teeny-weeny
zucchini

scenic
hygienic
unhygienic

phoenix
hygienics
Phoenix

meaning
cleaning
dry-cleaning
intervening
leaning
screening
spring-cleaning
well-meaning

> + You can add to this list by adding *-ing* to some words that rhyme with ***clean***, as in ***preening***

casino
albino
Angeleno
beano
cappuccino
Filipino
neutrino
palomino
Quentin Tarantino
Reno
Rudolph Valentino
San Marino
The Beano
vino

keenly
cleanly
meanly
obscenely
routinely
serenely

senior
Kenya
Monsignor

means
baked beans
jeans
Milton Keynes
New Orleans
Philippines
smithereens
teens

> + You can add to this list by adding *-s* to some words that rhyme with ***clean***, as in ***screens***

6.10

deep
asleep
beep
bleep
cheap
cheep
creep
dirt-cheap
heap
Jeep®
keep
knee-deep
leap
Meryl Streep
oversleep
peep
put to sleep
reap
seep
sheep
sleep
steep
sweep
Uriah Heep
weep

sleeper
barkeeper
beekeeper
bleeper
carpet-sweeper
creeper
doorkeeper
gamekeeper
gatekeeper
goalkeeper
housekeeper
innkeeper
keeper
minesweeper
reaper
shopkeeper
sweeper
the grim reaper
timekeeper
wicketkeeper

> + You can add to this list by adding *-er* to some words that rhyme with ***deep***, as in ***beeper***
>
> You can also make rhymes for these words by using ***her*** after some words that rhyme with ***deep***, as in ***keep her***

people
steeple
townspeople

cheapen
deepen
steepen

sleepy
creepy
weepy

sleeping
bookkeeping
creeping
goalkeeping
housekeeping
keeping
peacekeeping
safe-keeping
sweeping
timekeeping
weeping

+ You can add to this list by adding *-ing* to some words that rhyme with ***deep***, as in ***leaping***

6.11

crease
apiece
Bernice
breach of the peace
caprice
cease
centrepiece
decease
decrease
Dumfries
fleece
frontispiece
geese
Grease
grease
Greece
increase
lease
mantelpiece
masterpiece
mounted police
Nice
niece
obese
peace
piece
police
release
Rhys
War and Peace

recent
decent
indecent

recently
decently
indecently

rhesus
Croesus

+ You can also make rhymes for these words by using ***us*** after some words that rhyme with ***crease***, as in ***release us***

faeces
prostheses
theses

fleecy
greasy
St Francis of Assisi

leasing
ceasing
creasing
decreasing
fleecing
greasing
increasing
piecing
policing
releasing
unceasing

thesis
amniocentesis
prosthesis

seaside
Deeside
quayside
Teesside

east
beast
deceased
feast
least
northeast
north-northeast
priest
southeast
south-southeast
yeast

+ You can add to this list by adding ***-ed*** to some words that rhyme with ***crease***, as in ***released***

Easter
Batista
fashionista

6.12

seizure
freesia
Indonesia
Melanesia
Micronesia
Polynesia

→ Many English speakers pronounce some words in section **6.19** (eg *amnesia*) in such a way that they rhyme with these words

lesion
adhesion
cohesion
Fri(e)sian
Indonesian

6.13

leash
fiche
hashish
Kenny Dalglish
microfiche
niche
pastiche
quiche
unleash

Esher
Aisha
Nisha

completion
deletion
depletion
Grecian
secretion
Tahitian
Venetian

facetious
specious
unleash us

6.14

sweet
beat
beet
bittersweet
bleat
cheat
compete
complete
conceit
cracked wheat
Crete
deceit
defeat
delete
deplete
discreet
discrete
downbeat
Downing Street
eat
effete
ejector seat
elite
en suite
entreat
excrete
feat
feet
fleet
greet
heat
ill-treat
incomplete
indiscreet
maltreat
meat
meet
mete
mistreat
neat
obsolete
overeat
overheat
parakeet
peat
Pete
petite
pleat
preheat
receipt
repeat
replete
retreat
seat
secrete
sheet
sleet
street
suite
teat
the patter of tiny feet
treat
tweet
unseat
upbeat
wheat
white as a sheet

detail
retail

heater
Anita
beater
centilitre
centimetre
cheetah
eater
Gita
litre
Lolita
man-eater
meat-eater
meter
metre
millilitre
millimetre
Nita
Peter
peter
Rita
saltpetre
teeter
windcheater
world-beater

> + You can add to this list by adding *-er* to some words that rhyme with ***sweet***, as in ***neater***
>
> You can also make rhymes for these words by using ***her*** after some words that rhyme with ***sweet***, as in ***beat her***

beetle
Beatle
Beetle
betel
deathwatch beetle
decretal
f(o)etal

beaten
Buster Keaton
Cretan

eaten
Eton
moth-eaten
neaten
overeaten
sweeten
unbeaten
uneaten
weatherbeaten
wheaten
worm-eaten

treaty
entreaty
meaty
Nefertiti
sweetie
Tahiti

heated
conceited
deep-seated
pleated
repeated
undefeated

> + You can add to this list by adding *-(e)d* to some words that rhyme with ***sweet***, as in ***competed***

beating
cheating
fleeting
greeting
heating
man-eating
meat-eating
meeting
seating
self-defeating

> + You can add to this list by adding *-ing* to some words that rhyme with ***sweet***, as in ***repeating***

defeatist
elitist

defeatism
elitism

veto
burrito
Hirohito
incognito
Marshal Tito
mosquito
Quito
SEATO (= *South-East Asia Treaty Organization*)

sweetly
completely
discreetly
indiscreetly
neatly

sweetness
neatness

eats
Keats

> + You can add to this list by adding *-s* to some words that rhyme with ***sweet***, as in ***meets***

reach
beach
beech
beseech
bleach
breach
breech
each
impeach
leech
overreach
peach
preach
screech
speech
teach

teacher
creature
feature
preacher
schoolteacher

> + You can add to this list by adding *-er* to some words that rhyme with ***reach***, as in ***beseecher***
>
> You can also make rhymes for these words by using ***her*** after some words that rhyme with ***reach***, as in ***teach her***

teaching
beseeching
far-reaching
schoolteaching

> + You can add to this list by adding *-ing* to some words that rhyme with ***reach***, as in ***screeching***

6.15

breathe
bequeath
Meath
seethe
sheathe
teethe
unsheathe
Westmeath
wreathe

breather
bequeather
either
neither

teething
bequeathing

breathing
seething
sheathing
unsheathing
wreathing

6.16

teeth
beneath
buckteeth
Edward Heath
heath
Keith
sheath
underneath
wreath

> + You can also make rhymes for these words by using words in section **6.5** that rhyme with ***chief***

Aretha
ether
Ibiza

> + You can also make rhymes for these words by using ***her*** after some words that rhyme with ***teeth***, as in ***beneath her***

6.17

leave
achieve
believe
cleave
conceive
deceive
disbelieve
Eve
eve
Genevieve
grieve
heave
make-believe
naive
Niamh
overachieve
peeve
perceive
Rajiv
receive
relieve
reprieve
retrieve
sleeve
Steve
Tel Aviv
thieve
underachieve
weave
we've

fever
achiever
beaver
believer
cantilever
cleaver
deceiver
disbeliever
Eva
Geneva
hayfever
leaver
lever
overachiever
receiver
retriever
rheumatic fever
scarlet fever
unbeliever
underachiever
weaver

> + You can also make rhymes for these words by using ***her*** after some words that rhyme with ***leave***, as in ***believe her***

believable
achievable
conceivable
inconceivable
irretrievable
retrievable
unbelievable

evil
medieval
primeval
upheaval

even
Stephen
Steven
uneven

previous
devious

deviate
abbreviate
alleviate

weaving
grieving
heaving
receiving
thieving

bereaved
aggrieved
long-sleeved
preconceived
received
short-sleeved
unrelieved

> + You can add to this list by adding ***-d*** to some words that rhyme with ***leave***, as in ***believed***

achievement
bereavement
overachievement
underachievement

leaves
Anne of Cleves

as thick as thieves
eaves
Jeeves
sheaves
thieves

+ You can add to this list by adding *-s* to some words that rhyme with ***leave***, as in ***believes***

6.18

freeway
leeway
seaway

kiwi
wee(-)wee

6.19

freeze
antifreeze
Antipodes
appease
Balinese
Belize
breeze
Burmese
Cantonese
Celebes
cheese
Chinese
Congolese
deep-freeze
Denise
disease
displease
DTs
dungarees
ease
expertise
frieze
Gabonese
Guyanese
he's
Hebrides
Heloise
Hercules
Japanese
Javanese
jeez
journalese
Lebanese
lees
legalese
like chalk and cheese
Los Angeles
Louise
Maltese
manganese
Nepalese
officialese
overseas
Pekinese
please
Portuguese
Pyrenees
Rameses
re-freeze
seize
Senegalese
she's
Siamese
Sinhalese
sleaze
sneeze
squeeze
Sudanese
Taiwanese
tease
these
Togolese
trapeze
Ulysses
unease
unfreeze
valise
Valkyries
Viennese
Vietnamese
wheeze

+ You can add to this list by adding *-s* to some words that rhyme with ***tree***, as in ***agrees***

freezer
crowd pleaser
fridge-freezer
geezer
geyser
Julius Caesar
Louisa
Pisa
teaser
T(h)eresa
visa

+ You can add to this list by adding *-r* to some words that rhyme with ***freeze***, as in ***appeaser***

You can also make rhymes for these words by using ***her*** after some words that rhyme with ***freeze***, as in ***tease her***

weasel
diesel
easel
teasel

reason
off-season
season
treason

reasonable
seasonable
treasonable
unreasonable
unseasonable

reasoning
seasoning

amnesia
breezier

easier
queasier
sleazier

> ➔ Many English speakers pronounce some words in section **6.12** (eg *Polynesia*) in such a way that they rhyme with these words

easy
breezy
queasy
sleazy
sneezy
uneasy

easily
breezily
queasily
sleazily
uneasily

pleasing
appeasing
displeasing
easing
freezing
seizing
sneezing
squeezing
teasing
wheezing

pleased
diseased
displeased

> + You can add to this list by adding *-d* to some words that rhyme with ***freeze***, as in ***teased***

Section 7
-EAR-

All the words in this section use the sound **-ear-** (as in f*ear*, *wear*y, app*ear*) in their main stressed syllable

7.1

dear
adhere
all-clear
amenorrhoea
appear
atmosphere
auctioneer
austere
beer
Benazir
bier
bioengineer
biosphere
black marketeer
blear
Boadicea
brigadier
buccaneer
career
cashier
cashmere
cavalier
chandelier
cheer
clear
commandeer
Crimea
crystal-clear
deer
diarrhoea
disappear
Dorothea
dysmenorrhoea
ear
Edward Lear
endear
engineer
fear
gazetteer
gear
Golda Meir
gondolier
grenadier
Guinevere
hear
hemisphere
here
insincere
interfere
jeer
Kampuchea
Kashmir
King Lear
Korea
leer
lithosphere
Maria
mere
mishear
mountaineer
musketeer
mutineer
near
overhear
overseer
panacea
peer
persevere
pier
pioneer
profiteer
pyorrhoea
queer
racketeer
reappear
rear
revere
scrutineer
sear
seer
severe
shear
sheer
sincere
smear
sneer
Sofia
souvenir
spear
sphere
steer
stratosphere
Tangier
Tanzania
tear (= *a drop of moisture*)
tier
Tyne and Wear
unclear
veer
veneer
volunteer
Wear

we're
weir
Windermere
year
Zaire

7.2

weird
beard

+ You can add to this list by adding *-ed* to some words that rhyme with *dear*, as in *appeared*

7.3

tearful
cheerful
earful
fearful

7.4

real
ideal
ordeal
surreal
unreal

→ Many English speakers pronounce some words in section **6.7** (eg *deal*) in such a way that they rhyme with these words

really
clearly
dearly
half-yearly
ideally
merely
nearly
sincerely
yearly

+ You can add to this list by adding *-ly* to some words that rhyme with *dear*, as in *severely*

fearless
cheerless
peerless

realist
idealist
surrealist

realism
idealism
surrealism

realize
idealize

7.5

Vera
Elvira
era
lira
lire
Madeira

+ You can add to this list by adding *-er* to some words that rhyme with *dear*, as in *clearer*

You can also make rhymes for these words by using *her* after some words that rhyme with *dear*, as in *near her*

serum
theorem

+ You can add to this list by adding *'em* to some words that rhyme with *dear*, as in *near 'em*

clearance
adherence
appearance
coherence
disappearance
incoherence
interference
perseverance
reappearance

bacteria
Algeria
anterior
cafeteria
cheerier
criteria
diphtheria
drearier
eerier
exterior
hysteria
Iberia
inferior
interior
Lake Superior
Liberia
Nigeria
posterior
Siberia
superior
ulterior
wearier

serial
bacterial
cereal
ethereal
immaterial
imperial
magisterial
managerial
material
ministerial
venereal

materialism
imperialism

serialize
materialize

Nigerian
Algerian
criterion
Iberian
Liberian
Presbyterian
Shakespearean
Siberian
Zairean

serious
deleterious
imperious
mysterious

seriously
imperiously
mysteriously

weary
beery
bleary
cheery
dreary
eerie
eyrie
Kashmiri
Lake Erie
query
theory
world-weary

eerily
cheerily
drearily
wearily

hearing
clearing
earring
electioneering
endearing
engineering
God-fearing
interfering
jeering
mountaineering
orienteering
pioneering
racketeering
searing
sneering
steering

+ You can add to this list by adding *-ing* to some words that rhyme with ***dear***, as in ***appearing***

hero
Local Hero
Nero
Rio de Janeiro
Robert De Niro
sub-zero
zero

7.6

fierce
pierce

7.7

shears
Algiers
arrears
Britney Spears
in tears
Piers
Tangiers

+ You can add to this list by adding *-s* to some words that rhyme with ***dear***, as in ***appears***

Section 8
-ER-

All the words in this section use the sound **-er-** (as in h*er*b, G*er*man, em*er*ge) in their main stressed syllable

8.1

her
aver
blur
burr
concur
confer
connoisseur
defer
demur
deter
entrepreneur
err
fir
fur
incur
infer
inter
Louis Pasteur
masseur
myrrh
non sequitur
occur
per
prefer
purr
recur
refer
saboteur
sir
slur
spur
stir
transfer
voyeur
were
whirr

8.2

herb
blurb
curb
disturb
kerb
perturb
Serb
superb
verb

herbal
burble
gerbil
nonverbal
verbal

verbally
hyperbole
nonverbally

urban
bourbon
Durban
suburban
turban

sherbet
Herbert
turbot

Serbia
suburbia

disturbed
undisturbed
unperturbed

+ You can add to this list by adding ***-ed*** to some words that rhyme with ***herb***, as in ***perturbed***

8.3

work
berk
berserk
bodywork
Dirk
dirk
Dunkirk
F W de Klerk
handiwork
irk
jerk
Kirk
kirk
latticework
lurk
metalwork
needlework
overwork
paperwork
perk
quirk
rework

shirk
silverwork
smirk
Turk
wickerwork

worker
berserker
circa
coworker
Gurkha
shirker
tearjerker

> + You can also make rhymes for these words by using *-er* after some words that rhyme with ***work***, as in ***lurker***
>
> You can also make rhymes for these words by using ***her*** after some words that rhyme with ***work***, as in ***irk her***

workable
reworkable
shirkable
unworkable

jerky
Albuquerque
murky
perky
quirky
Turkey
turkey

working
hard-working
smirking

> + You can add to this list by adding *-ing* to some words that rhyme with ***work***, as in ***lurking***

circuit
short-circuit

> + You can also make rhymes for these words by using ***it*** after some words that rhyme with ***work***, as in ***jerk it***

8.4

heard
absurd
bird
blurred
Cape Verde
curd
Douglas Hurd
four-letter word
gird
herd
hummingbird
Kurd
ladybird
misheard
nerd
overheard
preferred
reword
Richard III
surd
the last word
third
undeterred
word

> + You can add to this list by adding *-red* to some words that rhyme with ***her***, as in ***stirred***

> → Many English speakers pronounce some words in section **19.2** (eg *assured*) in such a way that they rhyme with these words

murder
Gerda
girder

> + You can also make rhymes for these words by using ***her*** after some words that rhyme with ***heard***, as in ***preferred her***

hurdle
curdle
girdle

sturdy
birdie
hurdy-gurdy
nerdy
Verdi
wordy

verge
converge
dirge
diverge
emerge
merge
purge
scourge
Serge
serge
submerge
surge
urge

merger
perjure
verger

> + You can also make rhymes for these words by using ***her*** after some words that rhyme with ***verge***, as in ***purge her***

surgeon
burgeon
sturgeon
virgin

emergence
convergence
divergence

urgency
emergency
insurgency
resurgency

urgent
detergent
divergent
emergent
insurgent
resurgent

surgery
microsurgery
neurosurgery
perjury

8.5

turf
Astroturf®
serf
surf

+ You can also make rhymes for these words by using words in section **8.16** that rhyme with ***earth***

surfing
turfing
windsurfing

8.6

Luxembourg
erg
Gettysburg
Gothenburg
Heidelberg
Johannesburg
Nuremberg
St Petersburg

burgle
gurgle

8.7

curl
earl
furl
girl
hurl
mother-of-pearl
Pearl
pearl
purl
swirl
twirl
unfurl
whirl

surly
burly
curly
curly-wurly
early
Elizabeth Hurley
girlie
hurly-burly
pearly
Shirley

sterling
curling
hurling
Stirling

+ You can add to this list by adding *-ing* to some words that rhyme with ***curl***, as in ***swirling***

girlish
churlish

world
News of the World
underworld
unfurled

+ You can add to this list by adding *-ed* to some words that rhyme with ***curl***, as in ***hurled***

8.8

term
affirm
confirm
firm
full-term
germ
half-term
infirm
perm
reaffirm
sperm
squirm
worm

+ You can also make rhymes for these words by using words in section **8.9** that rhyme with ***turn***

murmur
Burma
Irma

+ You can add to this list by adding *-er* to some words that rhyme with ***term***, as in ***firmer***

thermal
geothermal

+ You can make rhymes for these words by using words in section **8.9** that rhyme with ***kernel***

German
Herman
sermon

vermin
determine
ermine
predetermine

terminate
exterminate
germinate

hermit
Kermit
permit (= *a licence*)

> You can also make rhymes for these words by using *it* after some words that rhyme with *term*, as in *confirm it*

confirmed
unconfirmed

> You can add to this list by adding *-ed* to some words that rhyme with *term*, as in *squirmed*

8.9

turn
about-turn
adjourn
Bannockburn
Bern(e)
burn
churn
concern
discern
earn
fern
intern
Jules Verne
Lake Lucerne
learn
overturn
pay-as-you-earn
return
spurn
stern
taciturn
tern
urn
yearn

> You can also make rhymes for these words by using words in section **8.8** that rhyme with *term*

learner
Bunsen burner
burner
earner
Smyrna

> You can add to this list by adding *-er* to some words that rhyme with *turn*, as in *sterner*
>
> You can also make rhymes for these words by using *her* after some words that rhyme with *turn*, as in *concern her*

returnable
discernible

kernel
colonel
eternal
external
fraternal
infernal
internal
journal
maternal
nocturnal
paternal

eternally
externally
fraternally
internally
maternally
nocturnally
paternally

sternum
laburnum

> You can add to this list by adding *'em* to some words that rhyme with *turn*, as in *burn 'em*

journey
attorney
Bernie
Ernie

turning
burning
concerning
discerning
learning
yearning

> You can add to this list by adding *-ing* to some words that rhyme with *turn*, as in *returning*

earnest
Ernest
The Importance of Being Earnest
sternest

furnish
burnish

eternity
fraternity
maternity
paternity

inferno
Salerno

concerned
hard-earned
unconcerned
unearned
well-earned

+ You can add to this list by adding *-ed* to some words that rhyme with ***turn***, as in ***burned***

adjournment
discernment
internment

learnt
burnt
weren't

8.10

slurp
burp
chirp
twerp
usurp

turpentine
serpentine

8.11

stirring
recurring
unerring

+ You can add to this list by adding *-ring* to some words that rhyme with ***her***, as in ***occurring***

8.12

verse
adverse
averse
coerce
converse
curse
disburse
disperse
diverse
hearse
immerse
intersperse
nurse
perverse
purse
rehearse
reimburse
reverse
terse
transverse
traverse
universe
worse

cursor
bursar
precursor
purser
vice versa

+ You can add to this list by adding *-r* to some words that rhyme with ***verse***, as in ***curser***

You can also make rhymes for these words by using ***her*** after some words that rhyme with ***verse***, as in ***curse her***

rehearsal
dispersal
reversal
universal

person
chairperson
non-person
salesperson
spokesperson
sportsperson
worsen

nursery
anniversary
bursary
cursory

mercy
Percy

subversive
discursive

tersely
adversely
conversely
perversely

first
burst
Damien Hirst
headfirst
thirst
versed
worst

+ You can add to this list by adding *-d* to some words that rhyme with ***verse***, as in ***cursed***

thirsty
Kirsty

8.13

commercial
controversial
infomercial
uncontroversial

version
assertion
aversion
coercion
conversion
desertion
diversion

excursion
exertion
immersion
incursion
insertion
Persian
perversion
reversion
submersion
subversion

8.14

dirt
advert (= *to refer*)
assert
avert
Bert
blurt
cert
convert
curt
desert (= *to leave*)
dessert (= *a sweet course*)
disconcert
divert
exert
extrovert
flirt
girt
hurt
inert
insert
introvert
invert
Kurt
miniskirt
overt
pert
pervert (= *to lead astray*)
reinsert
revert
shirt
skirt
spurt
squirt
subvert
underskirt
unhurt

deserter
Alberta
Roberta

> + You can add to this list by adding ***-er*** to some words that rhyme with ***dirt***, as in ***converter***
>
> You can also make rhymes for these words by using ***her*** after some words that rhyme with ***dirt***, as in ***hurt her***

turtle
hurtle
Myrtle
myrtle

certain
curtain
uncertain

dirty
flirty
Gertie
shirty
thirty

deserted
concerted
disconcerted
extroverted
introverted
inverted

> + You can add to this list by adding ***-ed*** to some words that rhyme with ***dirt***, as in ***converted***

furtive
assertive

hertz
deserts (= *what one deserves*)
just deserts
kilohertz
megahertz

> + You can add to this list by adding ***-s*** to some words that rhyme with ***dirt***, as in ***shirts***

search
besmirch
birch
church
lurch
perch
research

nurture
researcher

> + You can add to this list by adding ***-er*** to some words that rhyme with ***search***, as in ***lurcher***
>
> You can also make rhymes for these words by using ***her*** after some words that rhyme with ***search***, as in ***besmirch her***

searching
besmirching
birching
lurching
perching
researching

8.15

worthy
airworthy
blameworthy

newsworthy
noteworthy
praiseworthy
roadworthy
seaworthy
trustworthy
untrustworthy
unworthy

+ You can make rhymes for these words by using words in section **8.17** that rhyme with ***nervy***

8.16

earth
afterbirth
berth
birth
dearth
down-to-earth
Fort Worth
girth
Middle Earth
mirth
Perth
rebirth
unearth
worth

+ You can also make rhymes for these words by using words in section **8.5** that rhyme with ***turf***

Bertha
Eartha

8.17

nerve
conserve
curve
derv
deserve
observe
preserve
reserve
serve
swerve
unnerve
verve

fervour
observer
preserver
server

+ You can also make rhymes for these words by using ***her*** after some words that rhyme with ***nerve***, as in ***observe her***

servant
fervent
observant
unobservant

nervy
scurvy
topsy-turvy

+ You can make rhymes for these words by using words in section **8.15** that rhyme with ***worthy***

serving
conserving
curving
deserving
observing
preserving
reserving
swerving
undeserving
unnerving
unswerving

curved
reserved
undeserved
unobserved
unreserved

+ You can add to this list by adding ***-d*** to some words that rhyme with ***nerve***, as in ***observed***

8.18

hers
masseuse
secateurs

+ You can add to this list by adding ***-s*** to some words that rhyme with ***her***, as in ***occurs***

jersey
Jersey
Mersey
New Jersey

Section 9
-I-

All the words in this section use the sound **-i-** (as in sh*i*p, c*i*ty, adm*i*t) in their main stressed syllable

9.1

rib
ad-lib
bib
crib
drib
fib
glib
jib
nib
squib
women's lib

fibber
gibber
women's libber

+ You can add to this list by adding ***-ber*** to some words that rhyme with ***rib***, as in ***glibber***

dribble
nibble
quibble
scribble
Sibyl

ribbon
gibbon

Libya
Namibia
tibia

Libyan
amphibian
Namibian

exhibit
gibbet
inhibit
prohibit

9.2

quick
Arabic
arithmetic
arsenic
bishopric
Bolshevik
brick
candlestick
chick
click
crick
Dick
Dominic
double-quick
flick
get on someone's wick
get-rich-quick
heretic
hick
in good nick
kick
lick
Limerick
limerick
lunatic
maverick
Mick
Nick
nick
nonstick
pick
politic
prick
Reykjavik
rhetoric
Rick
rick
Roderick
sic
sick
slick
stick
thick
three-card trick
tic
tick
travel-sick
trick
turmeric
Vic
wick

flicker
bicker
liquor
nit-picker
picnicker
rainslicker
snicker
sticker

vicar
wicker

+ You can add to this list by adding *-er* to some words that rhyme with ***quick***, as in ***thicker***

You can also make rhymes for these words by using ***her*** after some words that rhyme with ***quick***, as in ***pick her***

despicable
applicable
explicable
inexplicable

fickle
nickel
pickle
prickle
sickle
tickle
trickle

chicken
grief-stricken
horror-stricken
no spring chicken
panic-stricken
poverty-stricken
quicken
sicken
stricken
terror-stricken
thicken

trickery
chicory
flickery
hickory

tricky
Billericay
brickie
dicky
Mick(e)y
mickey
Nicky
Nikki
piccy
picky
quickie
Ricky
sticky
Vicki

ticking
nit-picking

+ You can add to this list by adding *-ing* to some words that rhyme with ***quick***, as in ***picking***

ticket
cricket
picket
thicket
wicket

+ You can also make rhymes for these words by using ***it*** after some words that rhyme with ***quick***, as in ***pick it***

rickety
pernickety

pick-up
hiccup
stick-up

quickly
prickly
sickly
thickly
trickly

sickness
airsickness
carsickness
homesickness
quickness
seasickness
thickness
travel-sickness

fix
affix
Beatrix
crucifix
fiddlesticks
geopolitics
in the sticks
like a ton of bricks
MI6
mix
politics
six
Styx
transfix

+ You can add to this list by adding *-s* to some words that rhyme with ***quick***, as in ***picks***

mixer
elixir
fixer
sixer

vixen
Richard Nixon

mixed
fixed

+ You can add to this list by adding *-ed* to some words that rhyme with ***fix***, as in ***transfixed***

mixture
fixture

fiction
addiction
affliction
benediction
constriction

contradiction
conviction
crucifixion
depiction
dereliction
diction
eviction
friction
jurisdiction
non-fiction
prediction
Pulp Fiction
restriction

strict
addict
afflict
Benedict
conflict (= *to disagree*)
constrict
contradict
convict
depict
derelict
evict
inflict
Pict
predict
restrict

+ You can add to this list by adding *-ed* to some words that rhyme with ***quick***, as in ***picked***

victor
boa constrictor
depicter
inflicter
predictor
stricter
Victor

predictable
contradictable
convictable
inflictable
unpredictable

victory
contradictory
self-contradictory

addicted
restricted
self-inflicted
unrestricted

+ You can add to this list by adding *-ed* to some words that rhyme with ***strict***, as in ***predicted***

vindictive
addictive
restrictive

ubiquitous
iniquitous

antiquity
iniquity
ubiquity

gesticulate
articulate (= *to speak*)
matriculate

particular
curricular
extracurricular
perpendicular
vehicular

ridiculous
meticulous

9.3

lid
amid
bid
Billy the Kid
chid
did
El Cid
flip one's lid
forbid
grid
hid
inhabited
inhibited
kid
limited
Madrid
mid
outbid
outdid
overdid
prohibited
pyramid
quid
redid
rid
skid
slid
squid
talented
undid
uninhibited

bidder
consider
reconsider

+ You can also make rhymes for these words by using ***her*** after some words that rhyme with ***lid***, as in ***forbid her***

middle
diddle
fiddle
griddle
idyll
riddle
twiddle

hidden
bedridden
bidden
chidden
forbidden
midden
overridden
ridden
stridden

unbidden

hideous
fastidious
insidious
invidious
perfidious

bidding
forbidding

> + You can add to this list by adding *-ding* to some words that rhyme with *lid*, as in *kidding*

stupidity
acidity
fluidity
humidity
liquidity
rapidity
rigidity
solidity
timidity
validity

fiddler
riddler
tiddler

fiddly
tiddly
twiddly

kidney
Sidney
Sydney

bridge
abridge
anchorage
average
beverage
foliage
fridge
haemorrhage
heritage
lineage
midge
ridge

religious
irreligious
prestigious
prodigious
sacrilegious

rigid
frigid

pigeon
pidgin
smidgen
wigeon

fidget
Bridget
digit
midget

abridged
unabridged

> + You can add to this list by adding *-d* to some words that rhyme with *bridge*, as in *ridged*

residual
individual

9.4

stiff
biff
bored stiff
Cliff
cliff
if
niff
quiff
riff
sniff
tiff
whiff

> + You can also make rhymes for these words by using words in section **9.16** that rhyme with *pith*

differ
sniffer
stiffer

differed
Clifford

stiffen
griffin
gryphon

Tiffany
Epiphany

vociferous
coniferous

periphery
midwifery

jiffy
iffy
sniffy

terrific
horrific
Pacific
prolific
scientific
soporific
South Pacific
specific
unscientific

> + You can also make rhymes for these words by using words in section **9.16** that rhyme with *neolithic*

gift
adrift
drift
GIFT (= *gamete intrafallopian transfer*)
lift
rift
shift
shrift
sift
swift
thrift

uplift

drifter
grifter
shoplifter
snifter
swifter
weightlifter

> **+** You can also make rhymes for these words by using *her* after some words that rhyme with *gift*, as in *shift her*

shifty
fifty
nifty
thrifty

uplifting
drifting

> **+** You can add to this list by adding *-ing* to some words that rhyme with *gift*, as in *shifting*

shiftless
thriftless

9.5

dig
big
fig
gig
infra dig
jig
pig
prig
rig
sprig
swig
twig
wig
WYSIWYG

digger
disfigure
figure
four-figure
gold-digger
gravedigger
jigger
prefigure
rigour
snigger
transfigure
trigger
vigour

> **+** You can add to this list by adding *-ger* to some words that rhyme with *dig*, as in *bigger*

giggle
jiggle
niggle
squiggle
wiggle
wriggle

ligament
disfigurement

vigorous
rigorous

bigot
frigate

piggy
biggie
biggy
Twiggy

stigma
enigma

figment
pigment

indignant
malignant
non-malignant

signify
dignify

dignified
signified
undignified

digs
Bay of Pigs
Ronnie Biggs
syrup of figs

> **+** You can add to this list by adding *-s* to some words that rhyme with *dig*, as in *twigs*

9.6

still
Benny Hill
Bill
bill
Brazil
brazil
chill
chlorophyl(l)
Cruella De Vil
daffodil
dill
distil
downhill
drill
fill
frill
fulfil
Gil
gill
go downhill
goodwill
grill
grille
hill
if looks could kill
ill
instil
Jill
kill
Louisville
mill

morning-after pill
nil
overkill
overspill
over the hill
Phil
pill
quill
refill
Rhyl
run-of-the-mill
Seville
shrill
sill
skill
spill
stand still
stock-still
swill
thrill
till
trill
until
uphill
vaudeville
Will
will
windowsill

killer
Arthur Miller
Attila
Camilla
caterpillar
cedilla
Glenn Miller
gorilla
guer(r)illa
lady-killer
Manila
miller
painkiller
pillar
Priscilla
thriller
tiller
vanilla
villa
weedkiller

+ You can add to this list by adding *-er* to some words that rhyme with ***still***, as in ***chiller***

You can also make rhymes for these words by using ***her*** after some words that rhyme with ***still***, as in ***kill her***

syllable
monosyllable
refillable
tillable

villain
Bob Dylan
Dylan
Harold Macmillan

pillory
ancillary
artillery
capillary
distillery
Hilary
Sir Edmund Hillary

Phyllis
bacillus
villus

+ You can also make rhymes for these words by using ***us*** after some words that rhyme with ***still***, as in ***kill us***

dilatory
depilatory

familiar
Brasília
haemophilia
unfamiliar

Brazilian
Chilean
Gillian
Lil(l)ian
pavilion
reptilian
Sicilian

bilious
punctilious
supercilious

silly
arum lily
Billy
Caerphilly
Chile
chilli
chilly
filly
frilly
hillbilly
hilly
Lily
lily
Millie
Scilly
silly-billy
tiger lily
Tilly
water lily
Willie
willy-nilly

humiliate
affiliate
conciliate

idyllic
acrylic

silica
basilica

village
pillage
spillage

penicillin
Enniskillen

willing
chilling

filling
grilling
killing
schilling
shilling
spine-chilling
thrilling
unwilling

> + You can add to this list by adding *-ing* to some words that rhyme with ***still***, as in ***spilling***

willingness
thrillingness
unwillingness

billet
fillet
millet

> + You can also make rhymes for these words by using *it* after some words that rhyme with ***still***, as in ***spill it***

militate
debilitate
facilitate
rehabilitate

ability
accessibility
agility
availability
capability
civility
compatibility
credibility
debility
disability
durability
eligibility
facility
fallibility
feasibility
fertility
flexibility
fragility
futility
gullibility
hostility
humility
immobility
impossibility
improbability
inability
inaccessibility
incapability
incivility
incompatibility
ineligibility
inevitability
infallibility
infertility
inflexibility
instability
irresponsibility
liability
mobility
nobility
possibility
probability
profitability
reliability
respectability
responsibility
senility
stability
sterility
suitability
tranquillity
unavailability
unfeasibility
unprofitability
unreliability
unsuitability
utility
versatility
viability
virility
visibility
vulnerability

pillow
Amarillo
armadillo
billow
willow

willowy
billowy

bilberry
Tilbury

silk
buttermilk
ilk
milk
semi-skimmed milk
skimmed milk

silky
milky

build
gild
guild
rebuild
skilled
strong-willed
unfulfilled
unskilled
weak-willed

> + You can add to this list by adding *-ed* to some words that rhyme with ***still***, as in ***killed***

builder
bewilder
guilder
Hilda
Mat(h)ilda
St Kilda

building
gilding
rebuilding

skilful
unskilful
wilful

skilfully
unskilfully
wilfully

fulfilment
instilment

illness
shrillness
stillness

tilt
built
custom-built
gilt
guilt
hilt
jerry-built
jilt
kilt
lilt
purpose-built
quilt
rebuilt
silt
spilt
stilt
well-built
wilt

filter
kilter

+ You can also make rhymes for these words by using *her* after some words that rhyme with ***tilt***, as in ***jilt her***

zilch
filch

million
billion
civilian
pillion
trillion
vermilion

gills
battle of wills
Beverly Hills
green about the gills
no-frills
old as the hills

+ You can add to this list by adding ***-s*** to some words that rhyme with ***still***, as in ***bills***

9.7

slim
acronym
antonym
brim
dim
grim
gym
him
homonym
hymn
interim
Jim
Kim
limb
prim
pseudonym
rim
skim
swim
synonym
Tim
trim
whim

+ You can also make rhymes for these words by using words in section **9.8** that rhyme with ***skin***

simmer
dimmer
gimmer
glimmer
shimmer
slimmer
swimmer

+ You can add to this list by adding ***-mer*** to some words that rhyme with ***slim***, as in ***primmer***

women
persimmon

Jimmy
shimmy
Timmy

mimic
gimmick

image
scrimmage
spitting image

eliminate
discriminate (= *to make a distinction*)
incriminate

incriminating
discriminating
eliminating
undiscriminating

criminal
subliminal

slimming
swimming
trimming

+ You can add to this list by adding ***-ming*** to some words that rhyme with ***slim***, as in ***skimming***

limit
delimit

+ You can also make rhymes for these words by using ***it*** after some words that rhyme with ***slim***, as in ***trim it***

scimitar
perimeter

proximity
anonymity
equanimity
magnanimity
unanimity

timber
limber

nimble
cymbal
symbol
thimble

limbo
akimbo
bimbo
himbo

loose-limbed
semi-skimmed

+ You can add to this list by adding ***-(m)ed*** to some words that rhyme with ***slim***, as in ***trimmed***

nymph
lymph

dimly
grimly
primly

limp
blimp
chimp
crimp
imp
pimp
scrimp
shrimp
skimp
wimp

simper
whimper

+ You can add to this list by adding ***-er*** to some words that rhyme with ***limp***, as in ***crimper***

simple
dimple
pimple
wimple

impish
wimpish

simply
limply
pimply

stimulate
simulate

9.8

skin
adrenalin(e)
akin
amphetamine
Anne Boleyn
aspirin
Bedouin
begin
Benjamin
Berlin
bin
built-in
bulletin
Catherine
chin
din
discipline
feminine
fin
Finn
genuine
get under someone's skin
gin
glycerin
Glyn
grin
Gwyn
heroin
heroine
Ho Chi Minh
Huckleberry Finn
in
indiscipline
inn
insulin
kaolin
kin
lanolin(e)
lie-in
Lynn(e)
Madel(e)ine
mandolin
mannequin
masculine
medicine
melanin
moccasin
next-of-kin
origin
paraffin
PIN
pin
rub it in
run-in
self-discipline
shin
sin
spin
stand-in
terrapin
thin
tin
Turin
twin
underpin
violin
vitamin
wafer-thin
win
within

+ You can also make rhymes for these words by using words in section **9.7** that rhyme with ***slim***

dinner
beginner
Berliner
breadwinner
dog's dinner
inner
moneyspinner
prizewinner
sinner
thinner
winner

+ You can add to this list by adding ***-ner*** to some words that rhyme with ***skin***, as in ***grinner***

You can also make rhymes for these words by using ***her*** after some words that rhyme with ***skin***, as in ***spin her***

linear
Lavinia
non-linear
Sardinia
skinnier
tinnier
Virginia

aluminium
condominium

Sardinian
Argentinian
Palestinian
Virginian

skinny
cine
Ginny
Guinea
guinea
Mini
mini
Minnie
spinney
tinny
whinny
Winnie

clinic
cynic

clinical
cynical

winning
beginning
spinning

+ You can add to this list by adding ***-ning*** to some words that rhyme with ***skin***, as in ***grinning***

sinister
administer
minister
prime minister

finish
diminish
Finnish

finishing
diminishing

finished
diminished
undiminished
unfinished

minute
last-minute
up-to-the-minute

+ You can also make rhymes for these words by using ***it*** after some words that rhyme with ***skin***, as in ***bin it***

Trinity
affinity
divinity
femininity
infinity
masculinity
vicinity
virginity

minnow
winnow

think
blink
brink
chink
clink
drink
hyperlink
Inc
ink
kink
link
mink
pink
rethink
rink
shrink
sink
slink
stink
sync(h)
wink
zinc

thinker
drinker
freethinker
Inca
stinker
tinker

+ You can add to this list by adding ***-er*** to some words that rhyme with ***think***, as in ***blinker***

drinkable
undrinkable
unsinkable
unthinkable

sprinkle
crinkle
periwinkle
Rip Van Winkle
tinkle
twinkle
winkle
wrinkle

slinky
Helsinki
inky
kinky
minke
pinkie
stinky
Wee Willie Winkie

thinking
blinking
drinking
forward-thinking
hard-drinking
right-thinking
sinking
stinking

+ You can add to this list by adding *-ing* to some words that rhyme with ***think***, as in ***winking***

crinkly
twinkly
wrinkly

inkling
sprinkling
tinkling
twinkling
wrinkling

jinx
lynx
sphinx
tiddlywinks

+ You can add to this list by adding *-s* to some words that rhyme with ***think***, as in ***links***

distinction
extinction

distinct
extinct
index-linked
indistinct
succinct

+ You can add to this list by adding *-ed* to some words that rhyme with ***think***, as in ***linked***

tinned
close to the wind
dark-skinned
Gone With the Wind
rescind
Rosalind
tamarind
thick-skinned
thin-skinned
undisciplined
wind (= *a current of air*)

+ You can add to this list by adding *-(n)ed* to some words that rhyme with ***skin***, as in ***sinned***

hinder
Belinda
cinder
Clarinda
Linda
Lucinda
tinder

swindle
dwindle
kindle
rekindle
spindle

linden
Swindon

windy
Cindy
Hindi
indie
Rawalpindi
shindy

India
windier

indicate
syndicate (= *to publish by means of a syndicate*)
vindicate

spindly
Myra Hindley

fringe
binge
cringe
hinge
impinge
infringe
singe
syringe
tinge
twinge
whinge

ginger
binger
injure
whinger

stringent
astringent
contingent

dingy
stingy (= *miserly*)

cringing
binging

singeing
swingeing
whingeing

ring
anything
B B King
Beijing
bring
cling
everything
fling
king
left-wing
Martin Luther King
Ming
Nanking
Peking
ping
right-wing
sing
sling
spring
Stephen King
Sting
sting
string
swing
The Ring
thing
ting-a-ling
wing
wring

clingy
dinghy
springy
stingy (= *stinging*)
stringy
thingy

singing
mudslinging
stinging
upbringing
wringing

+ You can add to this list by adding *-ing* to some words that rhyme with ***ring***, as in ***swinging***

finger
bell-ringer
forefinger
humdinger
left-winger
linger
malinger
right-winger
singer
winger
wringer

+ You can add to this list by adding *-er* to some words that rhyme with ***ring***, as in ***swinger***

You can also make rhymes for these words by using ***her*** after some words that rhyme with ***ring***, as in ***bring her***

single
intermingle
jingle
mingle
shingle
tingle

bingo
by jingo
dingo
flamingo
gringo
lingo

distinguish
extinguish

thinly
Finlay

since
convince
evince
mince
Port-au-Prince
prince
quince
rinse
wince

mincer
pincer
rinser

mincing
convincing
evincing
rinsing
unconvincing
wincing

spinster
minster
York Minster

Winston
Princeton

insular
peninsula
peninsular

print
bint
Clint
dint
fingerprint
flint
glint
hint
imprint
mint
peppermint
reprint
skint
spearmint
splint
sprint
squint
stint
tint

winter
Harold Pinter
midwinter

printer
sinter
splinter
sprinter
teleprinter

Quintin
Bill Clinton

printing
unstinting

> You can add to this list by adding *-ing* to some words that rhyme with ***print***, as in ***squinting***

pinch
cinch
clinch
finch
flinch
half-inch
inch
lynch
the Grinch
winch

lynching
penny-pinching
unflinching

> You can add to this list by adding *-ing* to some words that rhyme with ***pinch***, as in ***flinching***

plinth
hyacinth
labyrinth

pinion
dominion
minion
opinion

sinew
continue
discontinue

sinuous
continuous
discontinuous

9.9

ship
apprenticeship
battleship
blip
brinkmanship
censorship
chairmanship
championship
chip
citizenship
clip
companionship
comradeship
craftsmanship
dictatorship
dip
directorship
drip
equip
fellowship
felt-tip
fibre-tip
fingertip
flip
gamesmanship
governorship
grip
guardianship
gyp
hip
horsemanship
kip
ladyship
leadership
lip
membership
microchip
nip
one-upmanship
outstrip
ownership
paperclip
partisanship
partnership
Pip
pip
quip
receivership
relationship
rip
round-trip
salesmanship
scholarship
seamanship
showmanship
silicon chip
sip
skip
slip
snip
sponsorship
sportsmanship
strip
tip
trip
unhip
unzip
whip
workmanship
zip

flipper
big dipper
clipper
day-tripper
dipper
Jack the Ripper
kipper
nipper
Pippa
skipper
slipper
stripper
The Yorkshire Ripper
zipper

> You can add to this list by adding *-per* to some words that rhyme with ***ship***, as in ***quipper***

You can also make rhymes for these words by using ***her*** after some words that rhyme with ***ship***, as in ***trip her***

ripple
cripple
nipple
tipple
triple

hippy
dippy
Mississippi
nippy
slippy
trippy
zippy

gripping
clipping
dripping
shipping
skipping

+ You can add to this list by adding ***-ping*** to some words that rhyme with ***ship***, as in ***slipping***

snippet
whippet

+ You can also make rhymes for these words by using ***it*** after some words that rhyme with ***ship***, as in ***slip it***

rip-off
tip-off

slip-on
clip-on
get a grip on

clipboard
chipboard
flipboard
shipboard

crippling
rippling
Rudyard Kipling
stripling
tippling

shipment
equipment

eclipse
apocalypse
ellipse
Mr Chips

+ You can add to this list by adding ***-s*** to some words that rhyme with ***ship***, as in ***trips***

tipsy
gipsy

lipstick
dipstick

description
conniption
conscription
decryption
Egyptian
encryption
inscription
prescription
subscription
transcription

script
clipped
conscript
crypt
decrypt
encrypt
manuscript
nondescript
transcript

+ You can add to this list by adding ***-ped*** to some words that rhyme with ***ship***, as in ***tripped***

cryptic
apocalyptic
diptych
styptic
triptych

stipulate
manipulate

9.10

squirrel
Cyril

stirrup
chirrup
syrup

Miriam
delirium

lyrical
empirical
satirical

lyricism
empiricism

9.11

kiss
abyss
amiss
antithesis
armistice
avarice
Beatrice
bliss
cannabis
Chris
chrysalis
cowardice
dismiss
edifice
emphasis

genesis
hiss
hit-or-miss
hypothesis
Indianapolis
liquorice
metamorphosis
metropolis
Minneapolis
Miss
miss
near miss
orifice
parenthesis
photosynthesis
precipice
prejudice
reminisce
remiss
Swiss
synthesis
this

Melissa
Clarissa
kisser

+ You can also make rhymes for these words by using *her* after some words that rhyme with ***kiss***, as in ***miss her***

whistle
bristle
dismissal
epistle
gristle
missal
thistle

listen
christen
glisten

cissy
Chrissie
missy
prissy

permissible
admissible
inadmissible
kissable
missable
unmissable

participate
anticipate
dissipate

explicit
elicit
illicit
implicit
licit
solicit

+ You can also make rhymes for these words by using *it* after some words that rhyme with ***kiss***, as in ***miss it***

solicitous
duplicitous
felicitous

publicity
authenticity
complicity
duplicity
eccentricity
elasticity
electricity
Felicity
felicity
hydroelectricity
multiplicity
simplicity

Mrs
missus

+ You can add to this list by adding *-es* to some words that rhyme with ***kiss***, as in ***misses***

risk
asterisk
brisk
compact disc
disc
disk
floppy disk
frisk
gold disc
hard disk
MiniDisc®
obelisk
platinum disc
silver disc
whisk

Biscay
risqué

discus
hibiscus
meniscus
viscous
whiskers

whisky
frisky
risky
whiskey

disco
Frisco
San Francisco

Christmas
isthmus

lisp
crisp
will-o'-the-wisp
wisp

mist
activist
amethyst
anarchist
arsonist
assist
atheist
bigamist
botanist
capitalist
catalyst

chauvinist
chiropodist
coexist
colonist
columnist
communist
conservationist
consist
conversationalist
cyst
desist
dramatist
economist
ecoterrorist
egoist
egotist
enlist
essayist
Eucharist
evangelist
exhibitionist
exist
existentialist
exorcist
expressionist
federalist
feminist
fist
gist
grist
hedonist
herbalist
hypnotist
imperialist
impressionist
individualist
industrialist
insist
journalist
list
Liszt
lobbyist
lyricist
masochist
Methodist
misogynist
monarchist
monetarist
motorist
naturalist
naturist
novelist
oboist
Oliver Twist
optimist
organist
pacifist
percussionist
persist
pessimist
pharmacist
philanthropist
physicist
physiotherapist
pianist
populist
pragmatist
prejudiced
psychiatrist
receptionist
resist
round the twist
satirist
saxophonist
scientist
separatist
socialist
soloist
strategist
subsist
symbolist
syndicalist
telephonist
televangelist
terrorist
The Exorcist
theorist
therapist
tobacconist
traditionalist
Trotskyist
tryst
twist
unionist
ventriloquist
vocalist
whist
wrist
Zionist

> + You can add to this list by adding ***-ed*** to some words that rhyme with ***kiss***, as in ***missed***

sister
blister
demister
half-sister
Mister
Mr
resistor
stepsister
transistor
twister
vista

> + You can also make rhymes for these words by using ***her*** after some words that rhyme with ***mist***, as in ***resist her***

pistol
Bristol
Crystal
crystal

piston
cistern

distance
assistance
braking distance
coexistence
existence
insistence
long-distance
middle-distance
outdistance
persistence
resistance
subsistence

distant
assistant
consistent
equidistant
existent
inconsistent
insistent
nonexistent
persistent
resistant
water-resistant

distantly
consistently
inconsistently
insistently
persistently

history
mystery
prehistory

Christine
pristine

misty
Agatha Christie
Christy
twisty

mystic
altruistic
artistic
atavistic
autistic
ballistic
characteristic
chauvinistic
egotistic
euphemistic
fatalistic
futuristic
holistic
humanistic
idealistic
impressionistic
jingoistic
journalistic
linguistic
logistic
masochistic
materialistic
moralistic
nationalistic
naturalistic
nihilistic
optimistic
pessimistic
realistic
sadistic
simplistic
statistic
stylistic
uncharacteristic
unrealistic
voyeuristic

mystical
egotistical
logistical
statistical

linguistics
ballistics
heuristics
logistics

+ You can add to this list by adding *-s* to some words that rhyme with ***mystic***, as in ***statistics***

twisted
computer-assisted
ham-fisted
tightfisted
unlisted

+ You can add to this list by adding ***-ed*** to some words that rhyme with ***mist***, as in ***resisted***

listing
existing

+ You can add to this list by adding ***-ing*** to some words that rhyme with ***mist***, as in ***assisting***

wistful
fistful

9.12

vision
circumcision
collision
decision
derision
division
envision
Eurovision
imprecision
incision
indecision
precision
provision
revision
subdivision
supervision
television

9.13

wish
cuttlefish
dish
fish
jellyfish
kettle of fish
swish

fisher
fissure
kingfisher
Letitia
militia
Patricia
swisher
Trisha
wellwisher

official
artificial
beneficial

extrajudicial
initial
judicial
prejudicial
sacrificial
superficial
unofficial

officially
artificially
beneficially
initially
superficially
unofficially

fission
abolition
acquisition
addition
admission
ambition
ammunition
apparition
attrition
audition
beautician
coalition
cognition
commission
competition
composition
condition
contrition
decomposition
definition
demolition
deposition
dietician
disposition
edition
electrician
emission
erudition
exhibition
expedition
exposition
extradition
fruition
ignition
imposition
inhibition
Inquisition
intermission
intuition
juxtaposition
magician
malnutrition
mathematician
Mauritian
mint condition
mission
mortician
musician
nutrition
obstetrician
omission
opposition
optician
paediatrician
partition
permission
petition
physician
politician
position
precondition
predisposition
premonition
preposition
presupposition
prohibition
proposition
recognition
remission
rendition
repetition
requisition
sedition
statistician
submission
superstition
supposition
suspicion
tactician
technician
theoretician
Titian
tradition
transition
transmission
tuition
volition

conditioner
commissioner
parishioner
petitioner

+ You can also make rhymes for these words by using ***her*** after some words that rhyme with ***fission***, as in ***audition her***

traditional
additional
conditional
nutritional
prepositional
transitional
unconditional

missionary
expeditionary

conditioning
air-conditioning
positioning

+ You can add to this list by adding ***-ing*** to some words that rhyme with ***fission***, as in ***auditioning***

reconditioned
air-conditioned

+ You can add to this list by adding ***-ed*** to some words that rhyme with ***fission***, as in ***auditioned***

efficiency
deficiency

efficient
coefficient
deficient
inefficient
insufficient
proficient
self-sufficient
sufficient

inefficiency
insufficiency
proficiency
sufficiency

efficiently
deficiently
inefficiently
insufficiently
proficiently
sufficiently

vicious
ambitious
auspicious
capricious
delicious
fictitious
inauspicious
injudicious
judicious
malicious
Mauritius
nutritious
officious
pernicious
propitious
seditious
superstitious
surreptitious
suspicious
unambitious
wish us

viciously
ambitiously
auspiciously
capriciously
deliciously
inauspiciously
injudiciously
judiciously
maliciously
officiously
perniciously
propitiously
seditiously
superstitiously
surreptitiously
suspiciously
unambitiously

dishy
fishy
swishy

initiate
officiate
propitiate

fishing
fly-fishing
overfishing

+ You can add to this list by adding ***-ing*** to some words that rhyme with ***wish***, as in ***swishing***

issue
a-tishoo
Mogadishu
reissue
The Big Issue
tissue

9.14

sit
acquit
admit
alit
baby-sit
befit
benefit
bit
Brad Pitt
Brit
candlelit
chit
close-knit
commit
composite
deficit
emit
favourite
fit
flit
git
grit
hit
hypocrite
Identikit®
infinite
Inuit
it
Jesuit
keep-fit
kit
knit
lit
mitt
nit
omit
op cit
opposite
outwit
permit (= *to allow*)
pit
plebiscite
quit
readmit
refit
remit
resit
skit
slit
spit
Split
split
submit
tightknit
tit
transmit
twit
two-bit
unfit
unlit
Whit

whit
wit
writ
zit

bitter
baby-sitter
bedsitter
embitter
fritter
glitter
gritter
house-sitter
litter
titter
transmitter
twitter
witter

> + You can add to this list by adding *-ter* to some words that rhyme with *sit*, as in *fitter*
>
> You can also make rhymes for these words by using *her* after some words that rhyme with *sit*, as in *acquit her*

hospitable
inhospitable
remittable

it'd
embittered

> + You can add to this list by adding *-ed* to some words that rhyme with *bitter*, as in *glittered*

little
acquittal
belittle
brittle
committal
it'll
noncommittal
remittal
skittle
spittle
whittle

bitterly
Italy

written
bitten
Britain
Briton
flea-bitten
frostbitten
handwritten
hard-bitten
kitten
mitten
overwritten
rewritten
smitten
underwritten
unwritten

Brittany
dittany
litany

pittance
admittance
remittance

obliterate
reiterate
transliterate

witty
bitty
city
committee
ditty
gritty
Kitty
kitty
nitty-gritty
pity
pretty
self-pity
sitting pretty
subcommittee
Walter Mitty

critic
anti-Semitic
arthritic
bronchitic
paralytic
parasitic
Semitic

critical
analytical
apolitical
hypercritical
hypocritical
Jesuitical
parasitical
political
uncritical

fitted
committed
halfwitted
hand-knitted
knitted
machine-knitted
quick-witted
slow-witted
uncommitted

> + You can add to this list by adding *-ted* to some words that rhyme with *sit*, as in *admitted*

mitigate
litigate

fitting
befitting
close-fitting
ear-splitting
hard-hitting
knitting
loose-fitting
side-splitting
sitting
splitting
tight-fitting

unremitting
unwitting

> + You can add to this list by adding *-ting* to some words that rhyme with ***sit***, as in ***admitting***

criticism
witticism

criticize
politicize

British
skittish

Britney
jitney
Whitney

witness
eyewitness
fitness

its
battle of wits
Biarritz
blitz
call it quits
double or quits
glitz
it's
quits
St Kitts
St Moritz
The Ritz

> + You can add to this list by adding *-s* to some words that rhyme with ***sit***, as in ***hits***

glitzy
ritzy

switch
bewitch
bitch
ditch
enrich
glitch
hitch
itch
kitsch
last-ditch
pitch
rich
Slobodan Milosevic
snitch
stitch
Switch®
ti(t)ch
twitch
which
witch

itchy
bitchy
kitschy
Richie
ti(t)chy
twitchy

situate
habituate

ritual
habitual

9.15

wither
dither
hither
slither
thither
whither
zither

withering
blithering

> + You can add to this list by adding *-ing* to some words that rhyme with ***wither***, as in ***slithering***

9.16

pith
Bessie Smith
forthwith
Ian Smith
kith
myth
silversmith
smith
Will Smith

> + You can also make rhymes for these words by using words in section **9.4** that rhyme with ***stiff***

neolithic
monolithic
mythic

> + You can also make rhymes for these words by using words in section **9.4** that rhyme with ***terrific***

9.17

give
forgive
Liv
live (= *to exist*)
outlive
relive
sieve
spiv
Viv

The following words will also tend to rhyme with these when they come at the end of a line:
ablative
additive
adjective
administrative

affirmative
alternative
appreciative
authoritative
commemorative
competitive
conservative
contemplative
cumulative
decorative
definitive
derivative
diminutive
figurative
fugitive
genitive
imaginative
imitative
imperative
indicative
infinitive
initiative
innovative
intuitive
investigative
iterative
laxative
legislative
lucrative
manipulative
negative
nominative
operative
palliative
pejorative
positive
preservative
prerogative
primitive
prohibitive
punitive
putative
qualitative
quantitative
relative
remunerative
repetitive
secretive
sedative
sensitive
speculative
superlative
talkative
transitive
untalkative
vituperative

river
deliver
giver
liver
quiver
shiver
sliver

+ You can also make rhymes for these words by using *her* after some words that rhyme with *give*, as in *outlive her*

livable
forgivable
relivable
unforgivable
unlivable

shrivel
civil
drivel
snivel
swivel
uncivil

equivalent
ambivalent

shrivelling
snivelling
swivelling

given
driven
forgiven
striven

carnivorous
herbivorous
omnivorous

+ You can also make rhymes for these words by using *us* after some words that rhyme with *river*, as in *deliver us*

shivery
delivery
livery
quivery

trivia
Bolivia
Olivia

trivial
convivial

Vivien
Bolivian
oblivion

oblivious
lascivious

privy
chiv(v)y
skivvy

vivid
livid

living
forgiving
giving
life-giving
misgiving
outliving
prizegiving
reliving
sieving
thanksgiving
unforgiving

rivet
privet
trivet

+ You can also make rhymes for these words by using *it* after some words that rhyme with ***give***, as in ***forgive it***

activity
captivity
conductivity
festivity
inactivity
insensitivity
Nativity
negativity
objectivity
proclivity
productivity
radioactivity
relativity
subjectivity

9.18

whizz
Buck's fizz
Cádiz
fizz
his
is
Liz
Ms
quiz
swizz
Viz
viz

wizard
blizzard
gizzard
lizard

sizzle
chisel
drizzle
fizzle
grizzle

prism
alcoholism
altruism
Americanism
anachronism
Anglicanism
Anglicism
animism
antagonism
aphorism
atheism
barbarism
behaviourism
Bolshevism
botulism
Briticism
capitalism
cataclysm
catechism
Catholicism
chauvinism
colloquialism
colonialism
commercialism
communism
consumerism
despotism
dynamism
egotism
embolism
eroticism
euphemism
evangelism
existentialism
exorcism
expressionism
favouritism
federalism
feminism
feudalism
gradualism
hedonism
heroism
Hinduism
hooliganism
humanism
hypnotism
impressionism
jingoism
journalism
Judaism
liberalism
magnetism
mannerism
masochism
mechanism
metabolism
Methodism
militarism
modernism
monetarism
mysticism
naturalism
nepotism
opportunism
optimism
organism
ostracism
pacifism
paganism
paroxysm
patriotism
pessimism
plagiarism
pluralism
pragmatism
professionalism
protectionism
Protestantism
radicalism
recidivism
regionalism
revisionism
rheumatism
romanticism
scepticism
schism
Scotticism
sensationalism
socialism
spiritualism
stoicism
symbolism
syndicalism
terrorism
tribalism
Trotskyism
vandalism
ventriloquism
witticism
Zionism

prison
arisen
imprison
risen

Tunisia
busier
dizzier
fizzier
frizzier
Kirg(h)izia

Parisian
Tunisian

dizzy
busy
fizzy
frizzy
Lizzie
tizzy
whizzy

visible
divisible
indivisible
invisible
risible

physical
metaphysical
non-physical
quizzical

visit
exquisite
is it?

Lisbon
Brisbane

drizzly
busily
dizzily
grisly
grizzly

sizzling
drizzling
fizzling
grizzling
Quisling
quisling

dismal
abysmal
baptismal

gizmo
machismo

Section 10
-IE-

All the words in this section use the sound **-ie-** (as in p*ie*, unt*ie*d, f*ie*ry) in their main stressed syllable

10.1

try
abaci
AI (= *artificial insemination; Artificial Intelligence*)
alibi
alkali
ally (= *to join together*)
amplify
anno Domini
apple pie
apply
awry
beautify
belie
bone-dry
bring-and-buy
Brunei
BSI (= *British Standards Institute*)
butterfly
buy
by
bye
bye-bye
cacti
CAI (= *computer-aided instruction*)
CBI (= *Confederation of British Industry*)
CDI (= *compact disc interactive*)
certify
cherry pie
clarify
codify
comply
crucify
cry
Dai
decry
deep-fry
defy
deify
demystify
deny
descry
Di
die
diversify
DIY
dragonfly
drip-dry
dry
DTI (= *Department of Trade and Industry*)
Dubai
dye
edify
electrify
exemplify
eye
falsify
FBI
fly
foci
freeze-dry
fry
Gemini
GI
glorify
goodbye
Guy
guy
hereby
hi
hi-fi
high
HMI (= *Her Majesty's Inspector*)
horrify
hue and cry
I
identify
imply
indemnify
intensify
I-spy
July
justify
knee-high
let fly
lie
liquefy
lullaby
lye
Madame Butterfly
magnify
magpie
mince pie
modify
multiply
mummify

my
mystify
nearby
NI (= *National Insurance*)
nigh
notify
nullify
NY (= *New York*)
occupy
ossify
oversimplify
Paraguay
passer-by
personify
petrify
pi
pie
ply
preoccupy
Private Eye
private eye
prophesy
pry
purify
putrefy
qualify
quantify
rabbi
reapply
rely
reply
reunify
rhombi
RNLI (= *Royal National Lifeboat Institution*)
RPI (= *retail price index*)
RSI (= *repetitive strain injury*)
rye
sanctify
satisfy
shallow-fry
Shanghai
shy
sigh
simplify
sky
Skye
sly
solidify
specify
spin-dry
spry
spy
stand by
stir-fry
stupefy
stye
sun-dry
supply
testify
Thai
the apple of someone's eye
The Catcher in the Rye
thesauri
thigh
tie
tie-dye
tumble-dry
typify
UDI (= *Unilateral Declaration of Independence*)
underlie
unify
untie
Uruguay
vie
whereby
why
WI
wry
Y

fire

acquire
admire
amplifier
aspire
attire
backfire
Bedfordshire
Benjamin Zephaniah
Berwickshire
Billy Liar
briar
Buckinghamshire
buyer
Cambridgeshire
campfire
Carmarthenshire
choir
Clackmannanshire
conspire
deep-fat fryer
deep-fryer
dehumidifier
Denbighshire
Derbyshire
desire
dire
drier
Dunbartonshire
entire
expire
first-time buyer
flier
friar
Gloucestershire
hairdryer
Herefordshire
Hertfordshire
high-flier
hire
humidifier
inquire
inspire
ire
Isaiah
Jeremiah
Kincardineshire
Kirkcudbrightshire
Lanarkshire
Lancashire
Leicestershire
liar
Lincolnshire
lyre
Messiah
mire
misfire
Monmouthshire
Morayshire

Northamptonshire
Nottinghamshire
occupier
owner-occupier
Oxfordshire
pacifier
pariah
Peeblesshire
Pembrokeshire
perspire
prior
pyre
quagmire
qualifier
quantifier
Renfrewshire
require
retire
rewire
Roxburghshire
sapphire
satire
Selkirkshire
shire
sire
spare tyre
spin-drier
spire
squire
Staffordshire
Stirlingshire
supplier
tire
transpire
trier
tumble-drier
Tyre
tyre
vampire
via
Warwickshire
washer-drier
Wigtownshire
wire
Worcestershire

+ You can add to this list by adding *-er* to some words that rhyme with ***try***, as in ***higher***

You can also make rhymes for these words by using ***her*** after some words that rhyme with ***try***, as in ***spy her***

liable
deniable
justifiable
non-viable
pliable
reliable
undeniable
unjustifiable
unreliable
unverifiable
verifiable
viable

reliably
deniably
justifiably
undeniably
unjustifiably
unreliably
unverifiably
verifiably

tired
awe-inspired
dog-tired
hired
inspired
oil-fired
retired
uninspired
wired

+ You can add to this list by adding *-d* to some words that rhyme with ***fire***, as in ***attired***

trial
denial
dial
mistrial
phial
redial
retrial
self-denial

violate
annihilate

violet
inviolate
triolet
ultraviolet
Violet

tireless
wireless

requirement
retirement

lion
Brian
cast-iron
dandelion
grappling iron
gridiron
Hawaiian
ion
iron
Mayan
Paraguayan
Ryan
soldering iron
Uruguayan
wrought-iron
Zion

Briony
Hermione
irony (= *like iron*)

science
alliance
appliance
compliance
defiance
reliance
self-reliance

giant
client
compliant
defiant
reliant
self-reliant

hirer
admirer
direr
inquirer
Ira
Myra

+ You can also make rhymes for these words by using ***her*** after some words that rhyme with ***fire***, as in ***hire her***

desirable
acquirable
undesirable

siren
Lord Byron

wiry
diary
enquiry
expiry
fiery
inquiry
priory

tiring
acquiring
admiring
aspiring
awe-inspiring
backfiring
conspiring
desiring
expiring
firing
hiring
inquiring
inspiring
misfiring
perspiring
requiring
retiring
rewiring
siring
squiring
uninspiring
untiring
wiring

bias
pious
Tobias

+ You can also make rhymes for these words by using ***us*** after some words that rhyme with ***by***, as in ***spy us***

quiet
diet
disquiet
riot

rioter
proprietor

+ You can add to this list by adding ***-er*** to some words that rhyme with ***quiet***, as in ***dieter***

piety
anxiety
impropriety
notoriety
propriety
satiety
sobriety
society
variety

dietary
podiatry
proprietary
psychiatry

psychiatrist
podiatrist

dying
crying
edifying
electrifying
flying
gratifying
high-flying
horrifying
low-flying
low-lying
lying
outlying
qualifying
stultifying
stupefying
terrifying
trying
underlying
unsatisfying

+ You can add to this list by adding ***-ing*** to some words that rhyme with ***try***, as in ***denying***

try-out
buyout
leveraged buyout

10.2

bribe
ascribe
circumscribe
describe
diatribe
gibe
imbibe
inscribe
prescribe
proscribe
scribe
subscribe
transcribe
tribe

fibre
imbiber
subscriber
Tiber

+ You can also make rhymes for these words by using *her* after some words that rhyme with ***bribe***, as in ***describe her***

Bible
libel
tribal

eyebrow
highbrow

10.3

like
alike
bike
businesslike
dislike
dyke
hike
Ike
ladylike
lookalike
Mike
mike
motorbike
pike
psych
soundalike
spike
sportsmanlike
statesmanlike
strike
trike
unalike
unbusinesslike
unlike
unsportsmanlike
workmanlike

striker
biker
Formica®
hiker
hitchhiker
mica

+ You can also make rhymes for these words by using *her* after some words that rhyme with ***like***, as in ***dislike her***

cycle
cervical
Michael
motorcycle
recycle

spiky
crikey
Nike
psyche

striking
biking
disliking
hiking
liking
spiking
Viking

10.4

side
abide
allied
alongside
Ambleside
applied
aside
astride
backside
beady-eyed
beside
betide
bide
bleary-eyed
Bonnie and Clyde
bride
chide
classified
Clyde
coincide
collide
confide
countryside
cried
cross-eyed
cyanide
decide
deep-fried
deride
dewy-eyed
dissatisfied
divide
doe-eyed
dried
eagle-eyed
fireside
fortified
fratricide
freeze-dried
fried
genocide
girl guide
glide
glorified
goggle-eyed
gratified
guide
herbicide
hide
homicide
horrified
Humberside
hydroxide
I'd
identified
implied
infanticide
insecticide
inside
Inverclyde
justified
matricide
Merseyside
Mr Hyde
nationwide

occupied
offside
outside
override
patricide
pesticide
Port Said
preoccupied
preside
pride
provide
rarefied
refried
reside
ride
riverside
satisfied
self-satisfied
shallow-fried
slide
sloe-eyed
snide
specified
spermicide
starry-eyed
stir-fried
Strathclyde
stride
subside
suicide
sun-dried
terrified
thorn in one's side
tide
tried
underside
unidentified
unjustified
unoccupied
unsatisfied
unspecified
untried
vied
waterside
wide

spider
cider
decider
Easy Rider
eider
glider
hang-glider
insider
joyrider
outrider
outsider
provider
rider

+ You can add to this list by adding *-r* to some words that rhyme with ***side***, as in ***wider***

You can also make rhymes for these words by using ***her*** after some words that rhyme with ***side***, as in ***beside her***

bridal
bridle
genocidal
homicidal
idle
idol
sidle
spermicidal
suicidal
tidal

widen
Leiden
Sidon

guidance
subsidence

strident
trident

tidy
bona fide
Friday
Heidi
Man Friday
untidy

guided
decided
divided
lopsided
misguided
one-sided
provided
undecided

+ You can add to this list by adding *-d* to some words that rhyme with ***side***, as in ***confided***

hiding
abiding
backsliding
biding
chiding
coinciding
colliding
confiding
deciding
deriding
dividing
gliding
guiding
hang-gliding
law-abiding
overriding
paragliding
presiding
providing
residing
riding
siding
sliding
striding
subsiding

guideline
sideline
tideline

10.5

life
afterlife

bane of one's life
Fife
for dear life
knife
long-life
paperknife
pocketknife
rife
strife
wife

cipher
decipher
Haifa
lifer

stifle
eyeful
rifle
trifle

hyphen
siphon

stifling
rifling
trifling

10.6

tiger
Eiger

10.7

smile
aisle
Anglophile
awhile
beguile
bibliophile
bile
camomile
Carlisle
compile
crocodile
defile
domicile
Europhile
file
francophile
guile
high-profile
I'll
infantile
isle
juvenile
Kyle
mercantile
mile
Nile
paedophile
pile
rank-and-file
reconcile
revile
rile
stile
style
tile
versatile
vile
volatile
while
worthwhile

Isla
Delilah
Islay
rottweiler

> + You can add to this list by adding *-r* to some words that rhyme with ***smile***, as in ***miler***
>
> You can also make rhymes for these words by using ***her*** after some words that rhyme with ***smile***, as in ***rile her***

nylon
pylon

island
Coney Island
Highland
Rhode Island
Thailand
Treasure Island

islander
Highlander

Highlands
islands

pilot
autopilot
copilot
eyelet
Pilate
twilit

shyly
drily
highly
Kylie
slyly
smiley
spryly
wily
wryly

mileage
silage

smiling
beguiling
compiling
defiling
filing
piling
profiling
reviling
riling
styling
tiling
whiling

styli
My Lai

skyline
by-line
try line

highlight
skylight
twilight

Lilo®
Shiloh

silo

child
great-grandchild
mild
Oscar Wilde
tiled
wild

> + You can add to this list by adding *-d* to some words that rhyme with ***smile***, as in ***riled***

wildly
mildly

wildness
mildness

wiles
Giles
Miles
piles

> + You can add to this list by adding *-s* to some words that rhyme with ***smile***, as in ***tiles***

10.8

time
all-time
chime
climb
crime
dime
extra-time
flex(i)time
full-time
Greenwich Mean Time
grime
half-time
I'm
in one's prime
lime
maritime
mime
mistime
overtime
pantomime
paradigm
part-time
prime
rhyme
rime
slime
sublime
summertime
thyme
wintertime

> + You can also make rhymes for these words by using words in section **10.9** that rhyme with ***line***

timer
climber
full-timer
Jemima
old-timer
part-timer
primer
rhymer

> + You can also make rhymes for these words by using ***her*** after some words that rhyme with ***time***, as in ***prime her***

slimy
blimey
grimy
limey
stymie

timing
chiming
climbing
miming
mistiming
non-rhyming
priming
rhyming

well-timed
ill-timed
unrhymed

> + You can add to this list by adding *-(e)d* to some words that rhyme with ***time***, as in ***climbed***

timely
sublimely
untimely

The Times
Radio Times
sign of the times

> + You can add to this list by adding *-s* to some words that rhyme with ***time***, as in ***rhymes***

10.9

line
align
alkaline
anodyne
aquiline
Argentine
asinine
assign
benign
borderline
brine
Caroline
Clementine
cloud nine
combine
concubine
confine
consign

Constantine
countersign
decline
define
design
dine
divine
endocrine
enshrine
entwine
fine
Frankenstein
incline
intertwine
landmine
lay it on the line
Liechtenstein
malign
mine
mulled wine
nine
off-line
on-line
outshine
Palestine
pine
porcupine
realign
recline
refine
resign
Rhine
shine
Shirley Valentine
shrine
sign
sine
spine
swine
tine
Torfaen
twine
Tyne
underline
undermine
valentine
vine
whine
wine

> + You can also make rhymes for these words by using words in section **10.8** that rhyme with *time*

liner
angina
Carolina
China
china
designer
Dinah
diner
eyeliner
hardliner
Indochina
miner
minor
mynah
one-liner
Regina
shiner

> + You can add to this list by adding *-(e)r* to some words that rhyme with *line*, as in *finer*
>
> You can also make rhymes for these words by using *her* after some words that rhyme with *line*, as in *malign her*

definable
assignable
combinable
inclinable
indefinable
refinable

final
doctrinal
intestinal
quarterfinal
semifinal
spinal
urinal
vinyl

finery
binary
refinery

minus
dryness
Highness
Linus
shyness
sinus

> + You can also make rhymes for these words by using *us* after some words that rhyme with *line*, as in *assign us*

tiny
briny
shiny
spiny
whiny

shining
assigning
combining
confining
consigning
declining
defining
designing
dining
divining
enshrining
entwining
inclining
intertwining
lining
mining
pining
reclining
refining

resigning
signing
underlining
undermining
whining
wining and dining

rhino
lino
wino

kind
behind
bind
blind
colour-blind
disinclined
find
grind
hind
humankind
lined
mankind
mastermind
mind
nonaligned
refined
remind
rewind
rind
unkind
unrefined
unsigned
unwind
wind (= *to twist*)

+ You can add to this list by adding *-(e)d* to some words that rhyme with ***line***, as in ***fined***

minder
baby-minder
binder
blinder
bookbinder
childminder
finder
grinder
kinda
kinder
organ-grinder
rangefinder
reminder
viewfinder
winder

+ You can also make rhymes for these words by using ***her*** after some words that rhyme with ***kind***, as in ***mind her***

minded
absent-minded
bloody-minded
broad-minded
evil-minded
fair-minded
feeble-minded
high-minded
like-minded
narrow-minded
open-minded
right-minded
simple-minded
single-minded
small-minded
strong-minded

+ You can add to this list by adding ***-ed*** to some words that rhyme with ***kind***, as in ***blinded***

binding
blinding
bookbinding
fact-finding
grinding
winding

+ You can add to this list by adding ***-ing*** to some words that rhyme with ***kind***, as in ***minding***

kindly
blindly
unkindly

kindness
blindness
unkindness

refinement
alignment
assignment
confinement
consignment

10.10

pipe
archetype
gripe
guttersnipe
hype
prototype
ripe
snipe
stereotype
stripe
swipe
tripe
type
unripe
wipe

viper
diaper
hyper
piper
sniper
The Pied Piper
wiper

+ You can add to this list by adding ***-r*** to some words that rhyme with ***pipe***, as in ***riper***

> You can also make rhymes for these words by using ***her*** after some words that rhyme with ***pipe***, as in ***swipe her***

disciple
archetypal

wiping
griping
hyping
piping
sniping
swiping
typing

striped
stereotyped

> + You can add to this list by adding ***-d*** to some words that rhyme with ***pipe***, as in ***swiped***

10.11

spiral
postviral
retiral
viral

virus
Cyrus
desirous
papyrus
retrovirus

> + You can also make rhymes for these words by using ***us*** after some words that rhyme with ***fire***, as in ***inspire us***

Irene
polystyrene

giro
Biro®
Cairo
tyro

10.12

ice
advice
concise
cut-price
device
dice
entice
half-price
imprecise
lice
mice
nice
paradise
precise
price
rice
sacrifice
slice
spice
splice
suffice
thrice
trice
twice
vice

de-icer
ISA

> + You can add to this list by adding ***-r*** to some words that rhyme with ***ice***, as in ***nicer***
>
> You can also make rhymes for these words by using ***her*** after some words that rhyme with ***ice***, as in ***entice her***

biceps
triceps

crises
Pisces

icy
dicey
pricey
spicy

bicycle
icicle
tricycle

icing
dicing
enticing
pricing
sacrificing
slicing
spicing
splicing
sufficing

crisis
Isis
midlife crisis

decisive
derisive
divisive
incisive
indecisive

nicely
concisely
imprecisely
precisely

iced
Antichrist
Christ
heist
overpriced
poltergeist

> + You can add to this list by adding ***-d*** to some words that rhyme with ***ice***, as in ***spliced***

10.13

white
acolyte
alight
all right
anthracite
apartheid
appetite
bite
black-and-white
blight
Bonfire Night
bright
brownfield site
byte
candlelight
cellulite
cite
copyright
delight
despite
dynamite
erudite
excite
expedite
extradite
Fahrenheit
fight
flight
fly-by-night
fright
gelignite
gigabyte
goodnight
greenfield site
Guy Fawkes Night
height
hermaphrodite
ignite
impolite
incite
indict
in-flight
invite
Isle of Wight
Israelite
Jacobite
kilobyte
kite
knight
landfill site
light
megabyte
meteorite
might
mite
Muscovite
night
not a pretty sight
off-white
outright
overnight
oversight
overwrite
parasite
plight
polite
quite
recite
reunite
rewrite
right
rite
satellite
sight
site
sleight
slight
smite
Snow White
snow-white
socialite
spite
sprite
stalactite
stalagmite
tight
tonight
too right
trite
Twelfth Night
underwrite
unite
uptight
watertight
write

writer
blighter
bullfighter
copywriter
fighter
firefighter
firelighter
ghostwriter
highlighter
lighter
mitre
prizefighter
screenwriter
scriptwriter
songwriter
speechwriter
typewriter
underwriter

+ You can add to this list by adding ***-(e)r*** to some words that rhyme with ***white***, as in ***brighter***

You can also make rhymes for these words by using ***her*** after some words that rhyme with ***white***, as in ***delight her***

excitable
indictable

vital
entitle
recital
subtitle
title

item
ad infinitum

+ You can add to this list by adding ***'em*** to some words that rhyme with ***white***, as in ***delight 'em***

frighten
brighten
Brighton
enlighten
heighten
lighten
tighten
whiten

frightened
enlightened
unenlightened

+ You can add to this list by adding *-ed* to some words that rhyme with ***frighten***, as in ***heightened***

mighty
almighty
blighty
flighty
nightie

sighted
clear-sighted
delighted
excited
far-sighted
long-sighted
near-sighted
overexcited
sharp-sighted
short-sighted
uninvited
united

+ You can add to this list by adding *-(e)d* to some words that rhyme with ***white***, as in ***slighted***

writing
backbiting
biting
bullfighting
citing
exciting
expediting
extraditing
fighting
handwriting
inciting
infighting
inviting
lighting
moonlighting
nail-biting
overwriting
reciting
reuniting
rewriting
sighting
siting
smiting
spiting
underwriting
unexciting
uninviting
uniting
whiting

+ You can add to this list by adding *-ing* to some words that rhyme with ***white***, as in ***slighting***

arthritis
appendicitis
bronchitis
conjunctivitis
cystitis
dermatitis
gastritis
gastro-enteritis
gingivitis
hepatitis
laryngitis
mastitis
meningitis
osteoarthritis
peritonitis
rheumatoid arthritis
sinusitis
tonsillitis

frightful
delightful
insightful
rightful
spiteful

frightfully
delightfully
insightfully
rightfully
spitefully

sightless
flightless

slightly
brightly
fortnightly
lightly
nightly
politely
rightly
sprightly
tightly
unsightly

excitement
incitement
indictment

lightning
unenlightening

+ You can add to this list by adding *-ing* to some words that rhyme with ***frighten***, as in ***enlightening***

brightness
impoliteness
lightness
politeness
tightness
whiteness

tights
human rights
see the sights
Wuthering Heights

> **+** You can add to this list by adding *-s* to some words that rhyme with ***white***, as in ***rights***

10.14

writhe
blithe
lithe
scythe

10.15

five
alive
arrive
Clive
connive
contrive
deprive
derive
dive
drive
hive
I've
jive
live (= *alive*)
MI5
overdrive
revive
skive
strive
survive
thrive

driver
diver
fiver
Ivor
pile-driver
saliva
screwdriver
skiver
skydiver
survivor
viva (= *an oral examination*)

> **+** You can add to this list by adding *-r* to some words that rhyme with ***five***, as in ***jiver***
>
> You can also make rhymes for these words by using ***her*** after some words that rhyme with ***five***, as in ***deprive her***

rival
arrival
revival
survival

liven
enliven
Ivan

contrivance
connivance

driving
arriving
conniving
contriving
depriving
deriving
diving
drink-driving
reviving
skiving
skydiving
striving
surviving
thriving

thrived
contrived
deprived

> **+** You can add to this list by adding *-d* to some words that rhyme with ***five***, as in ***arrived***

knives
chives
lives (= *existences*)
St Ives
wives

> **+** You can add to this list by adding *-s* to some words that rhyme with ***five***, as in ***drives***

10.16

highway
byway
fly way
my way

10.17

prize
acclimatize
advertise
advise
agonize
anaesthetize
analyse
antagonize
apologize
appetize
arise
authorize
baptize
booby-prize
bowdlerize
breathalyse
brutalize
burglarize
cannibalize
canonize
capitalize
capsize
carbonize
categorize
cauterize
centralize
characterize

chastise
circumcise
civilize
collectivize
colonize
comprise
compromise
computerize
conceptualize
counter-clockwise
crystallize
customize
decentralize
dehumanize
demilitarize
demise
demobilize
demoralize
deputize
despise
destabilize
devise
dies
disenfranchise
disguise
dramatize
economize
empathize
emphasize
enfranchise
enterprise
epitomize
equalize
eulogize
evangelize
excise
exercise
exorcize
extemporize
familiarize
fantasize
fertilize
finalize
franchise
fraternize
fries
galvanize
generalize
glamorize
guise
half-size
harmonize
high-rise
homogenize
hospitalize
humanize
hypnotize
hypothesize
idolize
immobilize
immunize
improvise
industrialize
institutionalize
internalize
ionize
itemize
jeopardize
king-size
legalize
liberalize
liquidize
Lord of the Flies
marginalize
maximize
mechanize
memorize
merchandise
mesmerize
miniaturize
minimize
mobilize
modernize
moisturize
monopolize
moralize
Morecambe and Wise
motorize
naturalize
neutralize
Nobel Prize
optimize
organize
ostracize
otherwise
overemphasize
oxidize
paralyse
pasteurize
patronize
pedestrianize
penalize
philosophize
photosynthesize
pixelize
plagiarize
polarize
popularize
pressurize
prioritize
prise
privatize
psychoanalyse
publicize
pulverize
queen-size
readvertise
recognize
reorganize
revise
revitalize
revolutionize
rhapsodize
rise
romanticize
sanitize
satirize
scrutinize
size
socialize
specialize
stabilize
standardize
sterilize
stigmatize
subsidize
summarize
supervise
surmise
surprise
symbolize
sympathize
synchronize
synthesize

systematize
tantalize
televise
terrorize
theorize
traumatize
trivialize
tyrannize
unionize
unwise
utilize
vaporize
verbalize
victimize
visualize
wise
worldly-wise

miser
advertiser
adviser
appetizer
Breathalyser
Eliza
equalizer
fertilizer
incisor
liquidizer
Liza
moisturizer
organizer
stabilizer
supervisor
sympathizer
synthesizer
tranquillizer
visor
womanizer

+ You can add to this list by adding *-r* to some words that rhyme with ***prize***, as in ***wiser***

You can also make rhymes for these words by using ***her*** after some words that rhyme with ***prize***, as in ***surprise her***

siz(e)able
advisable
inadvisable
recognizable
unrecognizable

advisory
supervisory

rising
acclimatizing
advertising
advising
agonizing
anaesthetizing
analysing
apologizing
appetizing
arising
authorizing
baptizing
bowdlerizing
breathalysing
brutalizing
burglarizing
cannibalizing
canonizing
capitalizing
capsizing
carbonizing
categorizing
cauterizing
centralizing
characterizing
chastising
circumcising
civilizing
collectivizing
colonizing
comprising
compromising
computerizing
conceptualizing
crystallizing
customizing
decentralizing
dehumanizing
demilitarizing
demobilizing
demoralizing
deputizing
despising
destabilizing
devising
disenfranchising
disguising
downsizing
dramatizing
economizing
empathizing
emphasizing
enterprising
epitomizing
equalizing
eulogizing
evangelizing
excising
exercising
exorcizing
extemporizing
familiarizing
fantasizing
fertilizing
finalizing
fraternizing
galvanizing
generalizing
glamorizing
harmonizing
homogenizing
hospitalizing
humanizing
hypnotizing
hypothesizing
idolizing
immobilizing
immunizing
improvising
industrializing
institutionalizing
internalizing
ionizing
itemizing
jeopardizing

legalizing
liberalizing
liquidizing
marginalizing
maximizing
mechanizing
memorizing
merchandising
mesmerizing
miniaturizing
minimizing
modernizing
moisturizing
monopolizing
moralizing
motorizing
nationalizing
naturalizing
neutralizing
optimizing
organizing
ostracizing
overemphasizing
oxidizing
paralysing
pasteurizing
patronizing
pedestrianizing
penalizing
philosophizing
photosynthesizing
pixelizing
plagiarizing
polarizing
popularizing
pressurizing
prioritizing
prising
privatizing
psychoanalysing
publicizing
pulverizing
readvertising
recognizing
reorganizing
revising
revitalizing
revolutionizing
rhapsodizing
romanticizing
sanitizing
satirizing
scrutinizing
sizing
socializing
specializing
stabilizing
standardizing
sterilizing
stigmatizing
subsidizing
summarizing
supervising
surmising
surprising
symbolizing
sympathizing
synchronizing
synthesizing
systematizing
tantalizing
televising
terrorizing
theorizing
traumatizing
trivializing
tyrannizing
unappetizing
uncompromising
unenterprising
unionizing
unsurprising
uprising
utilizing
vaporizing
verbalizing
victimizing
visualizing

proviso
Valparaíso

stylized
civilized
commercialized
disorganized
fossilized
galvanized
ill-advised
mechanized
middle-sized
motorized
organized
oversized
recognized
unauthorized
uncivilized
undersized
unrecognized
unsupervised
well-advised
westernized

+ You can add to this list by adding *-d* to some words that rhyme with ***prize***, as in ***surprised***

Section 11
-O-

All the words in this section use the sound **-o-** (as in d*o*g, p*o*cket, bey*o*nd) in their main stressed syllable

11.1

job
blob
Bob
bob
cob
corn on the cob
demob
fob
gob
hob
knob
lob
mob
rent-a-mob
Rob
rob
slob
snob
sob
swab
throb
yob

robber
clobber
cobber
slobber

+ You can add to this list by adding *-ber* to some words that rhyme with *job*, as in *sobber*

You can also make rhymes for these words by using *her* after some words that rhyme with *job*, as in *rob her*

wobble
bobble
cobble
gobble
hobble
nobble
squabble

robbery
slobbery
snobbery

Robert
The Hobbit

hobby
blobby
Bobby
bobby
knobby
lobby
nobby
Robbie
slobby

robin
bobbin
dobbin
Robin

sobbing
jobbing

+ You can add to this list by adding *-bing* to some words that rhyme with *job*, as in *throbbing*

wobbly
bobbly
knobbly
throw a wobbly

lobster
mobster

11.2

block
ad hoc
amok
Bangkok
baroque
bloc
chip off the old block
chock
chock-a-block
clock
cock
crock
culture shock
defrock
doc
dock

double-lock
electroshock
flock
frock
half-cock
hock
hollyhock
Jock
knock
loch
lock
mock
o'clock
Papa Doc
poppycock
rock
shock
shuttlecock
smock
sock
stock
unblock
unfrock
unlock
weathercock
wok

locker
Davy Jones's locker
docker
knocker
rocker
soccer

+ You can add to this list by adding *-er* to some words that rhyme with ***block***, as in ***mocker***

You can also make rhymes for these words by using ***her*** after some words that rhyme with ***block***, as in ***mock her***

mockery
crockery
rockery

vocative
evocative
locative
provocative

rocky
cocky
disc jockey
hockey
jockey
Rocky
stocky

shocking
interlocking
knocking
stocking

+ You can add to this list by adding *-ing* to some words that rhyme with ***block***, as in ***mocking***

pocket
locket
pickpocket
rocket
socket
sprocket

+ You can also make rhymes for these words by using ***it*** after some words that rhyme with ***block***, as in ***knock it***

knockout
lock-out

mock-up
cock-up
lockup

Cockney
David Hockney
mockney

box
Brer Fox
chatterbox
chickenpox
cox
equinox
Fort Knox
fox
Goldilocks
jack-in-the-box
mailbox
moneybox
orthodox
ox
paradox
tinderbox
unorthodox

+ You can add to this list by adding *-s* to some words that rhyme with ***block***, as in ***knocks***

oxen
coxswain
toxin

foxy
orthodoxy
poxy
proxy

shocked
cocked
concoct

+ You can add to this list by adding *-ed* to some words that rhyme with ***block***, as in ***knocked***

11.3

God
arthropod
bod
clod

cod
demigod
god
nod
odd
plod
pod
prod
quad
Rod
rod
shod
sod
squad
Sweeney Todd
Todd
trod
wad

fodder
dodder

> ➕ You can add to this list by adding ***-(d)er*** to some words that rhyme with ***God***, as in ***odder***

toddle
coddle
doddle
model
mollycoddle
supermodel
twaddle
waddle

sodden
downtrodden
modern
trodden
ultramodern

body
antibody
anybody
busybody
dogsbody
embody
everybody
Irrawaddy
nobody
Noddy
Roddy
shoddy
somebody
squaddie
wadi

melodic
periodic
rhapsodic
spasmodic

methodical
periodical

periodically
methodically
rhapsodically
spasmodically

full-bodied
able-bodied
disembodied
nodded
plodded
prodded

bodice
goddess

modest
immodest
oddest

oddity
commodity

oddly
godly
ungodly

lodge
bodge
dislodge
dodge
splodge
stodge

lodger
bodger
dodger
Roger
The Artful Dodger

> ➕ You can also make rhymes for these words by using ***her*** after some words that rhyme with ***lodge***, as in ***dodge her***

stodgy
dodgy
podgy
splodgy

logic
geologic
pedagogic

logical
anthropological
archaeological
astrological
bacteriological
biological
chronological
ecological
entomological
etymological
geological
gynaecological
ideological
illogical
meteorological
mythological
pathological
pedagogical
physiological
psychological
scatological
sociological
tautological
technological
terminological
theological
zoological

erogenous
androgynous
homogenous

module
nodule

11.4

off
browned-off
cough
doff
Gorbachev
hands-off
kalashnikov
knock it off
quaff
scoff
toff
trough
Vincent Van Gogh
well-off
whooping cough

+ You can also make rhymes for these words by using words in section **11.14** that rhyme with *froth*

offer
coffer
proffer

+ You can add to this list by adding *-er* to some words that rhyme with *off*, as in *scoffer*

oesophagus
sarcophagus

oesophagi
sarcophagi

waffle
offal

coffee
toffee

coffin
boffin

profit
prophet

+ You can also make rhymes for these words by using *it* after some words that rhyme with *off*, as in *scoff it*

soft
aloft
croft
loft
waft

lofty
softy

softly
softly-softly

11.5

dog
agog
analogue
bog
catalogue
clog
cog
demagogue
dialogue
duologue
flog
fog
frog
grog
hog
jog
log
monologue
slog
smog
snog
synagogue
underdog

joggle
boggle
goggle
toggle
woggle

foggy
doggy
groggy
soggy

photographer
autobiographer
biographer
cartographer
choreographer
cinematographer
geographer
lexicographer
pornographer
radiographer
stenographer

geography
autobiography
bibliography
biography
cartography
choreography
cinematography
ethnography
hagiography
mammography
photography
pornography
radiography
topography
typography

togs
go to the dogs
pop one's clogs
Reservoir Dogs

+ You can add to this list by adding *-s* to some words that rhyme with *dog*, as in *frogs*

11.6

doll
aerosol
alcohol
cholesterol

Interpol
loll
paracetamol
parasol
protocol
Sebastopol
Sol

collar
ayatollah
bet one's bottom dollar
blue-collar
dollar
Eurodollar
holler
hot under the collar
scholar
squalor
white-collar

apology
anthology
anthropology
archaeology
astrology
bacteriology
biology
biotechnology
cardiology
chronology
criminology
dermatology
ecology
endocrinology
entomology
ethnology
etymology
geology
graphology
gynaecology
ideology
meteorology
methodology
microbiology
mythology
nanotechnology
neurology
ophthalmology
ornithology
pathology
pharmacology
philology
phraseology
physiology
psychology
radiology
reflexology
seismology
sociology
tautology
technology
terminology
theology
urology
virology
zoology

psychologist
anthropologist
apologist
archaeologist
biologist
cardiologist
dermatologist
ecologist
endocrinologist
entomologist
escapologist
ethnologist
geologist
gynaecologist
musicologist
neurologist
ornithologist
pathologist
pharmacologist
philologist
radiologist
reflexologist
sociologist
zoologist

column
solemn

pollen
Colin

dollop
codswallop
lollop
scallop
trollop
wallop

jolly
brolly
collie
Dolly
dolly
folly
golly
Holly
holly
lolly
melancholy
Molly
Ollie
Polly
poly
trolley
volley
Wally
wally

frolic
alcoholic
apostolic
bucolic
carbolic
chocoholic
colic
metabolic
nonalcoholic
parabolic
shambolic
shopaholic
symbolic
vitriolic
workaholic

solid
squalid
stolid

college
acknowledge
knowledge
self-knowledge

qualify
disqualify
mollify

qualified
disqualified
mollified
overqualified
underqualified
unqualified

solace
Barnes Wallis
William Wallace

hydrolysis
electrolysis

polish
abolish
demolish

polished
abolished
demolished
unpolished

cosmopolitan
Cosmopolitan
metropolitan
Neapolitan

quality
equality
frivolity
inequality

follow
hollow
Sleepy Hollow
swallow
wallow

golf
minigolf
Rolf

Volga
Olga

solve
absolve
devolve
dissolve
evolve
involve
resolve
revolve

involved
unsolved

+ You can add to this list by adding *-d* to some words that rhyme with ***solve***, as in ***resolved***

soluble
dissoluble
indissoluble
insoluble
voluble

11.7

prom
aplomb
bomb
CD-ROM
from
intercom
mom
Peeping Tom
pom
ROM
the Somme
Tom
tom
Uncle Tom

+ You can also make rhymes for these words by using words in section **11.8** that rhyme with ***con***

comma
bomber

+ You can also make rhymes for these words by using ***her*** after some words that rhyme with ***prom***, as in ***from her***

commentary
promontory

promise
doubting Thomas
Thomas

commie
pommy
Tommy

comic
astronomic
atomic
economic
ergonomic
gastronomic
socioeconomic

comical
anatomical
astronomical
economical
gastronomical
uneconomical

economics
ergonomics
macroeconomics
microeconomics

+ You can add to this list by adding *-s* to some words that rhyme with ***comic***, as in ***socioeconomics***

dominate
nominate
predominate

nominal
abdominal
phenomenal

nominally
phenomenally

prominence
dominance
predominance

prominent
dominant

predominant

vomit
comet

thermometer
barometer
gasometer
kilometre
micrometer
milometer
speedometer
tachometer

geometry
trigonometry

romp
aide-de-camp
clomp
pomp
stomp
swamp
yomp

11.8

con
anon
automaton
Babylon
Bonn
Canton
carry-on
Ceredigion
Ceylon
chiffon
COMECON (= *Council for Mutual Economic Assistance*)
Dionne
Don
don
echelon
Elton John
emoticon
Eva Perón
foregone
futon
Gabon
goings-on
gone
hands-on
hanger-on
hangers-on
head-on
John
Lebanon
liaison
marathon
odds-on
on
outshone
polygon
roll-on
Ron
Saigon
scone
shone
spot-on
stick-on
swan
thereupon
Tucson
undergone
upon
wan
whereupon
woebegone
Yvonne

+ You can also make rhymes for these words by using words in section **11.7** that rhyme with *prom*

honour
belladonna
Con(n)or
dishonour
doner (= *kebab*)
Donna
goner
gonna
Honor
Madonna
madonna
wanna
wanner

+ You can also make rhymes for these words by using ***her*** after some words that rhyme with ***con***, as in ***on her***

Donald
Old MacDonald
Ronald

economy
agronomy
astronomy
autonomy
gastronomy
physiognomy
taxonomy

bonny
Bonnie
Connie
Donny
Johnny
Ronnie

tonic
bubonic
catatonic
chronic
demonic
electronic
embryonic
harmonic
histrionic
ironic
laconic
mnemonic
monophonic
moronic
Napoleonic
philharmonic
phonic
platonic
polyphonic
quadraphonic
sardonic
Slavonic

sonic
stereophonic
supersonic

Monica
harmonica
moni(c)ker
Veronica

conical
chronicle
ironical

electronics
histrionics
onyx

+ You can add to this list by adding *-s* to some words that rhyme with *tonic*, as in *mnemonics*

anonymous
eponymous
synonymous

astonish
admonish

astonishing
admonishing

astonished
admonished

bonnet
sonnet

+ You can also make rhymes for these words by using *it* after some words that rhyme with *con*, as in *on it*

honk
bonk
conk
honky-tonk
Mont Blanc
plonk

conquer
conker
reconquer

+ You can add to this list by adding *-er* to some words that rhyme with *honk*, as in *plonker*

wonky
donkey

pond
abscond
beyond
blond(e)
bond
correspond
fond
frond
James Bond
respond
second (= *to transfer*)
vagabond
wand

+ You can add to this list by adding *-ned* to some words that rhyme with *con*, as in *donned*

ponder
anaconda
Rhonda
Rhondda
squander
Wanda
wander
yonder

+ You can add to this list by adding *-er* to some words that rhyme with *pond*, as in *fonder*

You can also make rhymes for these words by using *her* after some words that rhyme with *pond*, as in *beyond her*

despondent
co-respondent
correspondent
respondent

bonding
corresponding

+ You can add to this list by adding *-ing* to some words that rhyme with *pond*, as in *responding*

song
along
belong
bong
ding-dong
evensong
gong
Hong Kong
King Kong
long
overlong
pong
prolong
prong
sarong
strong
thong
throng
wrong

→ Many English speakers pronounce some words in section **17.8** (eg *tongue*) in such a way that they rhyme with these words

longing
belonging

> **+** You can add to this list by adding *-ing* to some words that rhyme with ***song***, as in ***prolonging***

conga
conger
longer
stronger
Tonga

strongly
wrongly

ponce
ambiance
bonce
ensconce
once
response

consul
tonsil

conscious
Pontius
self-conscious
semiconscious
subconscious
unconscious
unselfconscious

font
détente
Nantes
Vermont
want

The Full Monty
Brontë

pronto
Toronto

poncho
honcho

bronze
bonze
mod cons
Mons
The Fonz

> **+** You can add to this list by adding *-s* to some words that rhyme with ***con***, as in ***dons***

11.9

top
alcopop
barbershop
belly-flop
blow one's top
bop
chop
cop
crop
drag-and-drop
drop
escalope
flop
fop
glottal stop
hop
lollipop
mop
Mrs Malaprop
non-stop
op
over-the-top
plop
pop
prop
Robocop
shop
slop
sop
stop
strop
swap
turboprop
whistle-stop

stopper
chopper
copper
cropper
dropper
grasshopper
improper
knee-high to a grasshopper
name-dropper
popper
proper
shopper
teeny-bopper
whopper

> **+** You can add to this list by adding *-per* to some words that rhyme with ***top***, as in ***hopper***
>
> You can also make rhymes for these words by using ***her*** after some words that rhyme with ***top***, as in ***stop her***

properly
improperly
monopoly
oligopoly

copier
choppier
floppier
photocopier
sloppier
soppier
stroppier

copy
carbon copy
choppy
floppy
jalop(p)y
photocopy
poppy
sloppy
soppy

stroppy

topic
microscopic
misanthropic
myopic
philanthropic
stereoscopic
telescopic
tropic

tropical
semitropical
subtropical
topical

soppily
choppily
floppily
sloppily
stroppily

shopping
chopping
hopping
name-dropping
showstopping
sopping
teleshopping
topping
whopping
window-shopping

+ You can add to this list by adding *-ping* to some words that rhyme with ***top***, as in ***cropping***

dropout
cop-out
stop-out

hops
copse

+ You can add to this list by adding *-s* to some words that rhyme with ***top***, as in ***shops***

option
adoption

opt
adopt
close-cropped
co-opt

+ You can add to this list by adding *-ped* to some words that rhyme with ***top***, as in ***cropped***

populate
copulate
depopulate

11.10

horror
begorrah
Sodom and Gomorrah

moral
amoral
Balmoral
Coral
coral
immoral
Laurel
laurel
quarrel
sorrel

warren
foreign
Lauren
sporran
Warren

Florence
abhorrence

torrent
abhorrent
warrant

oratory
exploratory

sorry
articulated lorry
Laurie
lorry
quarry

historic
meteoric
prehistoric
Warwick
Yorick

historical
categorical
metaphorical
rhetorical

horrid
florid
torrid

porridge
forage
Norwich

Doris
Boris
Horace
Maurice
morris
orris

forest
deforest
florist

forester
chorister

majority
authority
inferiority
minority
priority
seniority
superiority

borrow
morrow
sorrow
tomorrow

11.11

cross
across

albatross
Archbishop Makarios
boss
candyfloss
cos (= *lettuce*)
dental floss
DOS
doss
double-cross
dross
floss
gloss
Kate Moss
kudos
lacrosse
loss
Mikonos
moss
Ross
toss

tosser
crosser
dosser

+ You can also make rhymes for these words by using ***her*** after some words that rhyme with ***cross***, as in ***across her***

fossil
apostle
colossal
jostle

blossom
opossum
possum

+ You can add to this list by adding ***'em*** to some words that rhyme with ***cross***, as in ***across 'em***

glossy
bossy
mossy
posse

atrocity
animosity
curiosity
ferocity
generosity
monstrosity
pomposity
precocity
velocity
verbosity

Tosca
Oscar

phosphorus
Bosphorus

cost
accost
defrost
embossed
frost
lost
Pentecost
riposte

+ You can add to this list by adding ***-ed*** to some words that rhyme with ***cross***, as in ***tossed***

foster
Gloucester
impostor
roster

+ You can also make rhymes for these words by using ***her*** after some words that rhyme with ***cost***, as in ***lost her***

agnostic
acrostic
diagnostic

frosting
costing

+ You can add to this list by adding ***-ing*** to some words that rhyme with ***cost***, as in ***accosting***

rostrum
nostrum

11.12

gosh
awash
cosh
dosh
josh
mac(k)intosh
nosh
posh
quash
slosh
squash
tosh
wash

washer
dishwasher

+ You can add to this list by adding ***-er*** to some words that rhyme with ***gosh***, as in ***posher***

You can also make rhymes for these words by using ***her*** after some words that rhyme with ***gosh***, as in ***squash her***

11.13

spot
Aldershot

allot
apricot
bergamot
blot
Camelot
Captain Scott
carrycot
chimneypot
clot
cot
Dot
dot
flowerpot
forget-me-not
forgot
garrotte
got
go to pot
guillemot
hot
James Watt
jot
kilowatt
knot
lot
mailshot
megawatt
not
ocelot
overshot
plot
Pol Pot
polyglot
pot
red-hot
rot
Scot
shallot
shot
slot
snot
squat
SWAT
swat
swot
tie the knot
tot
trot
watt
what
white-hot
yacht

plotter
blotter
globetrotter
gotta
Harry Potter
jotter
otter
potter
ricotta
rotter
squatter
terracotta
totter
trainspotter
trotter

+ You can add to this list by adding *-ter* to some words that rhyme with ***spot***, as in ***hotter***

You can also make rhymes for these words by using ***her*** after some words that rhyme with ***spot***, as in ***got her***

bottle
Aristotle
throttle

mottled
bottled
throttled

bottom
rock-bottom

+ You can add to this list by adding ***'em*** to some words that rhyme with ***spot***, as in ***got 'em***

lobotomy
dichotomy
laparotomy

rotten
cotton
forgotten
gotten
ill-gotten
long-forgotten

botany
monotony

lottery
pottery
tottery

dotty
grotty
knotty
Lanzarote
potty
snotty
spotty
totty

neurotic
antibiotic
chaotic
despotic
erotic
exotic
hypnotic
idiotic
narcotic
patriotic
psychotic
quixotic
symbiotic
unpatriotic

robotics
macrobiotics
probiotics

+ You can add to this list by adding ***-s*** to some words that rhyme with ***neurotic***, as in ***antibiotics***

potted
besotted

> + You can add to this list by adding *-ted* to some words that rhyme with ***spot***, as in ***slotted***

cottage
pottage
wattage

yachting
cybersquatting
trainspotting

> + You can add to this list by adding *-ting* to some words that rhyme with ***spot***, as in ***trotting***

motto
blotto
grotto
lotto
Otto
risotto

motley
hotly

Scots
call the shots
culottes
Mary Queen of Scots

> + You can add to this list by adding *-s* to some words that rhyme with ***spot***, as in ***pots***

Scotsman
yachtsman

Scotswoman
yachtswoman

notch
blotch
botch
butterscotch
crotch
Scotch
scotch
swatch
watch

11.14

froth
broth
cloth
Goth
moth
tablecloth
tiger moth
wrath

> + You can also make rhymes for these words by using words in section **11.4** that rhyme with ***off***

11.15

novel
grovel
hovel

11.16

was
because
Cos
cos (= *because*)
Oz
Ros

closet
deposit
posit
was it?

Section 12
-OE-

All the words in this section use the sound **-oe-** (as in f*oe*, N*oe*l, mistlet*oe*) in their main stressed syllable

12.1

go
aglow
ago
although
archipelago
audio
below
bestow
blow
blow-by-blow
BO
Bordeaux
Borneo
bow (= *weapon*)
bravo
buffalo
bungalow
c/o
calico
cameo
CEO (= *chief executive officer*)
cheerio
CO (= *commanding officer*)
co (= *company*)
contraflow
crow
curio
doe
do(h)
domino
dough
dynamo
ebb and flow
Edgar Allan Poe
embryo
Eskimo
ex officio
Felixstowe
Flo
flow
FO (= *Foreign Office*)
foe
forego
fro
from top to toe
get-up-and-go
gigolo
glow
GMO (= *genetically modified organism*)
go-slow
GPO
grow
gung-ho
haricot
Hello!
hello
HMSO (= *Her Majesty's Stationery Office*)
hoe
Idaho
ILO (= *International Labour Organisation*)
indigo
Inspector Clouseau
ISO (= *International Standards Organization*)
Jericho
Jo
Joe
just so
know
KO
Kosovo
lo
low
Marilyn Monroe
MBO (= *management buyout*)
Michelangelo
mistletoe
Mo
Monaco
mow
NCO (= *non-commissioned officer*)
need-to-know
NGO (= *Non-Governmental Organization*)
no
no-show
O
oh
oho
ono (= *or near(est) offer*)
outgrow
overflow
overthrow
owe

patio
pedalo
piccolo
pistachio
PLO (= *Palestine Liberation Organization*)
PO (= *Post Office*)
pro
PTO
Punch and Judy show
radio
ratio
rodeo
roe
Romeo
row (= *a line; to propel a boat*)
San Antonio
Scorpio
sew
show
sloe
slow
snow
so
so-and-so
soh
sow (= *to scatter seed*)
status quo
stereo
stow
studio
the Alamo
though
throw
toe
tow
UFO
undergo
undertow
UNO (= *United Nations Organization*)
vertigo
video
VSO (= *Voluntary Service Overseas*)
WHO (= *World Health Organization*)
window
woe

mower
blower
boa
Boer
churchgoer
cinema-goer
flamethrower
grower
lawnmower
lower (= *further down*)
moviegoer
Noah
rower
Samoa
theatre-goer

> + You can add to this list by adding ***-er*** to some words that rhyme with ***go***, as in ***thrower***
>
> You can also make rhymes for these words by using ***her*** after some words that rhyme with ***go***, as in ***know her***

Joel
bestowal
Noel

stowaway
go away
throwaway

showy
blowy
Chloe
Joey
joey
snowy
Zoë

stoic
heroic

going
easy-going
flowing
glass-blowing
glowing
growing
ingrowing
knowing
ocean-going
ongoing
outgoing
owing
rowing (= *propelling a boat*)
seagoing
sewing
showing
thoroughgoing

> + You can add to this list by adding ***-ing*** to some words that rhyme with ***go***, as in ***throwing***

12.2

globe
disrobe
earlobe
lobe
probe
robe
strobe

crowbar
towbar

sober
Manitoba
October

noble
Chernobyl
global
Grenoble
ignoble

Toby
adobe

Gobi
goby
Nairobi

aerobic
agoraphobic
anaerobic
aqua(e)robic
claustrophobic
phobic
xenophobic

aerobics
agoraphobics
aqua(e)robics
claustrophobics
phobics
xenophobics

12.3

smoke
artichoke
awoke
Basingstoke
bespoke
beyond a joke
bloke
broke
choke
cloak
Coke®
coke
croak
evoke
folk
invoke
joke
masterstroke
oak
poke
provoke
revoke
soak
spoke
stoke
stroke
toke
woke
womenfolk
yoke
yolk

smoker
broker
choker
joker
mediocre
non-smoker
ochre
pawnbroker
poker
stockbroker
tapioca

> + You can add to this list by adding *-r* to some words that rhyme with ***smoke***, as in ***evoking***
>
> You can also make rhymes for these words by using ***her*** after some words that rhyme with ***smoke***, as in ***provoke her***

local
bifocal
focal
varifocal
vocal
yokel

broken
awoken
heartbroken
outspoken
plain-spoken
soft-spoken
spoken
token
unbroken
unspoken
well-spoken
woken

focus
crocus
hocus-pocus

> + You can also make rhymes for these words by using ***us*** after some words that rhyme with ***smoke***, as in ***choke us***

smoky
hokey-cokey
joky
okey-dokey
poky

Tokyo
Pinocchio

smoking
broking
choking
evoking
invoking
joking
no-smoking
poking
provoking
revoking
stoking
stroking
thought-provoking
toking
yoking

> + You can add to this list by adding *-ing* to some words that rhyme with ***smoke***, as in ***soaking***

coax
hoax

> + You can add to this list by adding *-s* to some words that rhyme with ***smoke***, as in ***strokes***

soaked
smoked
unprovoked

> + You can add to this list by adding *-(e)d* to some words that rhyme with ***smoke***, as in ***provoked***

12.4

code
abode
bode
commode
corrode
decode
discommode
download
encode
episode
erode
explode
goad
KO'd
load
middle-of-the-road
mode
node
ode
off-load
one for the road
overload
override
pigeon-toed
road
rode
sowed
strode
toad
unload

> + You can add to this list by adding ***-ed*** to some words that rhyme with ***go***, as in ***glowed***

soda
coda
freeloader
odour
pagoda
Rhoda
Skoda

> + You can add to this list by adding ***-(e)r*** to some words that rhyme with ***code***, as in ***decoder***
>
> You can also make rhymes for these words by using ***her*** after some words that rhyme with ***code***, as in ***goad her***

sodium
odium
podium
rhodium

custodian
Cambodian
melodeon
nickelodeon

odious
commodious
melodious
unmelodious

toady
Jodie
Miss Jean Brodie
roadie

loaded
colour-coded
outmoded

> + You can add to this list by adding ***-(e)d*** to some words that rhyme with ***code***, as in ***goaded***

loading
boding
coding
corroding
decoding
discommoding
encoding
eroding
exploding
foreboding

> + You can add to this list by adding ***-ing*** to some words that rhyme with ***code***, as in ***goading***

showdown
low-down
slow-down

Trojan
theologian

12.5

loaf
oaf

> + You can also make rhymes for these words by using by using words in section **12.16** that rhyme with ***both***

loafer
chauffeur
gopher
sofa

trophy
Sophie

12.6

rogue
brogue
en vogue
Vogue

vogue

yoga
ogre
toga

ogle
mogul

fogey
bogey

pogo
logo
Togo

12.7

hole
Adrian Mole
bankroll
bowl
buttonhole
cajole
camisole
casserole
coal
console
control
cubbyhole
dole
droll
enrol
extol
foal
goal
mole
Nat King Cole
Nicole
parole
patrol
pigeonhole
Pole
pole
poll
rigmarole
rock'n'roll
role
roll
scroll
self-control
Seoul
shoal
sole
soul
stole
stroll
toll
totem pole
troll
vole
watering hole
whole

polar
Angola
bowler
Coca-Cola®
cola
Francis Ford Coppola
Hispaniola
Lola
molar
potholer
roller
solar
steamroller
viola
Zola

+ You can add to this list by adding ***-(e)r*** to some words that rhyme with ***hole***, as in ***stroller***

You can also make rhymes for these words by using ***her*** after some words that rhyme with ***hole***, as in ***cajole her***

controllable
inconsolable
uncontrollable

stolen
Angolan
colon
semicolon
swollen

Poland
lowland
Roland

holier
lowlier
magnolia
Mongolia

linoleum
petroleum

Mongolian
Napoleon

holy
coley
goalie
guacamole
lowly
roly-poly
slowly
solely
Stromboli
unholy
wholly

polio
folio
portfolio

rolling
bowling
buttonholing
cajoling
casseroling
consoling
doling
pigeonholing
polling
potholing
tenpin bowling

+ You can add to this list by adding ***-(l)ing*** to some words that rhyme with ***hole***, as in ***controlling***

solo
Marco Polo
polo

cold
behold
bold
break the mould
centrefold
controlled
enfold
fold
foretold
gold
hold
hundredfold
ice-cold
manifold
marigold
mould
old
outsold
radio-controlled
remote-controlled
scold
sold
stone-cold
stranglehold
told
uncontrolled
unfold
unsold
untold
uphold
withhold

+ You can add to this list by adding *-((l)e)d* to some words that rhyme with ***hole***, as in ***strolled***

shoulder
beholder
boulder
cold-shoulder
folder
freeholder
holder
householder
leaseholder
moulder
officeholder
record-holder
shareholder
smallholder
smoulder
solder
stockholder
titleholder

+ You can add to this list by adding *-er* to some words that rhyme with ***cold***, as in ***older***

You can also make rhymes for these words by using ***her*** after some words that rhyme with ***cold***, as in ***hold her***

golden
beholden
embolden

mouldy
golden oldie
oldie

folding
holding
moulding
scolding
shareholding
smallholding

coldly
boldly

coldness
boldness

soulful
doleful

solely
wholly

soulless
goalless

coalman
patrolman

bolster
holster
upholster

bolt
colt
dolt
jolt
moult
revolt
smolt
thunderbolt
volt

molten
Bolton

12.8

home
aerodrome
chrome
chromosome
comb
dome
foam
gnome
honeycomb
Jerome
loam
metronome
monochrome
ohm
roam
Rome
tome

+ You can also make rhymes for these words by using words in section **12.9** that rhyme with ***bone***

coma
aroma

beachcomber
carcinoma
diploma
glaucoma
Homer
lymphoma
melanoma
misnomer
Oklahoma
Omagh
Paloma

+ You can add to this list by adding *-(e)r* to some words that rhyme with ***home***, as in ***roamer***

Roman
omen
roman
showman

foamy
hom(e)y
loamy
Salome

roaming
homing
Wyoming

+ You can add to this list by adding *-ing* to some words that rhyme with ***home***, as in ***foaming***

slo-mo
Lake Como
major-domo
Perry Como

12.9

bone
accident-prone
Al Capone
alone
Anglophone
atone
baritone
bemoan
blown
bridging loan
chaperone
clone
collarbone
Cologne
cologne
condone
cone
cornerstone
cortisone
crone
dethrone
disown
drone
eau de Cologne
entryphone
Eurozone
flown
francophone
full-blown
full(y)-grown
gramophone
groan
grown
hailstone
heart of stone
Home Alone
home-grown
hone
hydrocortisone
intone
Joan
known
loan
lone
marrowbone
megaphone
microphone
moan
monotone
mown
nuclear-free zone
outgrown
overblown
overgrown
overthrown
overtone
own
phone
postpone
prone
Rhone
saxophone
semitone
sewn
shown
Sierra Leone
Simone
skin and bone
sown
stone
Sylvester Stallone
telephone
testosterone
throne
thrown
tone
trombone
Tyrone
undertone
unknown
well-known
xylophone
zone

+ You can also make rhymes for these words by using words in section **12.8** that rhyme with ***home***

loner
Arizona
Barcelona
co-owner
Desdemona
donor
Fiona
homeowner
Iona
Jonah

krona
krone
kroner
landowner
Mona
owner
Pamplona
R(h)ona
shipowner
Shona
Verona
Winona

+ You can add to this list by adding *-(e)r* to some words that rhyme with ***bone***, as in ***moaner***

You can also make rhymes for these words by using ***her*** after some words that rhyme with ***bone***, as in ***phone her***

bonus
lowness
no-claims bonus
onus
slowness

+ You can also make rhymes for these words by using ***us*** after some words that rhyme with ***bone***, as in ***own us***

bonier
ammonia
Antonia
begonia
Catalonia
catatonia
Cephalonia
Estonia
Macedonia
moanier
Patagonia
phonier
pneumonia
stonier

colonial
ceremonial
matrimonial
neocolonial
testimonial

plutonium
harmonium
pandemonium

Estonian
Caledonian
draconian
Ionian
Macedonian

harmonious
acrimonious
ceremonious
erroneous
parsimonious
sanctimonious

pony
baloney
bony
crony
Joanie
macaroni
Marconi
moany
phon(e)y
stony
Toni
Tony

phone-in
serotonin

+ You can also make rhymes for these words by using ***in*** after some words that rhyme with ***bone***, as in ***grown in***

cloning
atoning
chaperoning
condoning
dethroning
droning
honing
intoning
landowning
phoning
postponing
stoning
telephoning
toning
zoning

+ You can add to this list by adding *-ing* to some words that rhyme with ***bone***, as in ***disowning***

kimono
no-no

stoned
state-owned
unchaperoned

+ You can add to this list by adding *-(e)d* to some words that rhyme with ***bone***, as in ***groaned***

only
lonely
read-only

atonement
postponement

don't
won't
wont

lazybones
feel it in one's bones
Indiana Jones
The Rolling Stones

Tom Jones

> You can add to this list by adding *-s* to some words that rhyme with ***bone***, as in ***moans***

12.10

hope
antelope
Bob Hope
cope
docusoap
dope
elope
envelope
grope
gyroscope
Hope
horoscope
isotope
kaleidoscope
microscope
misanthrope
mope
nope
periscope
pope
rope
scope
self-addressed envelope
slope
soap
stethoscope
telescope

no-hoper
interloper

> You can add to this list by adding *-r* to some words that rhyme with ***hope***, as in ***moper***

kopeck
OPEC (= *Organization of Petroleum-Exporting Countries*)

Utopia
Ethiopia
myopia

Utopian
Ethiopian

dop(e)y
rop(e)y
soapy

12.11

dose
bellicose
cellulose
close (= *near*)
comatose
grandiose
gross
lachrymose
morose
overdose
verbose

grocer
greengrocer
samosa

> You can add to this list by adding *-(e)r* to some words that rhyme with ***dose***, as in ***closer***

neuroses
diagnoses
prognoses
psychoses

hypnosis
arteriosclerosis
arthrosis
asbestosis
cirrhosis
diagnosis
doses
halitosis
myxomatosis
narcosis
neurosis
osmosis
osteoporosis
process
prognosis
psychosis
sclerosis
thrombosis
tuberculosis

explosive
corrosive

closely
grossly

post
boast
bottommost
coast
engrossed
first-past-the-post
furthermost
ghost
give up the ghost
host
inmost
innermost
most
outermost
roast
toast
uppermost
uttermost

> You can add to this list by adding *-(e)d* to some words that rhyme with ***dose***, as in ***grossed***

toaster
boaster
coaster
four-poster
poster

roaster
roller-coaster

postal
coastal

roasting
boasting
posting

> + You can add to this list by adding *-ing* to some words that rhyme with ***post***, as in ***coasting***

mostly
ghostly

12.12

closure
composure
disclosure
enclosure
exposure

explosion
corrosion
erosion
implosion

12.13

brochure
kosher
Nova Scotia

sociable
negotiable
non-negotiable
unsociable

notion
calamine lotion
cleansing lotion
commotion
demotion
devotion
emotion
hand lotion
locomotion
lotion
motion
ocean
potion
promotion

emotional
devotional
promotional
unemotional

ferocious
atrocious
precocious

12.14

note
afloat
anecdote
antidote
banknote
billy-goat
boat
coat
demote
denote
devote
dote
float
get someone's goat
gloat
goat
jump down someone's throat
misquote
moat
motorboat
nanny-goat
overcoat
overwrote
petticoat
promote
quote
remote
rewrote
rote
rowing boat
smote
stoat
throat
tote
undercoat
underwrote
unquote
vote
wrote

rota
boater
Dakota
iota
Minnesota
motor
promoter
quota
rotor
voter

> + You can add to this list by adding *-(e)r* to some words that rhyme with ***note***, as in ***floater***
>
> You can also make rhymes for these words by using ***her*** after some words that rhyme with ***note***, as in ***promote her***

total
anecdotal
subtotal
teetotal

rotary
notary
votary

notice
lotus

> + You can also make rhymes for these words by using ***us*** after some words that rhyme with ***note***, as in ***promote us***

throaty
coyote
floaty

noted
bloated
devoted
sugar-coated

+ You can add to this list by adding *-(e)d* to some words that rhyme with ***note***, as in ***coated***

coating
boating
demoting
denoting
devoting
doting
floating
misquoting
noting
promoting
quoting
toting
voting

+ You can add to this list by adding *-ing* to some words that rhyme with ***note***, as in ***gloating***

motive
automotive
emotive
locomotive
votive

photo
Kyoto
telephoto

oats
Captain Oates
compare notes

+ You can add to this list by adding *-s* to some words that rhyme with ***note***, as in ***votes***

coach
approach
broach
brooch
encroach
poach
reproach
roach

poachable
approachable
coachable
irreproachable
unapproachable

12.15

loathe
clothe

clothing
loathing
underclothing

betrothed
clothed
loathed
unclothed

clothes
loathes
underclothes

12.16

both
growth
loath
oath
sloth
undergrowth

+ You can also make rhymes for these words by using words in section **12.5** that rhyme with ***loaf***

12.17

stove
clove
cove
drove
grove
hove
mauve
Primus® stove
rove
strove
throve
treasure-trove
wove

over
Anna Pavlova
Casanova
changeover
clover
Dover
flyover
going-over
hangover
Jehovah
Land Rover
leftover
Moldova
moreover
once-over
ova
pavlova
pullover
pushover
Range Rover
rollover
stopover
turnover
voice-over
walkover

+ You can add to this list by adding *-r* to some words that rhyme with *stove*, as in *rover*

woven
Beethoven
cloven
disproven
Moldovan
proven

ovary
Madame Bovary

12.18

glow-worm
slow-worm

12.19

nose
arose
chose
close (= *to shut*)
come to blows
Comoros
compose
decompose
depose
diagnose
disclose
discompose
dispose
doze
enclose
expose
foreclose
froze
get up someone's nose
goes
hose
impose
interpose
juxtapose
KO's
misdiagnose
oppose
overexpose
pantyhose
pose
predispose
presuppose
propose
prose
repose
Rose
rose
superimpose
suppose
those
throes
transpose
tread on someone's toes

+ You can add to this list by adding *-s* to some words that rhyme with *go*, as in *blows*

rosé
exposé

poser
bulldozer
composer
Rosa

+ You can add to this list by adding *-r* to some words that rhyme with *nose*, as in *proposer*

You can also make rhymes for these words by using *her* after some words that rhyme with *nose*, as in *propose her*

frozen
chosen
re-frozen
well-chosen

cosy
dozy
nosey
posy
Rosie
rosy

closing
composing
decomposing
deposing
diagnosing
disclosing
discomposing
disposing
dozing
enclosing
exposing
foreclosing
hosing
imposing
interposing
juxtaposing
misdiagnosing
nosing
opposing
overexposing
posing
predisposing
presupposing
proposing
reposing
superimposing
supposing
transposing

closed
composed
disposed
exposed
ill-disposed
indisposed
supposed
underexposed
undisclosed
unopposed
well-disposed

+ You can add to this list by adding *-d* to some words that rhyme with *nose*, as in *proposed*

Section 13
-OW-

All the words in this section use the sound **-ow-** (as in t*ow*n, p*ow*er, all*ow*) in their main stressed syllable

13.1

now
allow
anyhow
bough
bow (= *to bend the body in respect*)
brow
cow
disallow
endow
Guinea-Bissau
how
kowtow
miaow
middlebrow
ow
plough
prow
row (= *an argument*)
sow (= *a female pig*)
vow
wow

power
bell-tower
bower
brainpower
cauliflower
cornflour
cornflower
cower
devour
Eisenhower
empower
flour
flower
glower
horsepower
hour
lower (= *to be overcast*)
man-hour
manpower
Mayflower
our
overpower
plain flour
scour
self-raising flour
shower
sour
staying power
sunflower
superpower
sweet-and-sour
tower
wallflower
watchtower
willpower

+ You can add to this list by adding *-er* to some words that rhyme with ***now***, as in ***endower***

You can also make rhymes for these words by using *her* after some words that rhyme with ***now***, as in ***allow her***

coward
high-powered
Howard
jet-powered
Noël Coward
solar-powered

+ You can add to this list by adding *-ed* to some words that rhyme with ***power***, as in ***glowered***

towel
avowal
bowel
dowel
Enoch Powell
Hywel
trowel
vowel

hourly
half-hourly
sourly

towering
empowering
overpowering

+ You can add to this list by adding *-ing* to

some words that rhyme with ***power***, as in ***glowering***

Maui
David Bowie

prowess
Powys

13.2

proud
aloud
avowed
bowed
cloud
crowd
loud
shroud
Stroud
thundercloud
Turin Shroud

\+ You can add to this list by adding ***-ed*** to some words that rhyme with ***now***, as in ***allowed***

powder
chowder
gunpowder
talcum powder

\+ You can add to this list by adding ***-er*** to some words that rhyme with ***proud***, as in ***louder***

You can also make rhymes for these words by using ***her*** after some words that rhyme with ***proud***, as in ***allowed her***

rowdy
cloudy
dowdy
Saudi

proudly
loudly

13.3

owl
cheek by jowl
cowl
foul
fowl
growl
howl
jowl
prowl
scowl
waterfowl
yowl

→ Many English speakers pronounce some words in section **13.1** (eg *towel*) in such a way that they rhyme with these words

prowler
howler

\+ You can add to this list by adding ***-er*** to some words that rhyme with ***owl***, as in ***scowler***

howling
growling

\+ You can add to this list by adding ***-ing*** to some words that rhyme with ***owl***, as in ***scowling***

13.4

town
bogged down
brown
clown
crown
Down
down
downtown
dressing down
dressing gown
drown
dumbing down
eiderdown
frown
gown
lie down
noun
one-horse town
on the town
put down
renown
run-down
tumbledown
upside down
uptown

brownie
Brownie
downy
towny

pound
abound
aground
all-round
around
astound
battleground
bound
compound (= *to add to*)
confound
expound
found
ground
hound
impound
leather-bound
merry-go-round

mound
profound
propound
rebound
renowned
resound
rewound
round
run-around
sound
stamping ground
surround
turnaround
ultrasound
underground
unsound
unwound
wound (= *past tense of wind*)

> + You can add to this list by adding *-ed* to some words that rhyme with ***town***, as in ***drowned***

bounder
all-rounder
flounder
founder
quarter-pounder
rebounder

> + You can add to this list by adding *-er* to some words that rhyme with ***pound***, as in ***rounder***
>
> You can also make rhymes for these words by using ***her*** after some words that rhyme with ***pound***, as in ***around her***

dumbfounded
ill-founded
unbounded
unfounded
well-founded

> + You can add to this list by adding *-ed* to some words that rhyme with ***pound***, as in ***grounded***

grounding
astounding
resounding
surrounding

> + You can add to this list by adding *-ing* to some words that rhyme with ***pound***, as in ***sounding***

soundings
surroundings

soundly
profoundly
roundly

boundless
groundless
soundless

foundry
boundary

lounge
scrounge

crowning
Robert Browning

> + You can add to this list by adding *-ing* to some words that rhyme with ***town***, as in ***drowning***

bounce
announce
denounce
flounce
mispronounce
ounce
pounce
pronounce
renounce
trounce

bouncer
announcer
denouncer

> + You can also make rhymes for these words by using ***her*** after some words that rhyme with ***bounce***, as in ***denounce her***

announcement
pronouncement

pronounced
unannounced

> + You can add to this list by adding *-d* to some words that rhyme with ***bounce***, as in ***announced***

count
account
amount
discount
dismount
fount
mount
paramount
recount
surmount
tantamount

counter
Brief Encounter
encounter
Geiger counter

> + You can also make rhymes for these

words by using ***her*** after some words that rhyme with ***count***, as in ***discount her***

countable
accountable
insurmountable
surmountable
unaccountable
uncountable

county
bounty

mounted
unaccounted

+ You can add to this list by adding ***-ed*** to some words that rhyme with ***count***, as in ***discounted***

mounting
accounting

+ You can add to this list by adding ***-ing*** to some words that rhyme with ***count***, as in ***discounting***

mountain
fountain
soda fountain

13.5

dowry
Lowry
Maori

13.6

mouse
clearing house
douse
fieldmouse
grouse
house (= *a home*)
house-to-house
in-house
jailhouse
Laos
louse
Mickey Mouse
nous
powerhouse
slaughterhouse
souse
spouse
Strauss
summerhouse

oust
joust

+ You can add to this list by adding ***-d*** to some words that rhyme with ***mouse***, as in ***groused***

13.7

out
about
all-out
bout
boy scout
Brussels sprout
burnt-out
carry-out
clapped-out
clout
devout
doubt
down-and-out
drought
flout
gout
grout
hand out
hang-out
layabout
lout
out-and-out
pout
roundabout
rout
sauerkraut
scout
self-doubt
shout
snout
spaced out
spout
sprout
stout
thought-out
throughout
tout
trout
turnabout
walkabout
way-out
well-thought-out
without
zonked out

outing
shouting

+ You can add to this list by adding ***-ing*** to some words that rhyme with ***out***, as in ***pouting***

whereabouts
have one's doubts
hereabouts
thereabouts

+ You can add to this list by adding ***-s*** to some words that rhyme with ***out***, as in ***sprouts***

pouch
couch
crouch
grouch

ouch
slouch
vouch

13.8

mouth
hand-to-mouth
Louth
south

13.9

drowse
arouse
blouse
browse
carouse
espouse
house (= *to provide accommodation for*)
rehouse
rouse

+ You can add to this list by adding **-s** to some words that rhyme with ***now***, as in ***cows***

tousle
arousal
carousal
espousal
spousal

drowsy
blowzy
lousy

rousing
arousing
browsing
carousing
drowsing
espousing
housing
rehousing

Section 14
-OR-

All the words in this section use the sound **-or-** (as in s*or*t, c*or*ner, aff*or*d) in their main stressed syllable

14.1

draw
abhor
adore
ambassador
Arkansas
ashore
at death's door
Aviemore
awe
Baltimore
before
boar
bore
brother-in-law
carnivore
caw
chore
claw
commodore
common-law
core
corps (= *a military body*)
corridor
daughter-in-law
Demi Moore
deplore
dinosaur
door
door-to-door
drawer
Ecuador
evermore
explore
father-in-law
flaw
floor
for
forbore
fore
foresaw
forswore
four
furthermore
galore
George Bernard Shaw
gnaw
gore
guarantor
guffaw
hard-core
herbivore
ignore
implore
inshore
jackdaw
jaw
labrador
Lahore
law
lore
louvre door
macaw
matador
metaphor
more
mother-in-law
Mysore
Nassau
next-door
Nineteen Eighty-Four
nor
oar
offshore
omnivore
or
ore
overawe
oversaw
paw
pinafore
pore
postwar
pour
prewar
rapport
raw
restore
roar
San Salvador
saw
score
semaphore
shore
Singapore
Sir Thomas More
sister-in-law
snore
soar
son-in-law
sophomore
sore
spore
squaw

stevedore
store
straw
superstore
swore
sycamore
thaw
Theodore
tore
toreador
tug-of-war
war
Wichita
withdraw
wore
you're
your

➔ Many English speakers pronounce some words in section **14.1** (eg *poor*) in such a way that they rhyme with these words

14.2

orb
absorb
daub

bauble
warble

floorboard
scoreboard

lawbreaker
jawbreaker

14.3

talk
Bob Hawke
chalk
Cork
cork
gawk
hawk
New York
pork
sparrowhawk
squawk
stalk
stork
tomahawk
tuning fork
uncork
walk
York

walker
baby-walker
deerstalker
hillwalker
jaywalker
Majorca
Minorca
sleepwalker
stalker
streetwalker
talker

+ You can add to this list by adding ***-er*** to some words that rhyme with ***talk***, as in ***corker***

You can also make rhymes for these words by using ***her*** after some words that rhyme with ***talk***, as in ***stalk her***

Majorcan
Minorcan

raucous
caucus

+ You can also make rhymes for these words by using ***us*** after some words that rhyme with ***talk***, as in ***stalk us***

chalky
gawky
Gorky
porky
walkie-talkie

walking
hillwalking
jaywalking
smooth-talking
talking

+ You can add to this list by adding ***-ing*** to some words that rhyme with ***talk***, as in ***stalking***

mawkish
hawkish

lawcourt
forecourt

forked
corked

+ You can add to this list by adding ***-ed*** to some words that rhyme with ***talk***, as in ***walked***

14.4

board
aboard
abroad
accord
across-the-board
afford
applaud
award
baud
bored
broad
chord
Claud(e)
cord

defraud
fjord
flawed
ford
fraud
harpsichord
hoard
horde
laud
lord
Maud(e)
motherboard
noticeboard
overboard
plasterboard
record (= *to register*)
reward
skirting board
sounding board
sword
tape-record
toward
umbilical cord
unexplored
untoward
ward

+ You can add to this list by adding *-ed* to some words that rhyme with ***draw***, as in ***explored***

→ Many English speakers pronounce some words in section **19.2** (eg *insured*) in such a way that they rhyme with these words

order
boarder
border
camcorder
disorder
hoarder
keyboarder
marauder
recorder
reorder
tape recorder
video recorder
warder

+ You can add to this list by adding *-er* to some words that rhyme with ***board***, as in ***broader***

You can also make rhymes for these words by using ***her*** after some words that rhyme with ***board***, as in ***toward her***

laudable
affordable
unaffordable

ordered
disordered

+ You can add to this list by adding *-ed* to some words that rhyme with ***order***, as in ***bordered***

warden
broaden
cordon
Gordon
Jordan
Lizzie Borden
Michael Jordan
traffic warden

mordant
discordant

Borders
marching orders
under starter's orders

+ You can add to this list by adding *-s* to some words that rhyme with ***order***, as in ***marauders***

cordial
primordial

accordion
Edwardian

gaudy
bawdy
Geordie

sordid
prerecorded
unrecorded

+ You can add to this list by adding *-ed* to some words that rhyme with ***board***, as in ***recorded***

inordinate
coordinate
insubordinate
subordinate

boarding
hoarding
marauding
recording
rewarding
snowboarding
unrewarding

+ You can add to this list by adding *-ing* to some words that rhyme with ***board***, as in ***applauding***

broadly
lordly

tawdry
Audrey

gorge
David Lloyd-George
forge
George

14.5

dwarf
Düsseldorf
swarf
wharf

+ You can also make rhymes for these words by using words in section **14.16** that rhyme with ***north***

awful
drawerful
lawful
unlawful

14.6

organ
Glamorgan
Gorgon

14.7

forehand
beforehand

warhead
forehead

storehouse
poorhouse

14.8

small
all
appal
awl
ball
basketball
bawl
befall
belle of the ball
Bengal
brawl
call
cannonball
Charles de Gaulle
crawl
Donegal
drawl
enthral
fall
firewall
forestall
free-for-all
gall
Gaul
hall
handball
haul
install
know-it-all
long-haul
mall
market stall
maul
Montreal
Nepal
off-the-wall
overall
overhaul
pall
Paul
recall
Saul
scrawl
Senegal
shawl
short-haul
sprawl
squall
stall
tall
trawl
volleyball
wall
wall-to-wall
warts and all
waterfall
wherewithal
withal

caller
crawler
footballer
hauler
kerbcrawler
Paula
trawler
what-d'ye-call-her

+ You can add to this list by adding ***-er*** to some words that rhyme with ***small***, as in ***taller***

You can also make rhymes for these words by using ***her*** after some words that rhyme with ***small***, as in ***call her***

sorely
Bengali
creepy-crawly
Nepali
Sir Walter Raleigh
squally

→ Many English speakers pronounce some words in section **19.3** (eg *poorly*) in such a way that they rhyme with these words

all-in
tarpaulin

+ You can also make rhymes for these words by using ***in*** after some words that rhyme with ***small***, as in ***crawl in***

calling
appalling
enthralling
galling
kerbcrawling
name-calling
sprawling

> + You can add to this list by adding *-ing* to some words that rhyme with ***small***, as in ***falling***

flawless
lawless

falcon
Balkan
peregrine falcon

bald
scald
so-called

> + You can add to this list by adding *-ed* to some words that rhyme with ***small***, as in ***called***

scalding
balding

false
waltz

fault
assault
default
exalt
malt
SALT
salt
somersault
vault
Walt

alter
altar
defaulter
falter
Gibraltar
halter
Malta
pole-vaulter
vaulter
Walter

> + You can also make rhymes for these words by using ***her*** after some words that rhyme with ***fault***, as in ***assault her***

faulty
Basil Fawlty
salty

vaulted
exalted
unsalted

> + You can add to this list by adding *-ed* to some words that rhyme with ***fault***, as in ***salted***

hallway
Galway

14.9

form
Benidorm
chloroform
conform
deform
dorm
inform
Norm
norm
perform
re-form
reform
storm
swarm
thunderstorm
transform
underperform
uniform
warm

> + You can also make rhymes for these words by using words in section **14.10** that rhyme with ***born***

format
doormat
re-format

former
dormer
informer
Norma
performer
reformer
transformer
trauma

> + You can add to this list by adding *-er* to some words that rhyme with ***form***, as in ***warmer***
>
> You can also make rhymes for these words by using ***her*** after some words that rhyme with ***form***, as in ***inform her***

normal
abnormal
formal
informal
paranormal
subnormal

normally
abnormally
formally
formerly
informally

formalize
normalize

foreman
doorman
longshoreman
Mormon
Norman
storeman

dormant
informant

enormous
ginormous

+ You can also make rhymes for these words by using *us* after some words that rhyme with ***form***, as in ***inform us***

formative
informative
normative

performing
barnstorming
brainstorming
heart-warming
housewarming

+ You can add to this list by adding ***-ing*** to some words that rhyme with ***form***, as in ***swarming***

deformity
conformity
enormity
uniformity

reformed
ill-informed
informed
malformed
uninformed
well-informed

+ You can add to this list by adding ***-ed*** to some words that rhyme with ***form***, as in ***stormed***

warmly
uniformly

14.10

born
adorn
at daggers drawn
borne
brawn
Capricorn
corn
Dawn
dawn
drawn
faun
fawn
forborne
forewarn
forlorn
forsworn
horn
lawn
leprechaun
Matterhorn
Mountains of Mourne
mourn
outworn
overdrawn
pawn
peppercorn
prawn
Quorn®
reborn
sawn
scorn
Sean
shorn
Siobhán
spawn
sworn
thorn
torn
unicorn
warn
waterborne
well-worn
withdrawn
worn
yawn

+ You can also make rhymes for these words by using words in section **14.9** that rhyme with ***form***

corner
fauna
fawner
fight one's corner
Lorna
mourner
sauna
yawner

+ You can also make rhymes for these words by using ***her*** after some words that rhyme with ***born***, as in ***mourn her***

scrawnier
brawnier
California
cornea
cornier
hornier
thornier

corny
brawny
horny
scrawny
tawny
thorny

morning
awning
midmorning

mourning
warning

+ You can add to this list by adding *-ing* to some words that rhyme with ***born***, as in ***adorning***

hornet
cornet

+ You can also make rhymes for these words by using ***it*** after some words that rhyme with ***born***, as in ***torn it***

mournful
scornful

haunt
daunt
flaunt
gaunt
jaunt
taunt
vaunt

haunted
undaunted

+ You can add to this list by adding ***-ed*** to some words that rhyme with ***haunt***, as in ***taunted***

daunting
haunting

+ You can add to this list by adding ***-ing*** to some words that rhyme with ***haunt***, as in ***taunting***

launch
haunch
paunch
staunch

14.11

warp
gawp

pauper
torpor

14.12

flora
Andorra
angora
aura
Aurora
Cora
Dora
explorer
Flora
Laura
Leonora
Nora(h)
Pandora
scorer
Thora

+ You can add to this list by adding ***-r*** to some words that rhyme with ***draw***, as in ***restorer***

→ Many English speakers pronounce some words in section **19.4** (eg *juror*) in such a way that they rhyme with these words

adorable
deplorable

oral
aural
choral
floral

forum
decorum
quorum

chorus
porous
Taurus
thesaurus

+ You can also make rhymes for these words by using ***us*** after some words that rhyme with ***draw***, as in ***bore us***

Maureen
chlorine
Noreen

Gloria
crematoria
euphoria
moratoria
Pretoria
sanatoria
Victoria

memorial
conspiratorial
dictatorial
editorial
equatorial
immemorial
pictorial
sartorial
territorial
tutorial

auditorium
crematorium
moratorium
sanatorium

historian
Dorian
Singaporean
Victorian

glorious
censorious
inglorious
laborious
meritorious
notorious
uproarious
victorious

➔ Many English speakers pronounce some words in section **19.4** (eg *furious*) in such a way that they rhyme with these words

gloriously
laboriously
notoriously
uproariously
victoriously

story
furore
glory
gory
hoary
knickerbocker glory
Lake Maggiore
multistorey
Rory
storey
Tory
West Side Story

boring
adoring
deploring
goring
ignoring
imploring
pouring
restoring
roaring
scoring
shoring
snoring
soaring
storing
warring

➔ Many English speakers pronounce some words in section **19.4** (eg *during*) in such a way that they rhyme with these words

+ You can add to this list by adding *-(r)ing* to some words that rhyme with ***draw***, as in ***flooring***

moron
boron
oxymoron

+ You can also make rhymes for these words by using ***on*** after some words that rhyme with ***draw***, as in ***pour on***

14.13

horse
coarse
course
discourse
divorce
endorse
enforce
force
gorse
hoarse
hobbyhorse
intercourse
Morse
recourse
reinforce
remorse
resource
rocking horse
sauce
source
soy sauce
tartar(e) sauce
tour de force
vaulting horse
watercourse

saucer
Chaucer

+ You can add to this list by adding ***-r*** to some words that rhyme with ***horse***, as in ***hoarser***

You can also make rhymes for these words by using ***her*** after some words that rhyme with ***horse***, as in ***force her***

morsel
dorsal

awesome
foursome

+ You can add to this list by adding ***'em*** to some words that rhyme with ***horse***, as in ***force 'em***

saucy
hors(e)y

corset
Dorset
faucet

+ You can also make rhymes for these words by using ***it*** after some words that rhyme with ***horse***, as in ***force it***

forceful
remorseful
resourceful
unremorseful

enforcement
endorsement
reinforcement

forced
exhaust
holocaust
unforced

+ You can add to this list by adding *-d* to some words that rhyme with ***horse***, as in ***enforced***

14.14

portion
abortion
apportion
caution
contortion
distortion
extortion
precaution
proportion

extortionate
proportionate

14.15

sort
abort
afterthought
Agincourt
alphasort
astronaut
besought
bought
brought
caught
cavort
consort
contort
cosmonaut
court
deport
distort
distraught
escort (= *to accompany*)
exhort
export
extort
fort
fought
fraught
hard-fought
heliport
import
juggernaut
life-support
naught
nought
ought
overwrought
port
purport
quart
report
resort (= *holiday destination*)
rethought
retort
self-taught
short
snort
sought
sport
support
taught
taut
thought
thwart
transport (= *to move*)
wart

water
aorta
backwater
breakwater
daughter
dishwater
exporter
freshwater
goddaughter
granddaughter
great-granddaughter
hot-water
importer
manslaughter
mortar
porter
quarter
rainwater
reporter
saltwater
slaughter
stepdaughter
supporter
transporter
underwater

+ You can add to this list by adding *-er* to some words that rhyme with ***sort***, as in ***shorter***

You can also make rhymes for these words by using ***her*** after some words that rhyme with ***sort***, as in ***taught her***

mortal
chortle
immortal
portal

mortally
quarterly

autumn
postmortem

+ You can add to this list by adding ***'em*** to some words that rhyme with ***sort***, as in ***caught 'em***

shorten
tauten

important
all-important
oughtn't
unimportant

watering
mouthwatering
quartering

headquarters
hindquarters

+ You can add to this list by adding *-s* to some words that rhyme with ***water***, as in *supporters*

vortex
cortex

courtier
consortia

forty
forte
haughty
naughty
sporty
UB40

nautical
aeronautical
cortical

sorted
assorted
distorted
unreported
unsupported

+ You can add to this list by adding *-ed* to some words that rhyme with ***sort***, as in *distorted*

mortify
fortify

sorting
sporting
supporting
unsporting

+ You can add to this list by adding *-ing* to some words that rhyme with ***sort***, as in *reporting*

vortices
cortices

supportive
abortive
sportive
unsupportive

auto
Oporto
quarto

shortly
portly

assortment
deportment

sports
quartz
shorts

+ You can add to this list by adding *-s* to some words that rhyme with ***sort***, as in *thoughts*

scorch
porch
torch

scorcher
torture

14.16

north
back and forth
forth
fourth
henceforth

+ You can also make rhymes for these words by using words in section **14.5** that rhyme with ***dwarf***

14.17

dwarves
wharves

14.18

doorway
Norway

14.19

lawyer
Tom Sawyer

14.20

pause
applause
Azores
because
cause
clause
corps (= *military bodies*)
gauze
indoors
Jaws
menopause
outdoors
out-of-doors
Rebel Without a Cause
Santa Claus
yours

+ You can add to this list by adding *-s* to some words that rhyme with ***draw***, as in *paws*

Section 15
-OI-

All the words in this section use the sound **-oi-** (as in c*oi*n, p*oi*nted, av*oi*d) in their main stressed syllable

15.1

boy
ahoy
alloy
annoy
blue-eyed boy
buoy
choirboy
corduroy
coy
deploy
destroy
employ
enjoy
Hanoi
Illinois
Joy
joy
Little Lord Fauntleroy
oi
ploy
pride and joy
redeploy
Roy
toy
Troy

soya
destroyer
employer
Goya
paranoia
sequoia

+ You can add to this list by adding *-er* to some words that rhyme with ***boy***, as in ***coyer***

You can also make rhymes for these words by using ***her*** after some words that rhyme with ***boy***, as in ***annoy her***

enjoyable
deployable
employable
unemployable
unenjoyable

loyal
disloyal
royal

loyally
disloyally
royally

royalist
loyalist

loyalty
disloyalty
royalty

buoyant
clairvoyant
flamboyant

cloying
annoying
soul-destroying

+ You can add to this list by adding *-ing* to some words that rhyme with ***boy***, as in ***enjoying***

15.2

void
asteroid
avoid
Celluloid®
devoid
Floyd
haemorrhoid
humanoid
Lloyd
overjoyed
paranoid
Pink Floyd
Polaroid®
self-employed
unemployed

+ You can add to this list by adding *-ed* to some words that rhyme with ***boy***, as in ***enjoyed***

15.3

oil
boil
broil
castor oil
coil
counterfoil
embroil
foil
hydrofoil
olive oil
Olive Oyl
parboil
recoil
soil
spoil
toil
uncoil

oily
doily

15.4

enjoyment
deployment
employment
redeployment
unemployment

15.5

join
adjoin
Battle of the Boyne
Boulogne
coin
enjoin
groin
loin
purloin
rejoin

point
anoint
appoint
ball-and-socket joint
boiling point
break-even point
clip joint
counterpoint
disappoint
freezing point
joint
jumping-off point
power point
sore point
strip joint
vantage point

pointed
appointed
disappointed
disjointed
self-appointed
well-appointed

+ You can add to this list by adding *-ed* to some words that rhyme with ***point***, as in ***jointed***

ointment
appointment
disappointment

15.6

voice
choice
James Joyce
Joyce
multiple-choice
rejoice
Rolls-Royce

foist
Ally McCoist
hoist
joist
moist
rejoiced
unvoiced
voiced

oyster
cloister

+ You can add to this list by adding *-er* to some words that rhyme with ***foist***, as in ***moister***

You can also make rhymes for these words by using ***her*** after some words that rhyme with ***foist***, as in ***hoist her***

15.7

exploit
adroit
Detroit
maladroit
quoit

loiter
exploiter
goitre

15.8

noise
poise

+ You can add to this list by adding *-s* to some words that rhyme with ***boy***, as in ***toys***

Section 16
-OO-

All the words in this section use the sound **-oo-** (as in b*oo*k, c*oo*ker, mist*oo*k) in their main stressed syllable

16.1

book
brook
Captain Cook
cook
copybook
crook
fishing hook
forsook
grappling hook
hook
look
mistook
nook
Osnabrück
overbook
overcook
overlook
overtook
partook
pocketbook
rook
shook
storybook
Tobruk
took
undercook
undertook

cooker
onlooker

+ You can add to this list by adding *-er* to some words that rhyme with ***book***, as in *looker*

You can also make rhymes for these words by using ***her*** after some words that rhyme with ***book***, as in ***took her***

cookery
rookery

cookie
bookie
fortune cookie
hook(e)y
rookie

cooking
bad-looking
booking
evil-looking
forward-looking
good-looking
inward-looking
nice-looking

+ You can add to this list by adding *-ing* to some words that rhyme with ***book***, as in ***looking***

hooked
double-booked
precooked
uncooked

+ You can add to this list by adding *-ed* to some words that rhyme with ***book***, as in ***overcooked***

16.2

good
adulthood
babyhood
brotherhood
could
fatherhood
hood
likelihood
livelihood
misunderstood
motherhood
neighbourhood
parenthood
Robin Hood
should
sisterhood
stood
understood
up to no good
withstood
wood

would

Buddha
do-gooder

+ You can also make rhymes for these words by using *her* after some words that rhyme with *good*, as in *understood her*

couldn't
shouldn't
wouldn't

woody
goody
goody-goody

16.3

full
Abdul
bull
dyed-in-the-wool
Istanbul
John Bull
like a red rag to a bull
pull
wool

The following words will also tend to rhyme with these when they come at the end of a line:
abominable
acceptable
accessible
adaptable
adjustable
admirable
admiral
affable
allowable
all-powerful
amenable
amiable
amicable
animal
apocryphal
appreciable
arguable
arsenal
audible
barnacle
basketful
bellyful
biblical
bicameral
bookable
bountiful
cannibal
capital
cardinal
carnival
cerebral
certifiable
charitable
classical
clavicle
cockerel
collapsible
colourful
combustible
comfortable
communal
communicable
companionable
compatible
conjugal
considerable
constable
contemptible
contestable
convertible
corpuscle
creditable
cubicle
culpable
cultural
cylindrical
demonstrable
detachable
digestible
digital
dispensable
disposable
disreputable
doggerel
ecumenical
electrical
elliptical
encyclical
enviable
ephemeral
episcopal
equable
evangelical
exceptional
execrable
fallible
fanciful
farcical
fathomable
feasible
federal
festival
fictional
flappable
forcible
formidable
fractional
funeral
general
gullible
guttural
habitable
hierarchical
horrible
hospital
identical
imaginable
impeccable
impenetrable
imperceptible
imperturbable
implacable
implausible
imponderable
impregnable
impressionable
inalienable
inapplicable
inaudible
inaugural

incompatible
incontestable
incontrovertible
incorrigible
incorruptible
indecipherable
indefatigable
indelible
indescribable
indigestible
indispensable
indistinguishable
indomitable
ineffable
inestimable
inevitable
inexhaustible
inexorable
inimical
inimitable
innumerable
insatiable
insufferable
insuperable
integral
interminable
interval
invincible
inviolable
invulnerable
irascible
irreconcilable
irredeemable
irremediable
irreplaceable
irresistible
irreversible
irrevocable
irritable
Ivan the Terrible
justifiable
knowledgeable
lackadaisical
lamentable
lateral
latitudinal
laughable
legible
lexical
liberal
likeable
Lionel
literal
longitudinal
lovable
magical
malleable
manageable
mandible
marginal
marital
marketable
marriageable
masterful
meaningful
medical
medicinal
memorable
merciful
mineral
minimal
miracle
miserable
monocle
multiple
municipal
musical
mythical
natural
nautical
navigable
negligible
negotiable
Newcastle
non-negotiable
nonsensical
notable
noticeable
numeral
objectionable
observable
obstacle
occasional
Oedipal
optical
optional
oracle
ordinal
original
palatable
palpable
paradoxical
participle
pastoral
peaceable
pedestal
perceptible
Percival
peripheral
perishable
personable
personal
pineapple
pinnacle
pitiable
pitiful
pivotal
plausible
plentiful
portable
Portugal
powerful
practicable
preferable
prodigal
proportional
provisional
purposeful
questionable
radical
reachable
receptacle
rechargeable
reciprocal
recoverable
regional
remarkable
renewable
reputable
reversible
sceptical
seasonal
seminal
serviceable

several
shovelful
skeletal
sorrowful
spectacle
stoical
structural
suggestible
surgical
susceptible
symmetrical
tangible
technical
temporal
tentacle
terminal
terrible
testicle
theatrical
unacceptable
unbeatable
uncomfortable
understandable
unfathomable
unflappable
ungovernable
unimaginable
unlovable
unnatural
unprintable
unpronounceable
unquestionable
unspeakable
untouchable
unverifiable
valuable
variable
vegetable
vehicle
venerable
verifiable
veritable
vertical
visceral
vulnerable
whimsical
wonderful

fully
bully
pulley
woolly

bullet
pullet
pull it

16.4

push
bush
George W Bush
shush

pushy
bushy
cushy

bushed
hard-pushed

+ You can add to this list by adding *-ed* to some words that rhyme with ***push***, as in ***shushed***

16.5

foot
afoot
barefoot
hotfoot
kaput
Lilliput
pussyfoot
put
soot
stay put
underfoot

footing
off-putting

+ You can add to this list by adding *-(t)ing* to some words that rhyme with ***foot***, as in ***pussyfooting***

butch
putsch

Section 17
-U-

All the words in this section use the sound **-u-** (as in cl*u*b, b*u*tter, beg*u*n) in their main stressed syllable

17.1

club
Beelzebub
blub
cub
dub
grub
hub
nub
pub
rub
scrub
shrub
snub
stub
sub
tub

rubber
blubber
clubber
grubber
scrubber

+ You can also make rhymes for these words by using ***her*** after some words that rhyme with ***club***, as in ***snub her***

blubbered
cupboard
walk-in cupboard

bubble
double
rubble
stubble
trouble

troubled
untroubled

+ You can add to this list by adding ***-d*** to some words that rhyme with ***bubble***, as in ***doubled***

shrubbery
rubbery

+ You can make rhymes for these words by using words in section **17.15** that rhyme with ***discovery***

chubby
grubby
hubby
scrubby
stubby
tubby

doubly
bubbly
grubbily
stubbly

publican
Republican
republican

17.2

luck
amuck
buck
Chuck
chuck
cluck
duck
fork-lift truck
lame duck
muck
pluck
potluck
Puck
ruck
snuck
struck
stuck
suck
thunderstruck
truck
tuck
unstuck
yu(c)k

pucker
bloodsucker
chukka
mucker
pukka
sucker

trucker
tucker
yucca

+ You can also make rhymes for these words by using *her* after some words that rhyme with *luck*, as in *chuck her*

chuckle
buckle
honeysuckle
knuckle
suckle

lucky
happy-go-lucky
Kentucky
mucky
plucky
unlucky
yucky

luckily
pluckily
unluckily

bucket
kick the bucket
Nantucket

+ You can also make rhymes for these words by using *it* after some words that rhyme with *luck*, as in *chuck it*

duckling
buckling
chuckling
knuckling
suckling
swashbuckling
ugly duckling

flux
Benelux
crux
de luxe
shucks
tux

+ You can add to this list by adding *-s* to some words that rhyme with *luck*, as in *bucks*

suction
abduction
conduction
construction
coproduction
deduction
destruction
induction
instruction
introduction
liposuction
obstruction
overproduction
production
reconstruction
reduction
reintroduction
reproduction
seduction
self-destruction
underproduction

duct
abduct
aqueduct
conduct (= *to lead*)
construct
deduct
induct
instruct
misconduct
obstruct
reconstruct
self-destruct
viaduct

+ You can add to this list by adding *-ed* to some words that rhyme with *luck*, as in *ducked*

instructor
abductor
conductor
semiconductor
superconductor

+ You can also make rhymes for these words by using *her* after some words that rhyme with *duct*, as in *abduct her*

deductible
conductible
indestructible
ineluctable
tax-deductible

constructive
counterproductive
destructive
inductive
instructive
obstructive
productive
reproductive
seductive
unproductive

succulent
truculent

17.3

mud
bad blood
blood
bud
cud
dud
flood
spud
stick-in-the-mud
stud

thud

shudder
judder
rudder
udder

cuddle
huddle
muddle
puddle

muddy
bloody
buddy
fuddy-duddy
ruddy
study
understudy

studied
cold-blooded
hot-blooded
red-blooded
warm-blooded

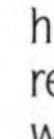
You can add to this list by adding *-(d)ed* to some words that rhyme with ***mud***, as in ***thudded***

budding
flooding

+ You can add to this list by adding *-(d)ing* to some words that rhyme with ***mud***, as in ***thudding***

cuddly
Dudley

judge
adjudge
begrudge
budge
drudge
fudge
grudge
misjudge
nudge
prejudge
sludge
smudge
trudge

budgie
pudgy

grudging
adjudging
begrudging
budging
drudging
fudging
judging
misjudging
nudging
prejudging
smudging
trudging
ungrudging

budget
low-budget

+ You can also make rhymes for these words by using *it* after some words that rhyme with ***judge***, as in ***budge it***

17.4

stuff
bluff
buff
cuff
duff
enough
fluff
gruff
guff
huff
muff
off-the-cuff
powder puff
puff
rebuff
rough
ruff
scruff
scuff
slough
snuff
tough

suffer
buffer
duffer

+ You can add to this list by adding *-er* to some words that rhyme with ***stuff***, as in ***tougher***

You can also make rhymes for these words by using *her* after some words that rhyme with ***stuff***, as in ***rebuff her***

shuffle
duffle
kerfuffle
muffle
reshuffle
ruffle
scuffle
snuffle
truffle

muffled
unruffled

+ You can add to this list by adding *-d* to some words that rhyme with ***shuffle***, as in ***ruffled***

puffy
fluffy
huffy
scruffy

stuffy
toughie

muffin
puffin
ragamuffin

> You can also make rhymes for these words by using *in* after some words that rhyme with ***stuff***, as in ***stuff in***

gruffly
roughly
toughly

gruffness
roughness
toughness

tuft
chuffed

> You can add to this list by adding *-ed* to some words that rhyme with ***stuff***, as in ***buffed***

17.5

drug
bug
chug
debug
Doug
dug
fug
hug
jitterbug
jug
litterbug
lug
mug
plug
pug
rug
shrug
slug
smug
snug
thug
trug
tug
unplug

mugger
rugger

> You can add to this list by adding *-ger* to some words that rhyme with ***drug***, as in ***snugger***
>
> You can also make rhymes for these words by using *her* after some words that rhyme with ***drug***, as in ***bug her***

struggle
juggle
smuggle
snuggle

buggy
druggie
Duggie
muggy

plughole
lughole

smuggler
juggler
struggler

ugly
smugly
snugly

17.6

dull
annul
cull
gull
Hull
hull
lull
Mull
mull
null
scull
skull
Solihull

duller
colour
discolour
off-colour
sculler
watercolour

> You can also make rhymes for these words by using *her* after some words that rhyme with ***dull***, as in ***lull her***

coloured
dullard
many-coloured
multicoloured
rose-coloured
self-coloured

gully
sully

gullet
mullet

> You can also make rhymes for these words by using *it* after some words that rhyme with ***dull***, as in ***annul it***

bulk
hulk
skulk
sulk

bulky
sulky

bulge
divulge
indulge
overindulge

culminate
fulminate

gulp
pulp

pulse
convulse
dulse
repulse

ulcer
Tulsa

> + You can also make rhymes for these words by using *her* after some words that rhyme with *pulse*, as in *repulse her*

repulsive
compulsive
convulsive
impulsive

compulsion
emulsion
expulsion
propulsion
repulsion
revulsion

cult
adult
catapult
consult
exult
insult
occult
result

consultant
exultant
resultant

mulch
gulch

culture
agriculture
horticulture
subculture
vulture

17.7

drum
become
bothersome
bum
burdensome
capsicum
cerebrum
chewing gum
chrysanthemum
chum
come
crumb
cumbersome
curriculum
dumb
glum
gum
hum
humdrum
kettledrum
laudanum
maximum
meddlesome
minimum
modicum
mum
numb
optimum
overcome
pendulum
platinum
plum
plumb
quarrelsome
rum
scrum
scum
slum
some
strum
succumb
sum
swum
thumb
tiresome
Tom Thumb
troublesome
tum
Tweedledum
wearisome

> + You can also make rhymes for these words by using words in section **17.8** that rhyme with ***run***

summer
bummer
comer
drummer
latecomer
midsummer
newcomer
plumber

> + You can add to this list by adding *-((m)e)r* to some words that rhyme with *drum*, as in *glummer*
>
> You can also make rhymes for these words by using *her* after some words that rhyme with *drum*, as in *overcome her*

summon
cumin

summery
flummery
Montgomery
mummery
summary

hummus
pumice

mummy
Brummie
chummy
dummy
gummy
plummy
scrummy
tummy
yummy

coming
becoming
forthcoming
have another think coming
homecoming
incoming
mind-numbing
oncoming
overcoming
plumbing
unbecoming
unforthcoming
up-and-coming

+ You can add to this list by adding *-(m)ing* to some words that rhyme with ***drum***, as in ***humming***

summit
plummet

+ You can also make rhymes for these words by using ***it*** after some words that rhyme with ***drum***, as in ***hum it***

number
cucumber
encumber
lumbar
lumber
outnumber
slumber

stumble
crumble
fumble
grumble
humble
jumble
mumble
rough-and-tumble
rumble
tumble

tumbling
bumbling
crumbling
fumbling
grumbling
humbling
jumbling
mumbling
rumbling
stumbling

jumbo
Colombo
Dumbo
mumbo jumbo

tumbler
fumbler
grumbler
humbler
mumbler

crumbly
humbly

lump
bump
chump
clump
dump
Forrest Gump
frump
gazump
grump
hump
jump
plump
pump
rump
slump
stump
sugar lump
sump
thump
trump

jumper
bumper
dumper

+ You can add to this list by adding ***-er*** to some words that rhyme with ***lump***, as in ***plumper***

You can also make rhymes for these words by using ***her*** after some words that rhyme with ***lump***, as in ***dump her***

crumple
rumple

rumpus
compass
encompass

bumpy
dumpy
frumpy
grumpy
jumpy
lumpy
stumpy

thumping
bungee jumping
dumping

+ You can add to this list by adding ***-ing*** to some words that rhyme with ***lump***, as in ***bumping***

trumpet
crumpet

> **+** You can also make rhymes for these words by using *it* after some words that rhyme with *lump*, as in *dump it*

pumpkin
bumpkin

mumps
dumps

> **+** You can add to this list by adding *-s* to some words that rhyme with *lump*, as in *bumps*

jump-start
bump-start

assumption
consumption
gumption
presumption
resumption

scrumptious
bumptious

sumptuous
presumptuous

17.8

run
aftersun
begun
bun
close-run
done
fun
great-grandson
gun
hard-won
hit-and-run
machine gun
megaton(ne)
none
nun
one
one-to-one
outdone
outrun
overdone
overrun
pun
redone
rerun
sawn-off shotgun
shotgun
shun
son
spun
stun
sub-machine gun
sun
The Sun
tommy gun
ton(ne)
twenty-one
undone
won

The following words will also tend to rhyme with these when they come at the end of a line:
abdomen
acumen
Alison
Amazon
Amundsen
Anglican
anyone
badminton
cardigan
chairwoman
charlatan
charwoman
cinnamon
citizen
Congressman
Corsican
cyclamen
David Livingstone
Dominican
Edison
Englishman
Englishwoman
everyone
Frenchman
Frenchwoman
Galveston
gentleman
Gilbert and Sullivan
heptagon
hexagon
highwayman
hooligan
hurricane
hydrogen
Imogen
Irishman
jettison
John Betjeman
Jonathan
Kosovan
Leif Eriksson
Lexington
Mendelssohn
Mexican
Michigan
Moldavian
Monaghan
nitrogen
octagon
ombudsman
Oregon
Oscar Peterson
oxygen
Pamela Anderson
pelican
pentagon
phenomenon
ptarmigan
puritan
quieten
sacristan
Samaritan
Scandinavian
silicon
simpleton
Shackleton
skeleton
Solomon

subaltern
talisman
UNISON
unison
Vatican
veteran
Welshwoman
Wimbledon
Zimbabwean

+ You can also make rhymes for these words by using words in section **17.7** that rhyme with ***drum***

runner
forerunner
frontrunner
gunner
gunrunner
roadrunner
stunner

+ You can also make rhymes for these words by using ***her*** after some words that rhyme with ***run***, as in ***stun her***

tunnel
Channel Tunnel
funnel
gunwale

funny
bunny
honey
money
runny
sonny
sunny
unfunny

stunning
cunning
gunrunning
running

+ You can add to this list by adding ***-ning*** to some words that rhyme with ***run***, as in ***shunning***

punnet
whodun(n)it

+ You can also make rhymes for these words by using ***it*** after some words that rhyme with ***run***, as in ***done it***

chunk
bunk
debunk
drunk
dunk
flunk
funk
gunk
hunk
junk
monk
preshrunk
punk
shrunk
skunk
slunk
spunk
stunk
sunk
trunk

uncle
carbuncle
great-uncle

drunken
Duncan
shrunken
sunken

chunky
clunky
flunkey
funky
hunky
junkie
monkey
punky

function
compunction
conjunction
dysfunction
injunction
junction
malfunction
T-junction
unction

functional
conjunctional
dysfunctional
multi-functional

puncture
acupuncture
juncture

fund
moribund
refund
Rosamund
rotund

+ You can add to this list by adding ***-ned*** to some words that rhyme with ***run***, as in ***stunned***

Sunday
Burundi
Lundy
Monday
sundae

thunder
asunder
blunder
down under
plunder
Stevie Wonder
under
wonder

bundle
trundle

abundant
overabundant
redundant

rundown
sundown

plunge
expunge
grunge
gunge
lunge
sponge

plunger
conjure
sponger

lung
among
Brigham Young
bung
clung
dung
far-flung
flung
hamstrung
highly strung
hung
Mao Zedong
overhung
rung
slung
sprung
strung
stung
sung
swung
tongue
wrung
young

hunger
fishmonger
gossipmonger
ironmonger
not getting any younger
warmonger
younger

jungle
bungle
fungal

dunce
experience
influence
once

hunt
affront
blunt
brunt
confront
front
grunt
punt
runt
shunt
stunt
upfront
waterfront

hunter
Billy Bunter
junta
punter

+ You can add to this list by adding *-er* to some words that rhyme with ***hunt***, as in ***blunter***

You can also make rhymes for these words by using ***her*** after some words that rhyme with ***hunt***, as in ***confront her***

stunted
hunted

+ You can add to this list by adding *-ed* to some words that rhyme with ***hunt***, as in ***affronted***

hunting
bunting
fox-hunting

+ You can add to this list by adding *-ing* to some words that rhyme with ***hunt***, as in ***grunting***

bunch
brunch
crunch
hunch
lunch
munch
Punch
punch
scrunch

luncheon
truncheon

crunchy
punchy
scrunchie

munchies
scrunchies

+ You can add to this list by adding *-es* to some words that rhyme with ***bunch***, as in ***hunches***

runway
one-way

bunion
Damon Runyon
onion

17.9

up
built-up
buttercup
cover-up
cup

follow-up
grown-up
jumped-up
made-up
mixed-up
pent-up
pick-me-up
pup
runner-up
stand up
stuck-up
summing-up
sup
washing-up

supper
cuppa
scupper
upper

supple
couple

comeuppance
twopence

puppy
guppy
yuppie

corruption
disruption
eruption
interruption

corrupt
abrupt
disrupt
erupt
interrupt

> + You can add to this list by adding ***-ped*** to some words that rhyme with ***up***, as in *supped*

17.10

thorough
borough
kookaburra

hurry
curry
flurry
Murray
scurry
Surrey
worry

hurried
curried
scurried
worried

flourish
nourish

nourishing
flourishing

furrow
burrow

17.11

fuss
abacus
adulterous
analogous
anomalous
asparagus
autonomous
barbarous
bigamous
blasphemous
blunderbuss
bus
cacophonous
cadaverous
calculus
cancerous
cantankerous
Caucasus
chivalrous
covetous
dangerous
diaphanous
discuss
Ephesus
exodus
fabulous
frivolous
gangrenous
garrulous
gelatinous
genius
gluttonous
Gus
hazardous
hippopotamus
Icarus
impetus
indigenous
infamous
ingenious
languorous
Lazarus
ludicrous
marvellous
minibus
miraculous
mischievous
monogamous
monotonous
mountainous
nebulous
Nic(h)olas
obstreperous
octopus
Oedipus
ominous
omnibus
onerous
Pegasus
perilous
plus
poisonous
ponderous
populace
populous
posthumous
precipitous
preposterous
pretentious
prosperous
pus
querulous
rapturous
rhinoceros
riotous

Romulus
ruinous
sarcophagus
scandalous
scrupulous
scurrilous
slanderous
sonorous
Spartacus
stimulus
suss
syllabus
terminus
tetanus
thunderous
thus
timorous
tinnitus
tremulous
truss
unscrupulous
us
uterus
venomous
villainous
Vilnius
Wenceslas

rustle
Bertrand Russell
bustle
hustle
muscle
mussel
Russell
tussle

muscles
Brussels

> + You can add to this list by adding *-s* to some words that rhyme with ***rustle***, as in ***tussles***

fussy
hussy
pussy (= *full of pus*)

russet
gusset

> + You can also make rhymes for these words by using ***it*** after some words that rhyme with ***fuss***, as in ***suss it***

dusk
busk
husk
musk
rusk
tusk

Tuscan
Etruscan

hustler
bustler
rustler

just
adjust
august
bite the dust
bust
concussed
crust
disgust
distrust
dry as dust
dust
entrust
gust
lust
mistrust
must
nonplussed
readjust
robust
rust
thrust
trust
unjust
upper-crust
wanderlust

> + You can add to this list by adding *-(s)ed* to some words that rhyme with ***fuss***, as in ***trussed***

cluster
adjuster
Augusta
bluster
duster
fluster
General Custer
knuckle-duster
loss adjuster
lustre
muster

> + You can also make rhymes for these words by using ***her*** after some words that rhyme with ***just***, as in ***trust her***

custard
mustard

> + You can add to this list by adding *-ed* to some words that rhyme with ***cluster***, as in ***flustered***

custom
accustom

> + You can add to this list by adding ***'em*** to some words that rhyme with ***just***, as in ***trust 'em***

dusty
crusty
gusty
lusty

musty
rusty
trusty

trusted
encrusted
maladjusted
well-adjusted

> You can add to this list by adding *-ed* to some words that rhyme with ***just***, as in ***dusted***

Justin
Dustin

> You can also make rhymes for these words by using ***in*** after some words that rhyme with ***just***, as in ***trust in***

trusting
disgusting
thrusting

> You can add to this list by adding *-ing* to some words that rhyme with ***just***, as in ***dusting***

bust-up
dust-up

lustful
distrustful
mistrustful
trustful

adjustment
entrustment
readjustment

industrious
illustrious

17.12

rush
blush
brush
crush
flush
gush
hush
lush
mush
plush
Portrush
scrubbing brush
slush
sweeping brush
tarred with the same brush
thrush

blusher
Byelorussia
Prussia
Russia
usher

> You can add to this list by adding *-er* to some words that rhyme with ***rush***, as in ***plusher***
>
> You can also make rhymes for these words by using ***her*** after some words that rhyme with ***rush***, as in ***crush her***

Russian
Byelorussian
concussion
discussion
percussion
Prussian
repercussion

slushy
gushy
mushy

crushing
gushing

> You can add to this list by adding *-ing* to some words that rhyme with ***rush***, as in ***blushing***

hushed
brushed

> You can add to this list by adding *-ed* to some words that rhyme with ***rush***, as in ***crushed***

17.13

nut
Brazil nut
but
butt
clean-cut
clear-cut
coconut
cut
do one's nut
glut
gut
halibut
hazelnut
hut
jut
low-cut
monkey nut
mutt
putt
rebut
rut
shut
slut
smut
strut
uncut
undercut

The following words will also tend to rhyme with these when they come at the end of a line:
accurate
adequate
advocate (= *a legal representative*)
affectionate
aggregate
animate (= *living*)
approximate (= *rough*)
articulate (= *fluent*)
aspirate
barbiturate
celibate
certificate
commensurate
compatriot
confederate
conglomerate
Connecticut
considerate
consulate
corporate
degenerate (= *degraded*)
delegate (= *a representative*)
deliberate (= *intentional*)
desolate
desperate
devil's advocate
disconsolate
disproportionate
doctorate
duplicate (= *a copy*)
effeminate
elaborate (= *ornate*)
electorate
estimate (= *a guess*)
expatriate
fortunate
graduate (= *a person with a degree*)
Harrogate
illiterate
immaculate
immoderate
inanimate
indeterminate
intimate (= *close*)
intricate
inveterate
moderate (= *not extreme*)
numerate
obstinate
passionate
patriot
precipitate
predicate (= *part of a sentence*)
profligate
separate (= *apart*)
surrogate
syndicate (= *a group of businesses*)
triplicate
ultimate

mutter
bread-and-butter
butter
Calcutta
clutter
cutter
flutter
gutter
nutter
putter
shutter
splutter
sputter
stutter
utter
woodcutter

+ You can also make rhymes for these words by using ***her*** after some words that rhyme with ***nut***, as in ***cut her***

scuttle
rebuttal
shuttle
subtle

utterly
subtly

button
belly-button
glutton
mutton
push-button
unbutton

nutty
putty
slutty
smutty

cutting
price-cutting

+ You can add to this list by adding ***-ting*** to some words that rhyme with ***nut***, as in ***jutting***

nuts
misery-guts

+ You can add to this list by adding ***-s*** to some words that rhyme with ***nut***, as in ***guts***

clutch
crutch
Dutch
hutch
much
overmuch
such
touch

touchy
duchy

touched
clutched
untouched

17.14

other
another
Big Brother
brother
godmother
grandmother
great-grandmother
half-brother
mother
smother
stepbrother
stepmother

brotherhood
motherhood

mother-in-law
brother-in-law

17.15

love
above
cupboard love
dove
glove
shove
tug-of-love

lover
cover
discover
Lady Chatterley's Lover
plover
recover
rediscover
uncover
undercover

+ You can also make rhymes for these words by using ***her*** after some words that rhyme with ***love***, as in ***above her***

oven
govern
misgovern

discovery
recovery

+ You can make rhymes for these words by using words in section **17.1** that rhyme with ***shrubbery***

loving
fun-loving
peace-loving
shoving

unloved
beloved
well-loved

+ You can add to this list by adding ***-d*** to some words that rhyme with ***love***, as in ***shoved***

17.16

buzz
does
fuzz

puzzle
guzzle
muzzle
nuzzle

cousin
dozen

fuzzy
buzzy
does he?
muzzy
scuzzy

Section 18
-UE-

All the words in this section use the sound **-ue-** (as in bl*ue*, cr*ue*l, aven*ue*) in their main stressed syllable

18.1

zoo
accrue
ado
anew
askew
Autocue®
avenue
ballyhoo
bamboo
barbecue
bill and coo
bird's-eye view
black and blue
blew
blue
boo
brand-new
brew
can-do
canoe
caribou
cashew
Catch-22
chew
clue
cock-a-doodle-doo
cockatoo
construe
coo
Corfu
coup
CPU (= *central processing unit*)
crew
Crewe
cue
dew
do (= *to perform*)
Drew
drew
due
EMU (= *European Monetary Union*)
ensue
eschew
EU
ewe
FAQ (= *frequently asked question*)
few
flew
flu
flue
GCHQ (= *Government Communications Headquarters*)
GHQ (= *general headquarters*)
glue
gnu
goo
grew
hew
hitherto
HQ
hue
Hugh
hullabaloo
imbue
in lieu
interview
IOU
IQ
Jew
K2
kangaroo
Kat(h)mandu
knew
lasso
loo
Lou
mew
misconstrue
moo
navy-blue
nearly-new
new
NVQ (= *national vocational qualification*)
outdo
outgrew
overdo
overdue
overshoe
overthrew
overview
pay-per-view
Peru
pew
phew
pooh-pooh
POW

Pru(e)
pursue
Q
queue
redo
rendezvous
renew
residue
retinue
revenue
review
revue
RFU (= *Rugby Football Union*)
royal-blue
rue
screw
set-to
shampoo
shoe
shoo
shrew
skew
sky-blue
slew
spew
stew
strew
subdue
Sue
sue
taboo
talking-to
tattoo
thank you
The Taming of the Shrew
The Who
threw
through
Timbuktu
to
to-do
too
true
two
U
undo
undue
unscrew
untrue
Vanuatu
VDU
view
W
Waterloo
well-to-do
WEU (= *Western European Union*)
whew
who
Winnie the Pooh
withdrew
woo
Xanadu
yew
you
you-know-who

fewer
brewer
evildoer
interviewer
pursuer
reviewer
sewer (= *a drain*)
skewer
viewer
wrongdoer

+ You can add to this list by adding ***-(e)r*** to some words that rhyme with ***zoo***, as in ***newer***

You can also make rhymes for these words by using ***her*** after some words that rhyme with ***zoo***, as in ***view her***

cruel
dual
duel
fuel
gruel
jewel
refuel
renewal

jeweller
crueller

gruelling
fuelling
refuelling

fluency
truancy

fluent
truant

chewy
gooey
GUI (= *graphical user interface*)
Hughie
Louis

fluid
Clwyd
druid

doing
canoeing
ensuing
undoing
wrongdoing

+ You can add to this list by adding ***-ing*** to some words that rhyme with ***zoo***, as in ***viewing***

Lewis
Jewess
St Louis

fewest
canoeist
Uist

+ You can add to this list by adding ***-(e)st*** to some words that rhyme with ***zoo***, as in ***truest***

suet
cruet

> You can also make rhymes for these words by using *it* after some words that rhyme with *zoo*, as in *view it*

gratuitous
circuitous
fortuitous

gratuity
ambiguity
continuity
incongruity
ingenuity
perpetuity
promiscuity

18.2

tube
boob
cube
Eustachian tube
Fallopian tube

Cuba
scuba
tuba
tuber

Cuban
Reuben

exuberance
protuberance

ruby
booby
newbie
Ruby

cubic
pubic

lugubrious
insalubrious
salubrious

18.3

duke
archduke
Faruq
fluke
gobbledygook
Luke
nuke
puke
rebuke
spook

snooker
bazooka
lucre
verruca

> You can also make rhymes for these words by using *her* after some words that rhyme with *duke*, as in *rebuke her*

Lord Lucan
toucan

mucus
Lucas
mucous

> You can also make rhymes for these words by using *us* after some words that rhyme with *duke*, as in *rebuke us*

spooky
fluk(e)y
Newquay

18.4

rude
allude
altitude
amplitude
aptitude
attitude
brood
certitude
collude
conclude
crude
delude
denude
dude
elude
exactitude
exclude
exude
feud
food
fortitude
gratitude
include
ineptitude
interlude
intrude
Jude
lassitude
latitude
lewd
longitude
magnitude
mood
multitude
nude
preclude
protrude
prude
pseud
rectitude
servitude
shrewd
solitude
stewed
subdued
verisimilitude
you'd

> You can add to this list by adding *-ed* to some words that rhyme with *zoo*, as in *viewed*

Tudor
Antigua and Barbuda
barracuda
Bermuda
intruder

+ You can add to this list by adding *-(e)r* to some words that rhyme with ***rude***, as in ***cruder***

You can also make rhymes for these words by using ***her*** after some words that rhyme with ***rude***, as in ***include her***

doodle
caboodle
canoodle
feudal
poodle

noodles
oodles

+ You can add to this list by adding *-s* to some words that rhyme with ***doodle***, as in ***poodles***

student
imprudent
prudent

moody
broody
Judy
Trudi(e)

including
alluding
colluding
concluding
deluding
eluding
excluding
exuding
intruding
precluding
protruding

+ You can add to this list by adding *-ing* to some words that rhyme with ***rude***, as in ***brooding***

judo
Cluedo®
escudo
Pierre Trudeau
pseudo

huge
centrifuge
Scrooge
stooge
subterfuge

18.5

proof
aloof
bulletproof
burglar-proof
fireproof
goof
hoof
oven-proof
pouf(fe)
reproof
roof
shatterproof
shower-proof
spoof
waterproof
weatherproof

+ You can also make rhymes for these words by using words in section **18.16** that rhyme with ***truth***

18.6

frugal
bugle
centrifugal
Dougal

18.7

pool
birthing pool
Blackpool
cagoule
cool
drool
fool
ghoul
joule
Liverpool
minuscule
misrule
molecule
mule
overrule
paddling pool
preschool
ridicule
rule
school
spool
stool
swimming pool
tool
uncool
vestibule
work-to-rule
you'll

ruler
Petula

+ You can add to this list by adding *-(e)r* to some words that rhyme with ***pool***, as in ***cooler***

You can also make rhymes for these words by using ***her***

after some words that rhyme with ***pool***, as in ***fool her***

Julia
peculiar
unrulier

truly
duly
Julie
newly
unduly
unruly

schooling
cooling
ruling

+ You can add to this list by adding *-ing* to some words that rhyme with ***pool***, as in ***drooling***

foolish
coolish
ghoulish

Zulu
Honolulu
lulu

18.8

room
Alec Douglas-Home
anteroom
assume
bloom
boom
broom
changing room
consume
doom
exhume
fume
gloom
groom
Khartoum
loom
perfume
plume
presume
resume
subsume
tomb
whom
womb
zoom

+ You can also make rhymes for these words by using words in section **18.9** that rhyme with ***moon***

bloomer
baby-boomer
consumer
humour
Montezuma
Nkrumah
puma
tumour

+ You can also make rhymes for these words by using ***her*** after some words that rhyme with ***room***, as in ***consume her***

human
Harry S Truman
inhuman
Paul Newman
subhuman
superhuman

numerous
humerus
humorous
humour us

gloomy
roomy

ruminate
illuminate

luminous
voluminous

booming
blooming
time-consuming
unassuming

+ You can add to this list by adding *-ing* to some words that rhyme with ***room***, as in ***grooming***

18.9

moon
afternoon
baboon
balloon
bassoon
boon
Brigadoon
buffoon
Cameroon
cartoon
change one's tune
cocoon
commune
croon
dragoon
dune
festoon
goon
Haroun
harpoon
hewn
High Noon
honeymoon
hot-air balloon
immune
impugn
inopportune
June
lagoon
lampoon
macaroon
maroon

monsoon
noon
opportune
platoon
pontoon
prune
rac(c)oon
Rangoon
saloon
soon
spoon
strewn
swoon
tablespoon
Troon
tune
tycoon
typhoon
Walloon

> + You can also make rhymes for these words by using words in section **18.8** that rhyme with ***room***

tuna
lacuna
lunar
schooner
tuner
Una

> + You can add to this list by adding ***-er*** to some words that rhyme with ***moon***, as in ***sooner***
>
> You can also make rhymes for these words by using ***her*** after some words that rhyme with ***moon***, as in ***lampoon her***

loony
moony
puny

tunic
Munich

newness
Eunice
Tunis

cartoonist
balloonist
bassoonist
harpoonist
opportunist

unity
community
disunity
immunity
impunity
opportunity

attuned
wound (= *to injure*)

> + You can add to this list by adding ***-(e)d*** to some words that rhyme with ***moon***, as in ***swooned***

tuneful
spoonful

junior
Tristan da Cunha

union
communion
reunion
Soviet Union

18.10

loop
cantaloup(e)
cock-a-hoop
coop
droop
drupe
dupe
group
Guadeloupe
hoop
nincompoop
recoup
regroup
scoop
sloop
snoop
soup
stoop
swoop
troop
troupe
whoop

snooper
paratrooper
pooper-scooper
stupor
super
super-duper
trooper

> + You can also make rhymes for these words by using ***her*** after some words that rhyme with ***loop***, as in ***dupe her***

scruple
pupil

loopy
droopy
groupie
Snoopy

stupid
Cupid

two-pin
lupin

oops
whoops

> + You can add to this list by adding ***-s*** to some words that rhyme with ***loop***, as in ***hoops***

18.11

truce
abstruse
abuse (= *maltreatment*)
Belarus
Bruce
deduce
deuce
diffuse (= *spread out*)
disuse
excuse (= *a justification*)
goose
ill-use (= *harsh treatment*)
induce
introduce
juice
loose (= *slack*)
mass-produce
misuse (= *improper use*)
moose
mousse
noose
obtuse
overuse (= *excessive use*)
produce
profuse
recluse
reduce
reproduce
Robert the Bruce
seduce
sluice
spruce
stew in one's own juice
use (= *the act of using*)

producer
juicer
Medusa
seducer

+ You can add to this list by adding *-r* to some words that rhyme with ***truce***, as in ***looser***

+ You can also make rhymes for these words by using ***her*** after some words that rhyme with ***truce***, as in ***introduce her***

gruesome
twosome

+ You can add to this list by adding ***'em*** to some words that rhyme with ***truce***, as in ***introduce 'em***

juicy
Lucy

exclusive
abusive
conclusive
conducive
effusive
elusive
inclusive
inconclusive
intrusive
obtrusive
unobtrusive

exclusively
abusively
conclusively
effusively
intrusively
obtrusively
unobtrusively

trousseau
do so
Robinson Crusoe

loosely
abstrusely
profusely

roost
boost
Proust
reduced
unused (= *unaccustomed to something*)
used (= *accustomed to something*)

+ You can add to this list by adding *-d* to some words that rhyme with ***truce***, as in ***produced***

rooster
booster
used to

+ You can also make rhymes for these words by using ***her*** after some words that rhyme with ***roost***, as in ***boost her***

acoustics
Pooh sticks

18.12

rouge
Bruges
luge

fusion
allusion
collusion
conclusion
confusion
contusion
delusion
disillusion
exclusion
illusion
infusion
intrusion
profusion
seclusion
transfusion

18.13

solution
absolution
circumlocution
constitution
contribution
counter-revolution
devolution
dilution
distribution
electrocution
elocution
evolution
execution
high-resolution
institution
locution
persecution
pollution
prosecution
prostitution
resolution
retribution
revolution
substitution

constitutional
institutional
unconstitutional

revolutionary
counter-revolutionary
evolutionary

18.14

shoot
absolute
acute
arrowroot
astute
attribute (= *a characteristic*)
bald as a coot
beaut
Beirut
birthday suit
boot
brute
Canute
chute
commute
compute
cute
depute
destitute
dilute
dispute
disrepute
dissolute
electrocute
execute
flute
fruit
hoot
impute
institute
irresolute
jute
loot
lute
minute (= *tiny*)
moot
mute
newt
overshoot
parachute
persecute
pollute
prosecute
prostitute
pursuit
recruit
refute
repute
resolute
root
route
salute
scoot
substitute
suit
toot
uproot

scooter
commuter
computer
hooter
looter
microcomputer
neuter
peashooter
persecutor
pewter
polluter
prosecutor
router
sharpshooter
six-shooter
suitor
troubleshooter
tutor

> + You can add to this list by adding *-(e)r* to some words that rhyme with ***shoot***, as in ***cuter***
>
> You can also make rhymes for these words by using ***her*** after some words that rhyme with ***shoot***, as in ***suit her***

suitable
disputable
executable
immutable
indisputable
inscrutable
irrefutable
substitutable
unsuitable

Luton
gluten
Isaac Newton

mutant
pollutant

duty
beauty
booty
Djibouti

fruity
heavy-duty
off-duty
snooty

cuticle
pharmaceutical

muted
convoluted
deep-rooted
ill-suited
undiluted
undisputed
unpolluted
unsuited

+ You can add to this list by adding *-(e)d* to some words that rhyme with *shoot*, as in *executed*

beautiful
dutiful

mutinous
glutinous

mutiny
scrutiny

shooting
computing
looting
microcomputing
parachuting
telecommuting

+ You can add to this list by adding *-ing* to some words that rhyme with *shoot*, as in *commuting*

Pluto
Benazir Bhutto

acutely
absolutely
astutely
dissolutely
minutely
resolutely

smooch
hooch
mooch

future
suture

+ You can add to this list by adding *-er* to some words that rhyme with *smooch*, as in *moocher*

18.15

smooth
booth
soothe

18.16

truth
forsooth
half-truth
long in the tooth
Ruth
sleuth
sooth
tooth
uncouth
untruth
youth

+ You can also make rhymes for these words by using words in section **18.5** that rhyme with *proof*

truthful
untruthful
youthful

ruthless
toothless

18.17

move
approve
disapprove
disprove
groove
improve
prove
remove
reprove
you've

mover
groover
Hoover®
manoeuvre
remover
Vancouver

+ You can also make rhymes for these words by using *her* after some words that rhyme with *move*, as in *remove her*

movable
approvable
disprovable
immovable
removable

approval
disapproval
removal

movie
groovy

moving
approving
disapproving
disproving
improving
proving
removing
reproving

improved
unmoved

+ You can add to this list by adding *-d* to some words that rhyme with ***move***, as in ***removed***

movement
improvement

18.18

two-way
thruway

18.19

ooze
abuse (= *to maltreat*)
accuse
amuse
blow a fuse
booze
bruise
choose
confuse
cruise
defuse
diffuse (= *to spread*)
disabuse
enthuse
excuse (= *to forgive*)
fuse
hypotenuse
ill-use (= *to treat harshly*)
infuse
lose (= *to misplace; to be beaten*)
mews
misuse (= *to use wrongly*)
Muse
muse
news
overuse (= *to use excessively*)
peruse
refuse (= *not to accept*)
reuse (= *to use again*)
ruse
snooze
suffuse
Syracuse
Ted Hughes
Toulouse
use (= *to utilize*)
whose

+ You can add to this list by adding *-s* to some words that rhyme with ***zoo***, as in ***blues***

user
accuser
boozer
bruiser
cruiser
loser

+ You can add to this list by adding *-r* to some words that rhyme with ***ooze***, as in ***abuser***

You can also make rhymes for these words by using ***her*** after some words that rhyme with ***ooze***, as in ***accuse her***

usable
excusable
inexcusable
reusable
unusable

refusal
bamboozle
perusal

choosy
boozy
floozy
Jacuzzi®
oozy
snoozy
Susie
woozy

oozing
abusing
accusing
amusing
boozing
bruising
choosing
confusing
cruising
defusing
diffusing
disabusing
enthusing
excusing
fusing
ill-using
infusing
losing
misusing
musing
overusing
perusing
refusing
reusing
snoozing
suffusing
using

fused
accused
bemused
confused
unused (= *not used*)
used (= *utilized*)

+ You can add to this list by adding *-d* to some words that rhyme with ***ooze***, as in ***amused***

Section 19
-UR-

All the words in this section use the sound **-ur-** (as in s*ure*, f*ur*y, sec*ure*) in their main stressed syllable

19.1

sure
allure
aperture
assure
boor
candidature
caricature
coiffure
cure
curvature
demure
discomfiture
dour
endure
ensure
expenditure
furniture
immature
impure
insecure
insure
legislature
liqueur
literature
lure
manicure
manure
mature
miniature
Moor
moor
nomenclature
obscure
overture
pedicure
poor
premature
procure
pure
reassure
reinsure
secure
signature
sinecure
temperature
tour
unsure

19.2

gourd
assured
insured
self-assured
uninsured

+ You can add to this list by adding *-(e)d* to some words that rhyme with ***sure***, as in ***obscured***

19.3

surely
demurely
immaturely
insecurely
maturely
obscurely
poorly
prematurely
purely
securely
slowly but surely

19.4

juror
insurer
Jura

+ You can add to this list by adding *-(e)r* to some words that rhyme with ***sure***, as in ***poorer***

You can also make rhymes for these words by using ***her*** after some words that rhyme with ***sure***, as in ***assure her***

curable
durable
endurable
incurable
insurable
procurable
unendurable

uninsurable

plural
extramural
mural
neural
rural

insurance
assurance
endurance
reassurance
reinsurance

Muriel
mercurial

prurient
luxuriant

furious
curious
incurious
luxurious
spurious

fury
brewery
Jewry
jury
Missouri
potpourri

Zurich
sulphuric

during
alluring
assuring
caricaturing
curing
enduring
ensuring
insuring
luring
manicuring
maturing
mooring
obscuring
procuring
reassuring
securing
touring

tourist
caricaturist
jurist
purist

+ You can add to this list by adding ***-(e)st*** to some words that rhyme with ***sure***, as in ***poorest***

boorish
Moorish

purity
immaturity
impurity
insecurity
maturity
obscurity
security
surety

Euro
bureau
euro
Truro

INDEX

B

C

Q

R

T